You're one step closer to getting your perfect computer

BUILDING YOUR OWN PC is best and only way to make sure that you get the perfect computer for you. Buying a pre-built model may cost you roughly the same amount of money, but you have to put up with the manufacturer's choice of components, which may not suit your particular needs.

When you build your own PC, you can make sure you have the right processor, memory, storage space, monitor and graphics card to suit you. In fact, building your own computer is like having a bespoke suit: it fits your needs perfectly.

Fortunately, doing the work yourself doesn't have to be difficult. Our step-by-step workshops and advice will help you choose the right components at the right price, build your computer and install your choice of operating system. With essential troubleshooting tips and advice at the back, you can start building your own PC with absolute confidence.

The book is bang up to date with the latest technology, including Windows 7, Microsoft's best operating system yet. With a full guide to its new features, we'll help you use your new computer, too.

The main thing you'll get from building your own computer is the satisfaction that you've got exactly what you want, rather than just another box. So, whether you want a powerful gaming PC, a Linux computer for browsing the web, a way of sharing storage space or a Media Center PC for recording your favourite TV programmes, your perfect computer is within your reach.

Happy building!

David Ludlow, Editor
david_ludlow@dennis.co.uk

Contents

From choosing the right kit to putting it all together and installing your software, our step-by-step guides will help you build the perfect PC

Chapter 1
ESSENTIALS

Find out what kit you'll need before you start building your PC, and learn some essential skills

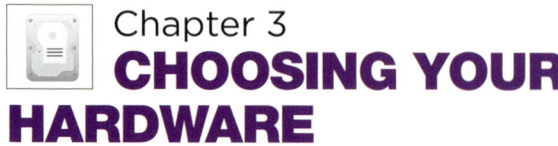

Chapter 2
CHOOSING AN OPERATING SYSTEM

Find out how Microsoft's latest operating system compares to previous versions of Windows, as well as the free open-source alternative, Linux

Chapter 3
CHOOSING YOUR HARDWARE

We explain what to look for when choosing the kit for your new build

Chapter 4
BUILDING YOUR PC

Step-by-step guides to creating the perfect PC

Chapter 5
POWER ON

Take control of how your computer works

Chapter 6
INSTALLING AN OPERATING SYSTEM

Everything from configuration to installing drivers

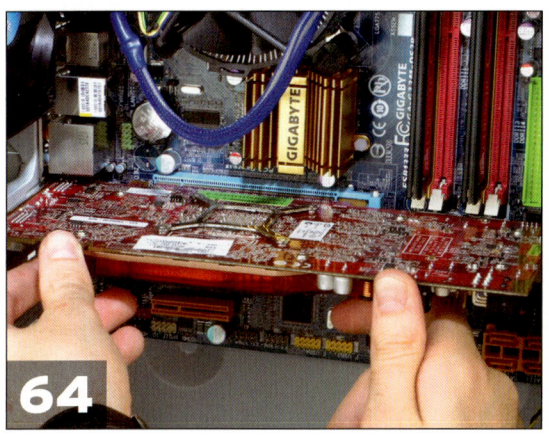

Chapter 7
WINDOWS 7

Your complete guide to Microsoft's latest release

Chapter 8
NEW PC ESSENTIALS

Our pick of the best free software around

Chapter 9
TROUBLESHOOTING

Having problems? Don't panic – here are our tips and tricks to get your PC running smoothly

JARGON-BUSTER

CHAPTER 1

ESSENTIALS

BEFORE YOU RUSH out and buy the bits for your new computer, there are some essential things that you need to know. Here, we'll show you what tools you'll require, the kind of workspace you should work on, the skills that you'll need and how to download the latest drivers for your new kit.

IN THIS CHAPTER

PC builder's

CAREFUL PREPARATION IS the key to every successful build, and the very first step is to get together the basic tools for the job. Over the next two pages, we'll show you how to put together a PC builder's toolkit that costs just a few pounds, but contains a range of hardware and software, which you can use again and again to tackle any build or future upgrade project with confidence.

WHAT YOU'LL GET WITH YOUR KIT

When you buy the components for your new PC, they will include a number of essential items. Your motherboard manual will have details of your motherboard's specifications and features, and an explanation of its ports and connectors. It'll also give you help with BIOS options and updates, and talk you through any bundled utility programs.

Your motherboard's box will contain all the data cables that you'll need to connect your hard disks and optical drives. There will be more cables than you need, so keep the other ones spare for future upgrades. Check the box carefully for any additional ports, such as rear-mounted USB, FireWire and eSATA. These will be easy to fit and your motherboard's manual will explain how.

Your case should have a manual that tells you how to take it apart and how to fit your components inside. Your case will generally ship with the screws that you'll need to fit your motherboard and other peripherals. If your case requires hard disks and optical drives to be fitted on runners, look for these in an accessory box either inside the packaging or the case itself.

If you're installing a graphics card, look inside its box carefully. Here you'll probably find DVI-to-VGA adaptors, which you'll need if you have a monitor with analogue inputs only; Molex-to-PCI Express power adaptors, which you'll need if your power supply doesn't have the necessary power connector; and, if your card supports it, DVI-to-HDMI adaptors. In the case of ATI graphics cards, this last item is really important. You have to use the ATI DVI-to-HDMI adaptor in order to get the sound working correctly; a standard adaptor will only deliver the picture.

Look inside all the component boxes for driver CDs. You can use these to get your hardware installed, although it's best to follow our guide on downloading the latest drivers on page 12 before you start building.

OPERATING THEATRE

A computer is useless without an operating system, so make sure that you've got your Windows or Linux disc handy before you begin building your computer.

A Windows install CD is made by Microsoft, bears a holographic Microsoft logo and has all the files needed to install the operating system. You can also use this CD to recover damaged Windows installations if you have trouble later on.

Your software box should also contain the licence key that you'll need to install Windows. You'll need this key when you install your operating system and if you ever have to reinstall Windows or contact Microsoft for support. It's critical, therefore, that you keep this key somewhere safe; without it, you'll need to buy a new copy of the software. Our complete guide to installing Windows 7 on page 78 explains everything.

You will have to create a Linux installation CD before you build your computer. This is easy to do, and our guide to installing Linux on page 92 explains everything you need to know.

SAVE IT FOR LATER

When you build your PC, you'll find that you may be left with some spare parts, such as blanking plates for expansion cards and extra drive rails for more hard disks. We recommend that you keep these parts somewhere safe, as you may need them should you decide to upgrade your computer in the future. It's also worth keeping any spare screws, as you never know when they'll come in handy.

TOOL UP

Building a PC isn't a particularly complicated procedure, and you'll need only a few tools to complete the job successfully. The picture opposite shows you the most common tools that you'll need, and you shouldn't need anything more specialised. Our guide to essential building skills on page 10 will show you how to use these tools, and our guide to your workspace on page 8 shows you the kind of area in which you should work.

ESSENTIAL TOOLS

No 2 crosshead screwdriver	£1.50
Long-nose pliers	£4.50
Multi-head screwdriver	£9
Total	**£15**

www.screwfix.com

OPTIONAL TOOLS

Torch	£6
Cable ties	£3
www.screwfix.com	
4GB flash drive	£9
www.pcnextday.co.uk	
Thermal paste	£3
Anti-static wristband	£3
www.lambda-tek.com/componentshop	
Total	**£24**
TOTAL AMOUNT	**£39**

toolkit

RECOMMENDED
Hardware tools

MULTI-HEAD SCREWDRIVER A ratchet or electric screwdriver with a wide range of fitments should cover anything that a standard crosshead screwdriver can't. Choose one with a range of hex sockets that includes at least 5, 6 and 7mm sizes.

CABLE TIES (not pictured) Great for tidying the inside of your PC, or to clip groups of wires or loose components out of the way while you work. Longer ties are more expensive but more versatile, and you can snip off any extra length.

ANTI-STATIC BAG Use a large anti-static bag as a safe surface for working on any sensitive components. Smaller bags are ideal for storing or transporting components. Most PC parts arrive in anti-static packaging, so don't throw them away.

MEDIUM CROSSHEAD SCREWDRIVER This can be used for almost every screw inside a PC, allowing you to fit or adjust all the major components. Choose one with a long shaft so that you can reach recessed screws.

TORCH This can be particularly useful when connecting a PC under a desk or making adjustments inside its case. A torch will also help you to read text on those components inside your PC that are labelled with small text or simply stamped with information.

FINE PLIERS You can use these to remove and fit jumpers, hold parts in tight spaces and help extract bits that are reluctant to move. You can also use them to cut wires or cable ties, and twist out metal blanking plates from a drive bay.

ANTI-STATIC WRISTBAND Wearing this reduces the chances that static electricity will damage sensitive components such as your expansion cards, motherboard, memory or processor.

STORAGE DEVICE A simple USB flash memory device lets you transfer any drivers or patches you need from another PC. A larger hard disk device is perfect for taking full backups if you're transferring data and programs from another PC.

THERMAL PASTE You may need this for the trouble-free installation of a new processor or graphics card heatsink, or when transferring a processor to a new motherboard. Make sure that you don't buy thermal adhesive by mistake.

Your workspace

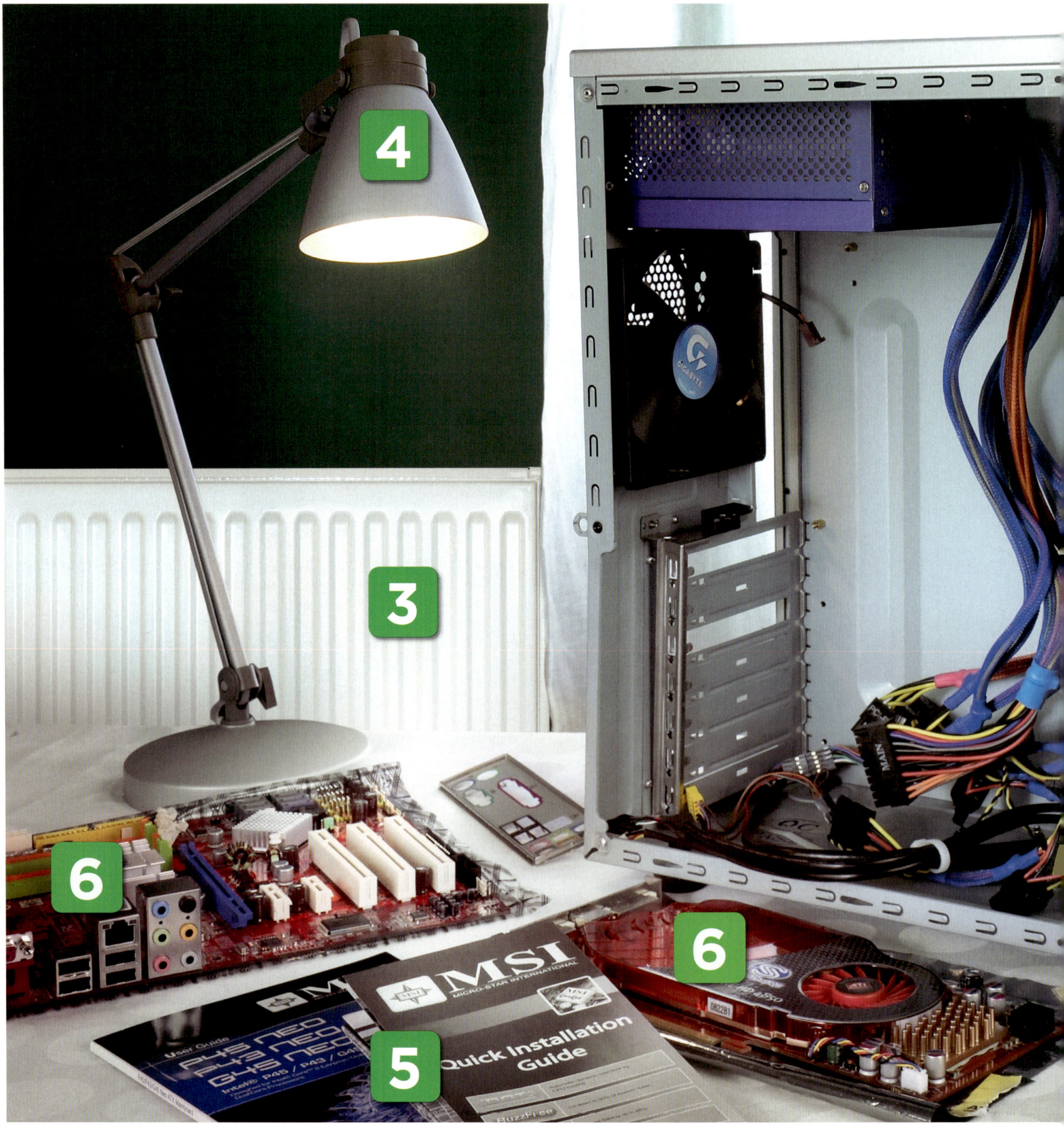

1 DESK

You need a clear desk or table to work on your PC. As cases can have sharp edges, put down a cloth before you start work to prevent scratches. If you haven't got a suitable cloth, lining your desk with paper should do the job.

2 PLASTIC CUP

Screws and clips from inside your case can easily get lost. A plastic cup is a handy way of storing everything so you don't lose them.

3 RADIATOR

It's good to work near a radiator, so you can touch an unpainted part of it to discharge static. Alternatively, wear an anti-static wristband.

4 LAMP

A desk lamp will help make sure that you have enough light inside your PC.

5 MANUALS

Keep any manuals that came with your kit handy, as they'll help you build your PC correctly.

6 COMPONENTS

Keep your components in or on top of their anti-static bags until you're ready to use them.

Essential skills

BEFORE YOU UNWRAP all the shiny new components you've bought and start shoving them into your case, there are some safety lessons to learn, along with some key skills that will make building your PC much easier. Without these, you run the risk of damaging your computer before you've even turned it on. The worst part is that most of the time, you'll be unable to tell that you've caused any damage until you turn on your PC for the first time. At this point, tracking the problem down can be a real nightmare. We'll take you through the main pitfalls you'll face when building a new computer and, more importantly, how to avoid them.

STATIC

We all know about static electricity: it's the charge that builds up when we walk across a carpet and discharges when we touch someone else. This little flash of electricity may not seem very powerful, but it's potentially fatal for sensitive electronic components. Get a build-up of static and touch your processor, and you may have destroyed one

of the most expensive parts of your computer before you've even started.

Fortunately, avoiding problems isn't that hard. If you've got one, wear an anti-static wrist strap. This will prevent static electricity from building up, making it safe to touch any component in your computer. If you haven't got one, don't panic, as there are other ways around the problem. Try to work near a radiator. To discharge any build-up of static, simply touch the unpainted part of the radiator. You're then safe to work.

Finally, all computer components come in anti-static bags to protect them. Don't remove any component from its bag until you're ready to fit it.

MAGNETIC SCREWDRIVER

Inside your PC, you'll find that there are lots of parts of your case that are awkward to reach to screw components into place. The easiest way to deal with this problem is to use a magnetic screwdriver. Simply place the screw into the screwdriver and then manoeuvre the screw towards its destination. The opposite is true when removing screws, as a gentle action should mean that a screw comes away attached to the screwdriver, rather than dropping to the floor.

Don't worry about magnetically sensitive devices inside your PC. A magnetic screwdriver isn't powerful enough to cause any damage or wipe any data.

THE RIGHT SCREWS

While the right screwdriver can make your job easier, it's essential to use the right screws to prevent damage. Put a screw that's too long into a hard disk, for example, and you could damage a circuit board and break the whole thing. Where possible, you should use the screws that come with the device, as these are guaranteed to work. Failing that, if your case has special fittings for devices, such as rails for hard disks and optical drives, the correct screws should have been fitted.

Of the different types of screws that are used, the small stubby ones are for hard disks and optical drives, the long screws are for holding expansion cards in place, while the screws with the flat heads are for fitting the motherboard and for some case panels. At all times, make sure that you don't overtighten screws, or you could cause damage. The idea is to tighten screws to the point where your components are held snugly in place.

⬆ Prevent the build-up of static by wearing an anti-static wrist strap

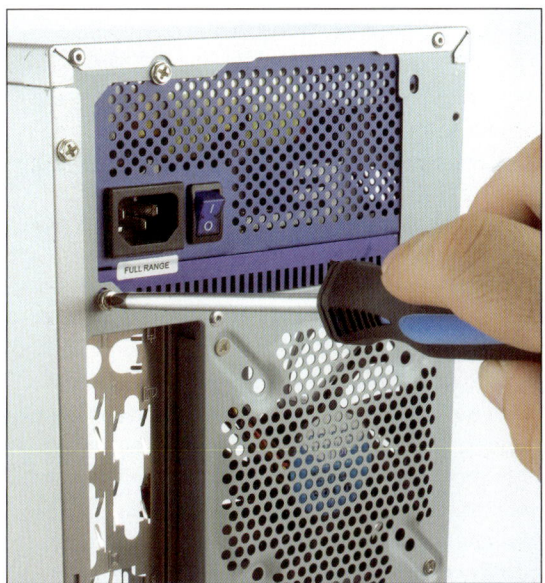

⬆ Choose the right screw for the right job

⬆ Check that the cables are all plugged in

THE RIGHT AMOUNT OF FORCE

When you plug components such as expansion cards, memory and a processor into your motherboard, it can be difficult to know how much force you should apply. Our tips should help you get it right. First, make sure that you've lined up your components correctly with the slot or socket – our step-by-step guide to building your PC on pages 42 to 67 will show you how to do this.

Next, make sure that you're applying equal pressure across the device to move it into position. Processors should drop into place with little pressure, memory needs a firm push to click it into place, while expansion cards need a fair push. If you're getting a lot of resistance, stop what you're doing and start over again.

POWER CABLES

When building a PC, it's important to remember you're dealing with an electrical device. Before you plug the power in and turn on your computer, check that you've plugged in all the power cables properly, particularly on the motherboard. Loose connections can cause problems.

The fans inside a PC can cause problems, too, particularly if you've got power cables near them. Make sure that all power-carrying cables are clipped out of the way of fans so that you don't cut through them. Power connectors plug in only one way, so if you can't get one in make sure that it's

the right way round. Forcing a connector in the wrong way will damage your devices irreparably.

Before you plug in your power cable, make sure that your power supply is set to the correct voltage. Some supplies, although rarely seen today, have a switch that changes the input voltage from 110V (US) to 230V (UK). If you've accidentally set it to 110V, the supply will be damaged and your motherboard may be affected, too.

TAKE YOUR TIME

The best tip that we can give is to follow each step carefully and take your time. Building a PC isn't a race and, as you're dealing with lots of expensive components, it's best to get it right the first time around. Our step-by-step help will guide you through every step you need to take, while our troubleshooting guides on pages 128 to 157 will help you fix any problems that you may run into.

➜ A magnetic screwdriver is a PC builder's best friend

Finding and installing drivers

ANY NEW HARDWARE that you buy will come with a driver disc, so that you can install it easily. Some motherboards even have fancy installation wizards that automatically detect which drivers you need and install them automatically. However, while this sounds straightforward, the drivers that you get on the disc are usually out of date.

If you've already got a computer, then your first job is to go on to the internet and download the latest driver files, saving them to a USB key or external hard disk. If you haven't got access to a PC, don't worry. Simply use the drivers that came on the disc until you've got a working computer, and then follow these instructions to download the latest drivers and install them afterwards. Thanks to the internet, getting drivers is incredibly easy and shouldn't take too long.

MOTHERBOARDS

The motherboard is the main part of your PC and it comes with plenty of built-in features, including onboard sound, networking, storage drivers and potentially even graphics. Windows will have drivers for many of these things, but if you want the best performance and the best range of features, you'll need the latest drivers.

You can get everything for your motherboard from the manufacturer's website: you'll find the address in your motherboard's manual. If not, then use a search engine to find the URL.

Once you're on the website, there should be a link for Support. Just keep following the links for motherboards and drivers. Eventually, you'll get to a point where you'll need to enter the details of your motherboard to locate the driver download page for your model. It's vital you get exactly the right model in order to get the correct drivers for your computer. If you can't find the details on the box or in the manual, then the motherboard's name is usually written on the board itself.

After you've entered your motherboard's details, you'll be presented with a long list of drivers divided by type, such as graphics or networking. For each heading, download one driver, making sure that you select the latest version. Most driver packages cater for all versions of Windows, but check the details to ensure that you download the correct driver.

GRAPHICS CARDS

If you're using onboard graphics, you'll be able to find the latest drivers on the motherboard

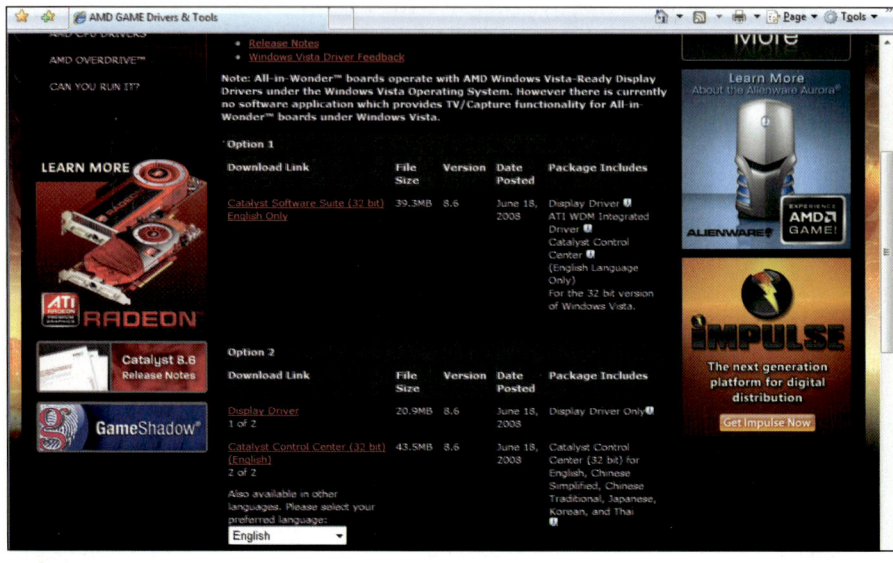

↑ ATI gives you a choice of files to download, but the full Catalyst Control Suite is the best choice for new computers

↑ You'll need to perform several file downloads to get the latest motherboard drivers

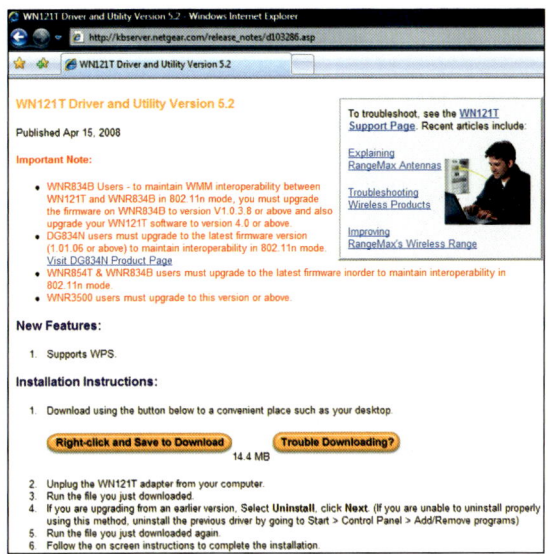

↑ You can find the latest drivers for all your devices on the internet

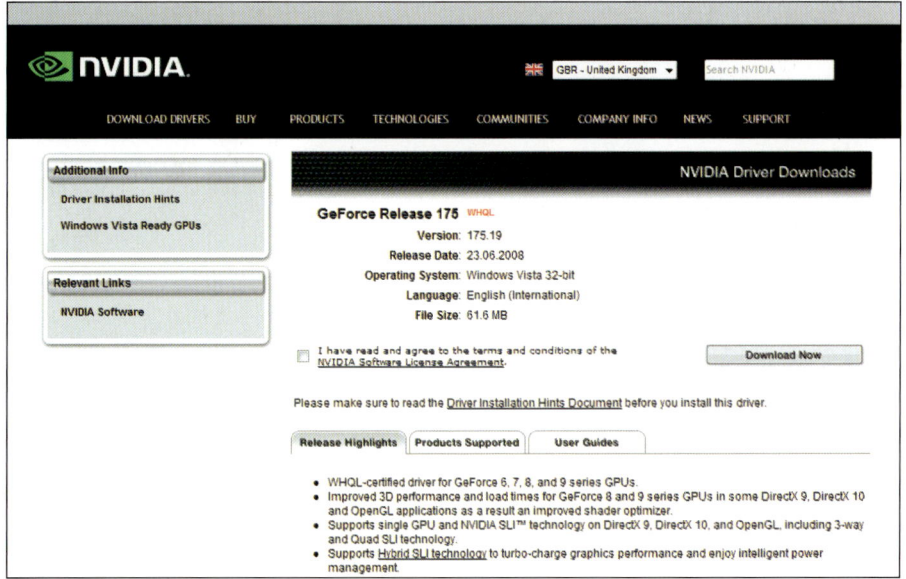

↑ Nvidia has a unified driver architecture, so a single download is all you need

manufacturer's website. If you're using a dedicated graphics card, you should download the drivers directly from ATI's or Nvidia's sites. This will ensure that you get the best performance and stability from your graphics card.

NVIDIA

Nvidia uses a unified driver package, so one download will work for most of its graphics cards. This makes installation simple. Visit *www.nvidia.com* and select Download Drivers from the Download Drivers menu in the top-left of the screen. Select the type of card (GeForce for consumer graphics cards) and the series of card that you have, such as 9xxx series for a GeForce 9600 GT. Select your language as English (UK) and click Search. Tick the box to accept the licence agreement and click Download.

It's important to select your graphics card model, as not every driver package has the driver for every graphics card. If you download the wrong package, your card won't install.

ATI

ATI has a similar unified driver architecture to Nvidia. Visit *http://support.amd.com/us/Pages/AMDSupportHub.aspx* and click the Download graphics drivers link under Support & Drivers. On the next page, select which operating system you'll be installing, select Radeon from the list (consumer graphics cards are all Radeon models), and then select your card. Click Go to be taken to the driver page. The Catalyst Software Suite includes the driver and the Catalyst Control Panel for configuring settings. Make sure you select your

model from the list, or you may get a version of the driver that doesn't support your card.

OTHER DEVICES

If you're installing other hardware, such as a wireless network adaptor, TV tuner, sound card or printer, you'll need to download the latest drivers for these, too. In a similar way to the procedure we've described above, you'll need to visit the manufacturer's website and follow the links until you get to where you can select which device you want to download drivers for. Check a device's manual for full details on the manufacturer's website. If you can't find any information, a Google search for the manufacturer's name should bring up the details you need. Remember to make sure that you get the right driver for your device and for the OS that you require.

REGULAR CHECKS

Once you have the latest drivers, your job isn't done. You should regularly check manufacturers' websites and see if updates are available. Typically, graphics card drivers are updated monthly, while other devices are updated less regularly.

Driver updates fix known problems and can help your PC become more stable and perform better. It's worth going back to a manufacturer's site to check for updates if you're suffering a problem, as a new driver can often fix this.

Manufacturers' websites are also useful if you want help with a product. You can also find manuals for download, which can be really helpful if you lose your printed version and need to check a detail or plan an upgrade.

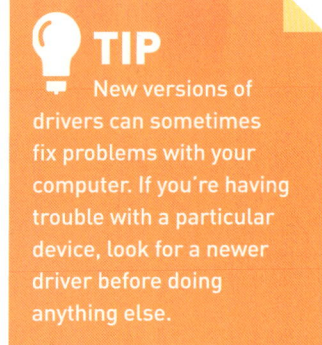

TIP
New versions of drivers can sometimes fix problems with your computer. If you're having trouble with a particular device, look for a newer driver before doing anything else.

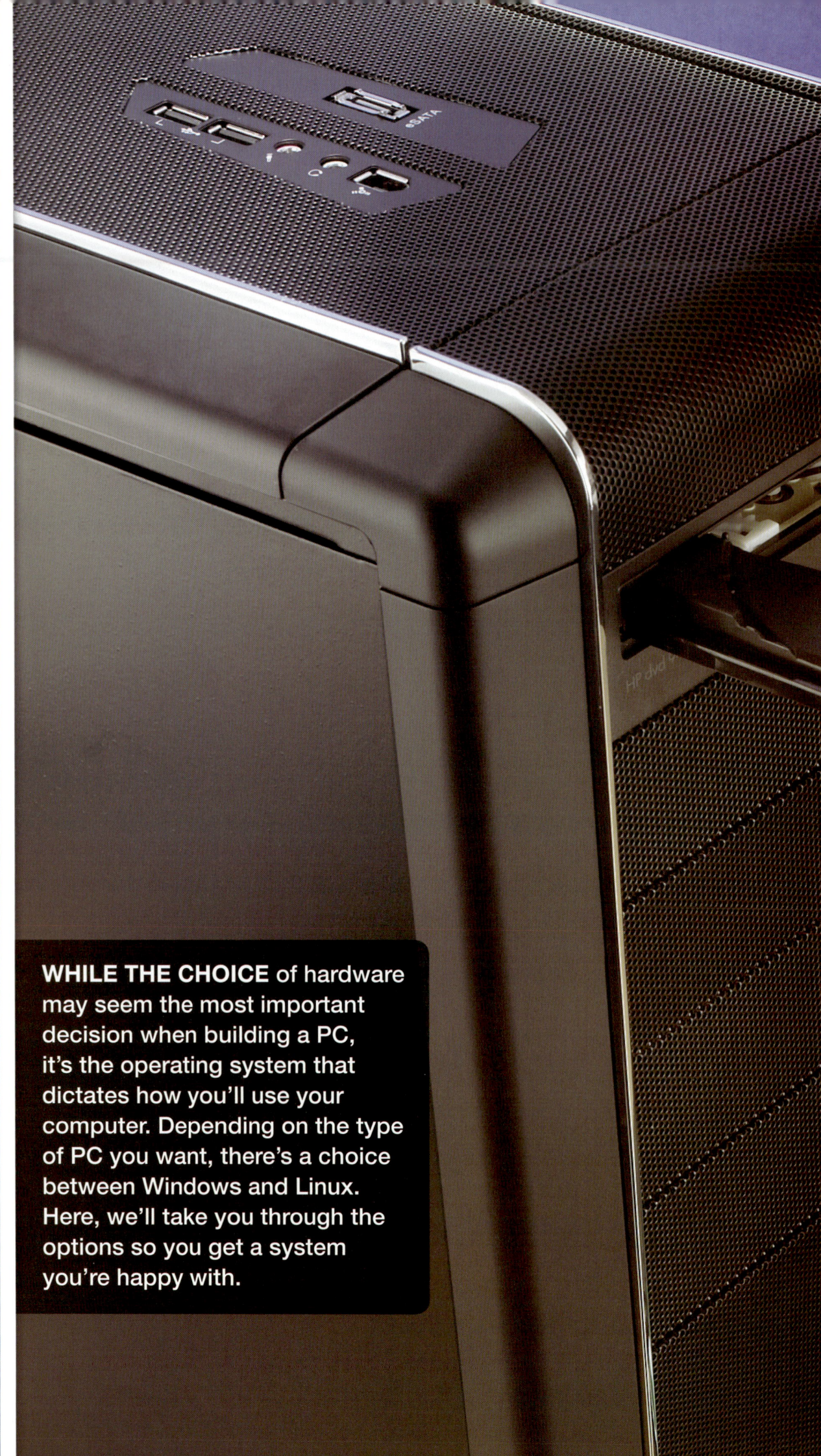

CHAPTER 2

CHOOSING YOUR OPERATING SYSTEM

WHILE THE CHOICE of hardware may seem the most important decision when building a PC, it's the operating system that dictates how you'll use your computer. Depending on the type of PC you want, there's a choice between Windows and Linux. Here, we'll take you through the options so you get a system you're happy with.

IN THIS CHAPTER

Windows 7

WINDOWS 7 IS Microsoft's latest operating system, and the early impressions of it are that it's everything that Windows Vista should have been. This makes it the ideal choice for any new PC, to the point where we now feel comfortable recommending that you shouldn't bother with Vista or XP unless you have an old copy of either of these two operating systems that you really want to use. With Windows 7 you're buying an operating system that's going to enjoy Microsoft's full support for the next few years.

When Windows Vista was first released, it had several compatibility problems. In particular, some hardware didn't have drivers for Vista, and some older software refused to run on the operating system. With Windows 7, this isn't the case: everything that worked on Vista – which is practically everything now – will work on Windows 7, so you can buy it safe in the knowledge that you won't have any compatibility problems.

Security has been beefed up, and Windows 7 also loads much faster and is less sluggish than Windows Vista. All round, it's a much better operating system. You're sure to be happy with your choice if you choose Windows 7.

FRIENDLY FIRE

Not all the new features are hidden under the surface. A lot of work has been put into making Windows easier to use and better to look at. This shouldn't be underestimated, as Windows 7's look and flash graphics mean it's a lot friendlier and make XP and even Vista look dated.

The new Windows management interface lets you quickly resize windows, see your desktop and choose which application you want to switch to.

Vista's sidebar has gone, but you can still run the same Gadgets (small applications for a specific job, such as showing the current weather, displaying post-it notes and showing you the current time). There are loads of Gadgets to choose from, with both official Microsoft and third-party applications available.

Those used to Vista will be pleased that there's still the built-in search, which makes it easier to find your files and programs. Simply click on the Start menu and start to type, and you'll be presented with a list of files and programs that contain your search terms. This search integrates with email (Windows Mail in Vista), so all your important information is incredibly easy to find. If you want Vista to search other email clients, such as Mozilla's Thunderbird or scan new file types, you can download iFilters (*http://ifilter.org*) to add these capabilities.

Windows 7 adds a lot more features besides, including Homegroups for easier networking, Blu-ray disc burning and full image-based backup in every edition. For more information, see our full guide to Windows 7 on page 106.

VERSION THERAPY

While Windows Vista had a relatively simple choice of just two versions – Home and Professional – Windows Vista comes in three major retail versions: Home Premium, Professional and Ultimate. The main benefit over Vista is that each edition contains the same features as the lower version, plus some more options. You can even use Windows Anytime Upgrade to upgrade your existing edition without having to reinstall the operating system.

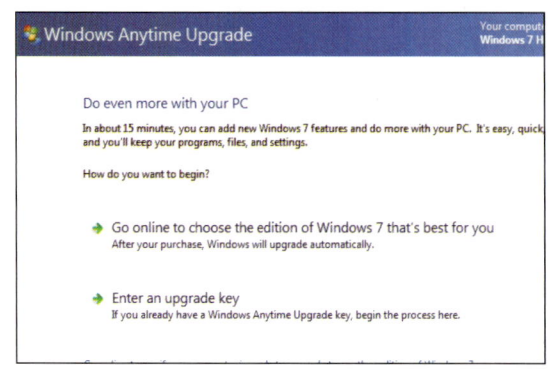

⬆ You can upgrade your version of Windows 7 without having to reinstall all your programs and files

⬆ Media Center is the easy way to view photos, videos and pictures, and record TV programmes

We think that Windows 7 Home Premium is the best version for home users. Professional, as the name implies, has extra features for businesses, while Ultimate has all the features of both other editions plus the BitLocker drive encryption feature. Both versions are relatively expensive compared to Windows 7 Home Premium, though, and we don't think that they're worth the extra cash. You can use Microsoft's website to make sure that the version you've chosen has all the features you need (*http://windows.microsoft.com/en-US/windows7/products/compare-editions*).

Finally, you also get a choice between the 32-bit and 64-bit versions of Windows. The 64-bit version of Windows can handle more system memory (the 32-bit version is limited to using a maximum of around 3.5GB). However, there are fewer drivers for it and not all software is guaranteed to work with the 64-bit version. Unless you're intent on sticking tons of memory in your new PC, stick with the 32-bit version.

UNDER CONTROL

One of the key benefits of Windows 7 is that it comes with Windows Media Center. This application lets you watch and control you music, videos and photos using a remote control (which costs around £15) using a TV-friendly interface. If you add a TV tuner (from around £15), you can even turn your PC into a hard disk recorder, complete with the best and completely free electronic programming guide (EPG).

It's incredibly easy to configure and the updated version supports the Red Button for interactive digital TV and Freesat HD broadcasts; two things that Vista's Media Center didn't support.

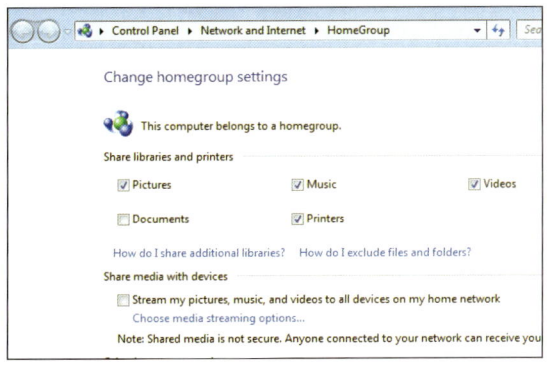

↑ Networking is even easier with Windows Homegroups

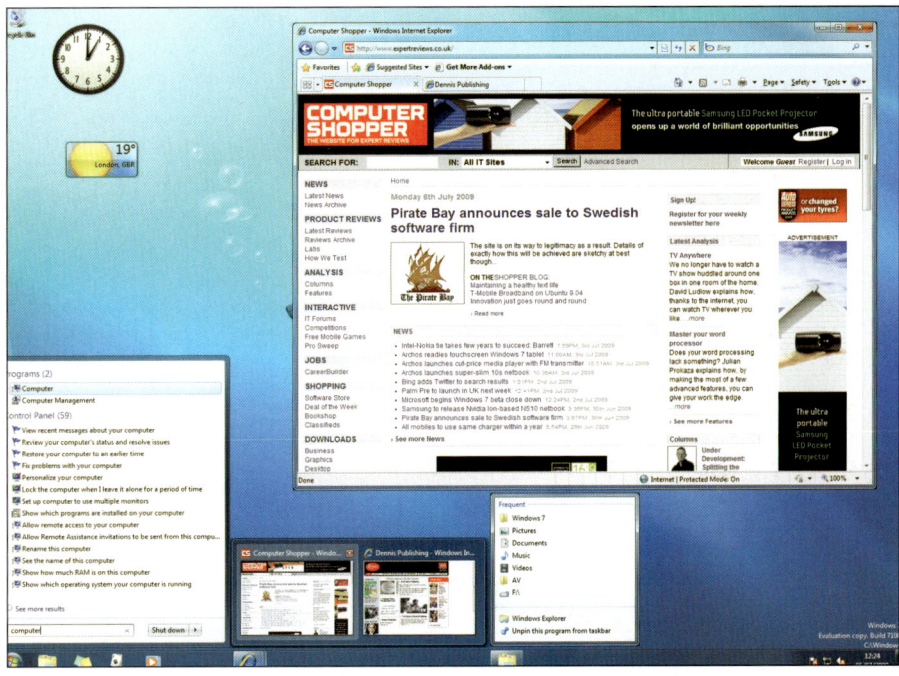

↑ Windows 7's new interface makes the operating system even easier to use

GOING STREAMLINE

Microsoft stuffed Vista full of extras such as the Windows Photo Gallery for organising photos. While some of these applications were useful, they just added to the general bloat of the operating system. With Windows 7, Microsoft has gone for a more streamlined operating system and any extra applications are optional: you can either download similar applications to Vista's from Windows Live or install other third-party applications instead.

POWER UP

Windows 7 will work with any computer on which Windows Vista would run. It needs a fairly decent specification and we strongly recommend that you have a PC with at least 2GB of memory in order to get the best experience. This means that Windows 7's not ideal if you want to build a budget PC; you may want to consider using Linux instead.

You may also find that some older hardware such as printers and scanners won't have drivers for Windows 7, but this is unlikely to be a problem for most people. If you have a particular bit of kit that you want to keep using and you can't find Windows 7 or Vista drivers, then XP could be a better choice if you've got a copy. For everyone else, Windows 7's the operating system we've all been waiting for.

TIP

The Original Equipment Manufacturer (OEM) version of Windows 7 can be bought with any new bit of hardware and is designed for people building a new computer. You don't get any telephone support, but the OEM versions are considerably cheaper than the full boxed products, and cheaper than the upgrade version.

Windows 7 editions

SETTING ASIDE ENTERPRISE options, which are only available on corporate licences, there are just four versions of Windows 7. Three are available both to upgraders and pre-installed on new PCs, while Starter is only sold with netbooks, and is designed to give you most of the Windows 7 experience without over-taxing the slow processors in low-end machines. This leaves netbook makers with little excuse to carry on bundling the older, cheaper Windows XP.

The three remaining editions are also available in 'N' versions. These are identical but for the omission of Microsoft's Windows Media Player, and have been made available to resolve an EU competition law dispute. Since they cost the same and have fewer features, they're not a good buy.

So you're left with a simple choice between Home Premium, Professional and Ultimate. If you're buying a new PC, it's most likely to come with Home Premium, but the supplier may be able to offer higher editions on request. For those buying just the software, there's a choice of full or upgrade packs. The upgrade is suitable for any PC running a licensed copy of Windows XP or Vista; you'll only need the full version for a machine that's never had Windows before, such as an Apple Mac (recent models can run Windows in addition to the Mac OS), or one whose copy of XP or Vista was obtained illegally and thus won't pass the upgrade

check. If you bought a Vista PC during the summer of 2009, you may have received a voucher for a completely free upgrade to Windows 7.

Going for an upgrade pack doesn't mean you can't opt for a 'clean' install of Windows 7, to start from scratch rather than updating your existing Windows. You get the same install options as anyone else; the only difference is that you must first boot up in Windows XP or Vista so the software can ensure your version is genuine.

FAMILY PACK

For the first time, Microsoft is issuing a Family Pack for Windows 7. This is designed to make it easier and cheaper for a whole household to upgrade its PCs from previous versions of Windows, which makes a lot of sense when so many of the new features, such as HomeGroup, are aimed at homes with multiple computers all running Windows 7. The Family Pack costs around £130 and covers three machines. It's an upgrade rather than a full version – logically enough, since if you were buying a new computer you'd get Windows 7 pre-installed – and will only be available for Home Premium.

If you have three or even two PCs, this saves you money, and you can still upgrade to a higher edition later if you prefer, through Anytime Upgrade. Microsoft has said the Family Pack will

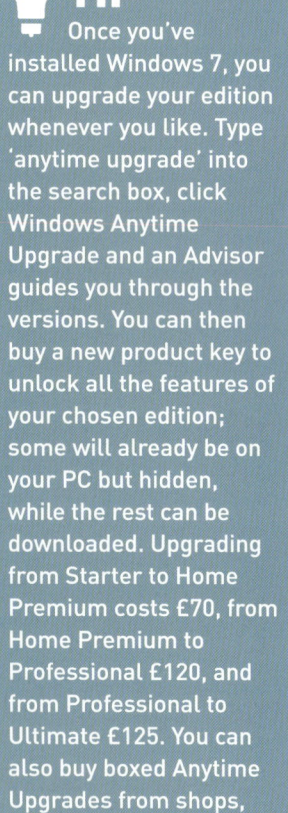

TIP
Once you've installed Windows 7, you can upgrade your edition whenever you like. Type 'anytime upgrade' into the search box, click Windows Anytime Upgrade and an Advisor guides you through the versions. You can then buy a new product key to unlock all the features of your chosen edition; some will already be on your PC but hidden, while the rest can be downloaded. Upgrading from Starter to Home Premium costs £70, from Home Premium to Professional £120, and from Professional to Ultimate £125. You can also buy boxed Anytime Upgrades from shops, which may be cheaper.

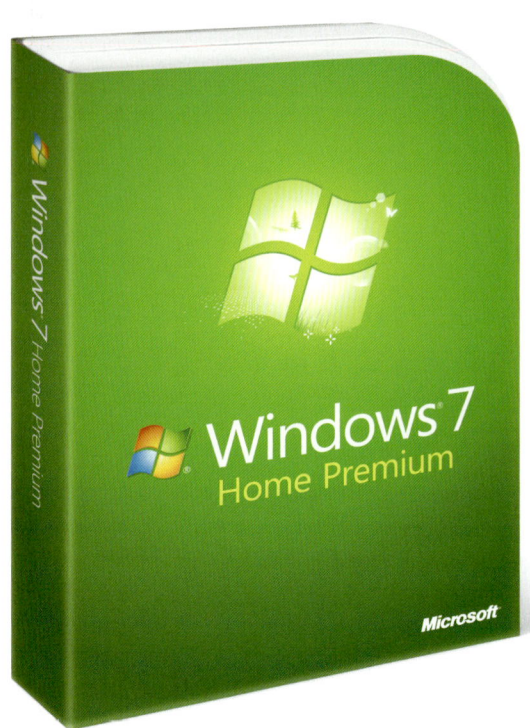

be available in 'limited quantities', but at the time of writing there's no sign of it running out.

STARTER EDITION

Windows 7 Starter Edition is only available pre-installed on new PCs, invariably low-cost netbooks. Some of the omissions, such as see-through windows and Taskbar previews, are justifiable on performance grounds. Others, including media streaming, Media Center and the ability to change your desktop background, seem a bit mean. Nor is there support for multiple displays, so although you can plug your netbook into a monitor (assuming it has a suitable output), you can't use both screens at once.

Although Starter is a perfectly respectable operating system, we think most people will find it frustrating to use on a regular basis. If you have the choice, go for Home Premium instead. Or try Starter first and get an Anytime Upgrade later.

HOME PREMIUM

As with Windows Vista, Home Premium is the version that consumers – as opposed to business users – are most likely to encounter. As such, it contains new tools and options that will appeal to home users and anyone who uses their PC for entertainment purposes.

Prime among these is the revamped Windows Media Center. This can be used as a full-screen entertainment system and can even be operated entirely with a remote control from the comfort of your sofa. It also works with Media Center Extender devices, such as Logitech's Squeezebox Duet and Microsoft's own Xbox 360 console, so your PC can be your home's entertainment hub.

We've also been impressed by the much-improved Windows Media Player, now in version 12. This is a superb way to control a large music and video collection, thanks to its intuitive interface and media-streaming abilities.

The latest Windows Aero interface, which is only partially supported in Windows 7 Starter Edition, is fully installed in Premium, and it's not just there to look pretty but to make using your computer more intuitive. It's the little touches – such as easy ways to manage windows, and some excellent desktop themes – that make it a superior environment to Vista. If you're fortunate enough to have a touchscreen PC, things go a step further thanks to a full set of multitouch features.

Windows 7 editions compared

	STARTER	HOME PREMIUM	PRO	ULTIMATE
Official price	N/A	£150	£220	£230
Street price*	N/A	£89	£159	£169
Official upgrade price	N/A	£80	£190	£200
Upgrade street price*	N/A	£75	£149	£151
Family Pack (three PCs) upgrade price	N/A	£150	N/A	N/A
Family Pack (three PCs) upgrade street price	N/A	£130	N/A	N/A
USER INTERFACE				
Aero Glass	🟠	🟢	🟢	🟢
Aero Peek	🟠	🟢	🟢	🟢
Aero Snaps	🟢	🟢	🟢	🟢
Aero Shake	🟠	🟢	🟢	🟢
Instant Search	🟢	🟢	🟢	🟢
Live Preview	🟠	🟢	🟢	🟢
Windows Flip 3D	🟠	🟢	🟢	🟢
Multi-Touch	🟠	🟠	🟢	🟢
BUNDLED APPS & SERVICES				
Windows Live Essentials (download)	🟢	🟢	🟢	🟢
Windows Fax and Scan	🟢	🟢	🟢	🟢
Gadgets	🟢	🟢	🟢	🟢
Paint, Calculator and WordPad	🟢	🟢	🟢	🟢
Windows Media Player	🟢	🟢	🟢	🟢
Remote Media Experience	🟠	🟢	🟢	🟢
HomeGroup	🟢**	🟢	🟢	🟢
Device Stage	🟢	🟢	🟢	🟢
ENTERTAINMENT				
Basic games	🟢	🟢	🟢	🟢
Premium games	🟠	🟢	🟢	🟢
Media Center Extender support	🟠	🟢	🟢	🟢
Windows Media Center	🟠	🟢	🟢	🟢
SECURITY & BACKUP				
BitLocker	🟠	🟠	🟠	🟢
AppLocker	🟠	🟠	🟠	🟢
Backup scheduling	🟠	🟠	🟢	🟢
Backup to network	🟠	🟠	🟢	🟢
Encrypting File System	🟠	🟠	🟢	🟢
Complete PC Backup & Restore	🟠	🟠	🟢	🟢
Windows Defender	🟢	🟢	🟢	🟢
Windows Firewall	🟢	🟢	🟢	🟢
Biometric support	🟠	🟢	🟢	🟢
PERFORMANCE				
64-bit processor support	🟠	🟢	🟢	🟢
Maximum RAM supported (32-bit)	4GB	4GB	4GB	4GB
Maximum RAM supported (64-bit)	—	16GB	192GB	192GB
DirectX 11	🟢	🟢	🟢	🟢
Dual processor support	🟠	🟢	🟢	🟢
Windows XP Mode	🟠	🟠	🟢	🟢
Mobility Center	🟠	🟢	🟢	🟢
Presentation Mode	🟠	🟠	🟢	🟢
Virtual Hard Disk booting	🟠	🟠	🟠	🟢
NETWORKING				
Offline Files & Folders	🟠	🟠	🟢	🟢
Remote Desktop	🟢**	🟢**	🟢	🟢
Windows Server Domain	🟠	🟠	🟢	🟢
DirectAccess	🟠	🟠	🟠	🟢

*Street prices correct in September 2010   **Can join but not create/organise

More powerful options are still missing from Home Premium, though: there's no BitLocker disk encryption, no Remote Desktop, and no Windows XP Mode to get the oldest and fussiest programs working (though most XP software will still run). The Backup and Restore Center is limited to local hard disk or DVD backups, which may be fine for most users but lacks the full versatility available with the Professional and Ultimate editions.

Most personal users will be well served by Home Premium, but we recommend that power users, corporates and tweakers consider Ultimate.

PROFESSIONAL EDITION

Windows 7 Professional is aimed at businesses, but may also appeal to ambitious home users looking for more power than Home Premium offers. The enhanced Backup and Restore Center allows you to schedule automatic backups, and the Encrypting File System, which adds a layer of protection for sensitive files, offers more complex algorithms that are almost impossible to hack.

Also in the Professional edition, Windows XP Mode is an ingenious 'virtual machine' that lets you run Windows XP alongside Windows 7 so seamlessly that you can forget which one each program is using. This will suit organisations that have invested in XP software that won't run correctly under Windows 7. It relies on Microsoft Virtual PC, which you can add as a free download.

Corporate users will be pleased with several other Professional features, too, including Presentation Mode, which can reset your desktop wallpaper to a default image, specify a preset volume level and prevent your screensaver from appearing – an instant way to set up your PC for the boardroom. Windows Server domain compatibility makes it easy to connect to other PCs running a recent version of Windows over a LAN or WAN.

Every feature in Home Premium is also included, including Aero, touchscreen support, Media Player 12 and (unlike with the old Vista Business) Windows Media

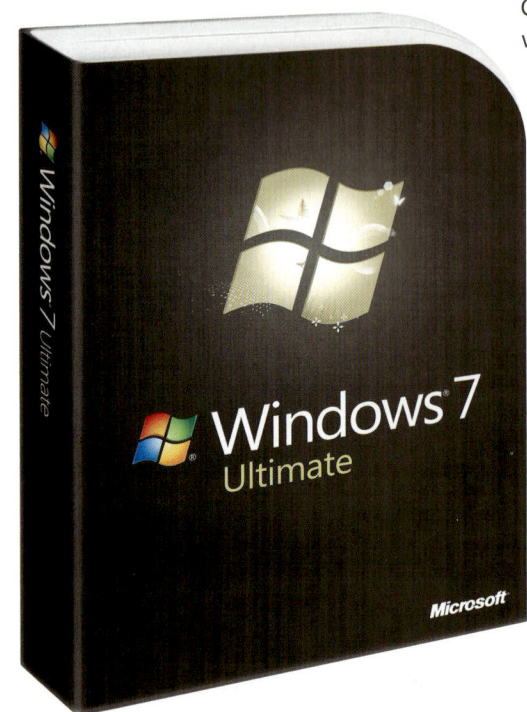

Center. Couple this with a raft of technical, security and networking enhancements and it's clear that, if work is on your mind, Professional Edition is probably the way to go.

Except that for hardly any more money you could go for an even better version…

ULTIMATE EDITION

Living up to its title, the Ultimate edition contains every new enhancement from Home Premium and Professional plus extras on top. In particular, the AppLocker and BitLocker security tools are unique to this version (along with Enterprise, basically the same product with a different type of licence). The former restricts which applications can run on a network, and the latter offers full-disk encryption to ensure no-one can get their hands on your data. BitLocker to Go also enables encryption of USB sticks and other portable devices, ensuring your data stays confidential if a drive is misplaced.

Other technical improvements include tools to run software in a Unix subsystem and DirectAccess for seamless connections between computers on a network. You can switch Windows between 35 languages, which isn't possible in Home Premium or Professional. Support for the VHD file format, which can preserve the complete contents and structure of a physical hard disk, is also reserved for Ultimate users.

While there's no sign of Vista's 'Ultimate Extras', the Ultimate edition of Windows 7 excels by matching the other editions and adding a host of features that will please enthusiasts, tweakers and IT managers. If you're looking for supreme power and every feature on the block, Windows 7 Ultimate is for you – and it's effectively the same price as Professional, give or take a few pounds.

32-BIT v 64-BIT WINDOWS

Windows comes in 32- or 64-bit versions to suit different setups. Essentially, if you want to use more than 3GB of RAM you need 64-bit. The only downside is that a few older programs and peripherals may not work; before upgrading an older PC, you also need to check its processor is compatible. Both 32- and 64-bit are supplied when you buy Windows 7 off the shelf, but you'll need to decide which to install, and when buying a PC with Windows 7 pre-installed you'll only get one or the other. Unlike switching editions, there's no easy way to move between 32- and 64-bit later.

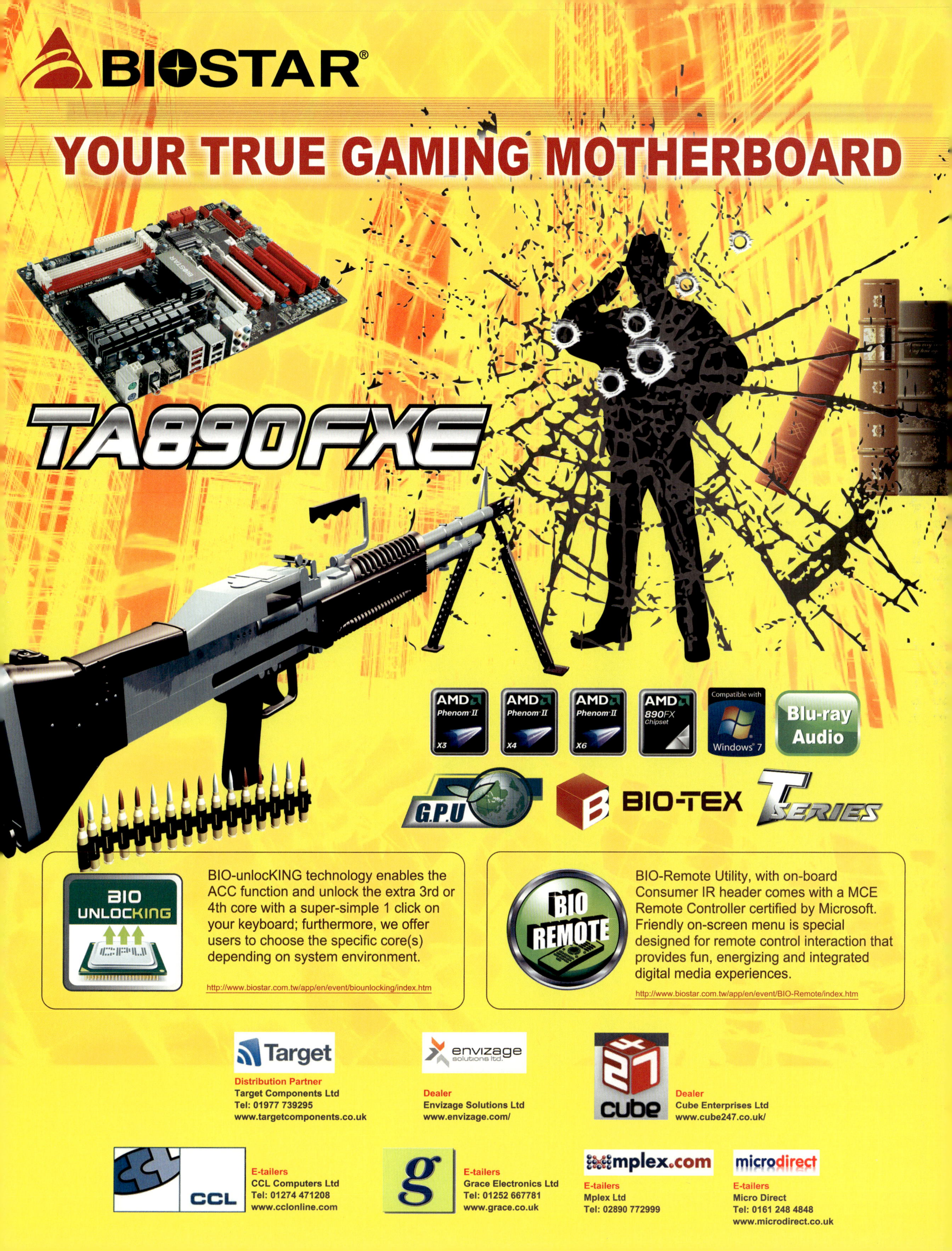
BIOSTAR®
YOUR TRUE GAMING MOTHERBOARD
TA890FXE
AMD Phenom II X3
AMD Phenom II X4
AMD Phenom II X6
AMD 890FX Chipset
Compatible with Windows 7
Blu-ray Audio
G.P.U
BIO-TEX
T SERIES
BIO UNLOCKING
BIO-unlocKING technology enables the ACC function and unlock the extra 3rd or 4th core with a super-simple 1 click on your keyboard; furthermore, we offer users to choose the specific core(s) depending on system environment.
http://www.biostar.com.tw/app/en/event/biounlocking/index.htm
BIO REMOTE
BIO-Remote Utility, with on-board Consumer IR header comes with a MCE Remote Controller certified by Microsoft. Friendly on-screen menu is special designed for remote control interaction that provides fun, energizing and integrated digital media experiences.
http://www.biostar.com.tw/app/en/event/BIO-Remote/index.htm
Target
Distribution Partner
Target Components Ltd
Tel: 01977 739295
www.targetcomponents.co.uk
envizage solutions ltd.
Dealer
Envizage Solutions Ltd
www.envizage.com/
24 7 cube
Dealer
Cube Enterprises Ltd
www.cube247.co.uk/
CCL
E-tailers
CCL Computers Ltd
Tel: 01274 471208
www.cclonline.com
g
E-tailers
Grace Electronics Ltd
Tel: 01252 667781
www.grace.co.uk
mplex.com
E-tailers
Mplex Ltd
Tel: 02890 772999
microdirect
E-tailers
Micro Direct
Tel: 0161 248 4848
www.microdirect.co.uk

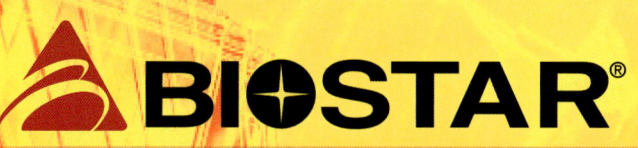

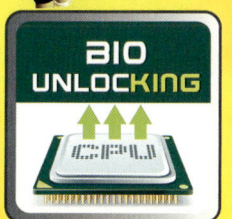

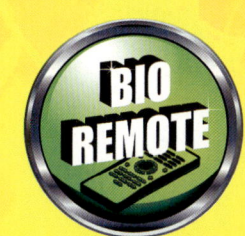

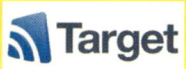

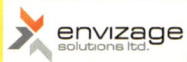

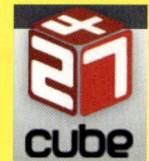

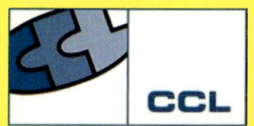

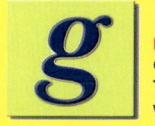

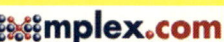

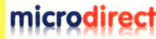

Linux

LINUX HAS A reputation for being tricky to use and something that only those that like to mess around with command lines should even bother with. While to a certain degree this reputation is justified, Linux has come on leaps and bounds in the past few years, and is now arguably just as easy to install as Windows. It's also being used by many companies in mainstream laptops. The current bunch of netbooks, including Asus's Eee PC and Acer's Aspire One, all run a version of Linux with a simplified menu stuck on top.

Linux, then, can be just as good a choice as Windows. Here we'll examine why you might want to install Linux on your new PC.

OPEN BORDERS

The main benefit of Linux is that it's free. As an open-source product, Linux costs nothing no matter what you use it for. The result has been that different companies have taken Linux and modified it to create their own versions, or distributions (distros), of the operating system.

The downside is that there are lots of different versions to choose from, each with its own slightly different installation routine and slightly different way of working. While this can be confusing, we recommend Ubuntu (*www.ubuntu.com*). This manages to strike a good balance between ease of use and power, and is a popular choice within the Linux community.

A FAMILIAR ENVIRONMENT

If you decide to install Linux, you'll find that you end up with a desktop that doesn't look a million miles away from Windows. In fact, from the

desktop you can select Computer from the Places menu and browse through your files using a Windows Explorer-style file manager. All the familiar drag-and-drop functions are available, and you can even create files and folders in the same way as with Windows. Using Linux from this point of view, therefore, is just as easy as using Windows.

As well as sharing a similar way of managing files, you'll find that Linux also shares a lot of applications with Windows, such as the free OpenOffice office suite and the Firefox web browser. What you may find surprising, though, is that using Ubuntu to install these applications is actually easier than it is with Windows. Using the Add/Remove Programs application you can browse additional software to install from an easy-to-use menu. Ubuntu then automatically downloads any applications you want to install. Try to do that with Windows.

That said, there's no getting away from the fact that your Windows applications won't install on Linux. While you'll be able to find free open-source equivalents for most of your Windows applications, not every type of application will be listed. You may be lucky enough to find an application to download from the web, but there's no standard installation routine for Linux, so installing a new application can sometimes be difficult.

STAYING UP TO DATE

Just as with Windows, Ubuntu is at risk from malicious hackers looking to exploit security vulnerabilities in the operating system. Fortunately, Ubuntu also has its own free updates. A message

DETAILS

Ubuntu Desktop Edition

WEB
www.ubuntu.com

PRICE
Free

GOOD FOR
Budget PC, mid-range PC

MINIMUM REQUIREMENTS
700MHz processor, 384MB RAM, 8GB hard disk space

PROS Free; simple application installation **CONS** Hardware support not as good as in Windows; poor games support

VERDICT
As it's completely free, Ubuntu is an attractive choice where cost is a primary concern. Even where this isn't the case, if you want a PC for the internet and office work, Ubuntu's great.

↑ The Linux desktop is similar to Windows

↑ Installing new applications is incredibly easy

pops up when new updates are ready to be installed. Clicking on it lets you select the updates you want to install, which are then downloaded automatically from the internet and installed on your computer. Ubuntu is therefore just as easy to use and keep updated as Windows is.

HARDWARE COMPATIBILITY

While you'll find that Ubuntu will install flawlessly on most computers, there are times when you'll have hardware that won't work properly as there aren't any drivers for it. Wireless network adaptors are a good example of hardware with which you can have problems. A fair number of hardware manufacturers make Linux drivers available on their websites. What you don't get, though, is a simple installation file to run. Instead, installing drivers can be a real pain. Fortunately, if you search the internet for help, you'll find lots of friendly sites and forums that can talk you through installation.

In general, before choosing to install Linux, you may be best off running Ubuntu from a CD first to see if you like the look and feel of the operating system. If you do decide to use it on your new PC, check that drivers are available for the hardware and peripherals that you'll want to use.

CONFIGURE IT OUT

Finally, although Linux has improved in leaps and bounds, there will be the odd times when it proves to be a bit tricky to deal with. Installing drivers is one such area, but there are other things that are difficult. Trying to troubleshoot problems in Linux can become very difficult, and sometimes there's no choice but to revert to a command line to get

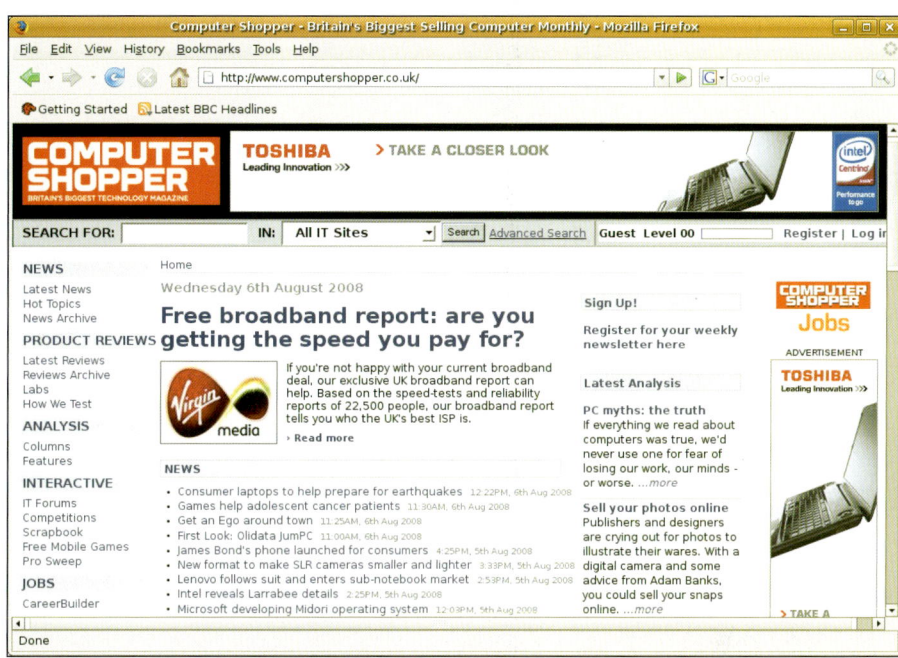

▲ Familiar applications such as Firefox are the same in Linux as in Windows

something done. This shouldn't put you off, however, and if you're interested in tinkering with your new computer and want to learn some new skills, Linux is a good way to go.

CHARMED LIFE

It's hard not to be taken in by Linux's charms, especially as it's free. With Firefox and OpenOffice being so easy to install from within Ubuntu, it's a great choice for a budget or mid-range PC whose primary job is going to be browsing the internet, sending email and using office documents.

If you want a wider choice of applications, have lots of peripherals and other hardware, then Windows works out better. If you're building a higher-end PC, particularly if gaming is a consideration, you should also use Windows.

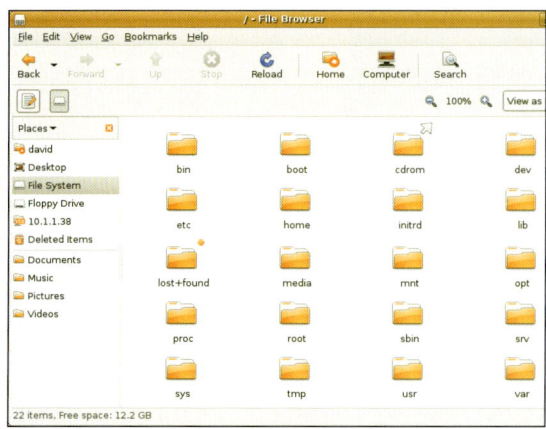

▲ Linux's file browser is similar to Windows Explorer

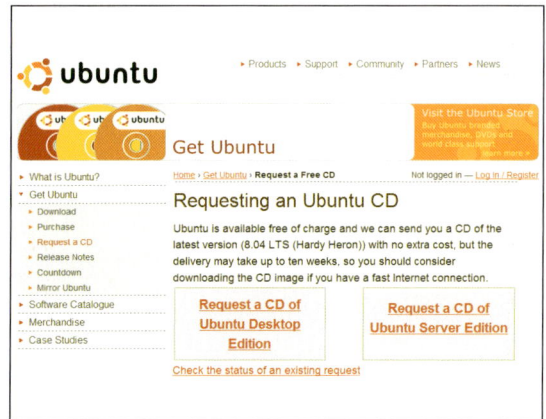

▲ Linux is free, so it's great for a budget PC

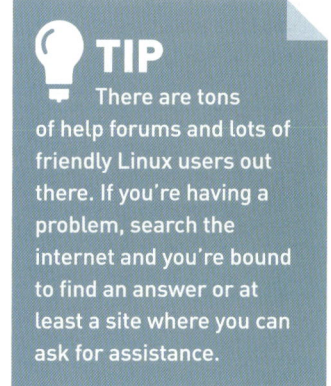

TIP
There are tons of help forums and lots of friendly Linux users out there. If you're having a problem, search the internet and you're bound to find an answer or at least a site where you can ask for assistance.

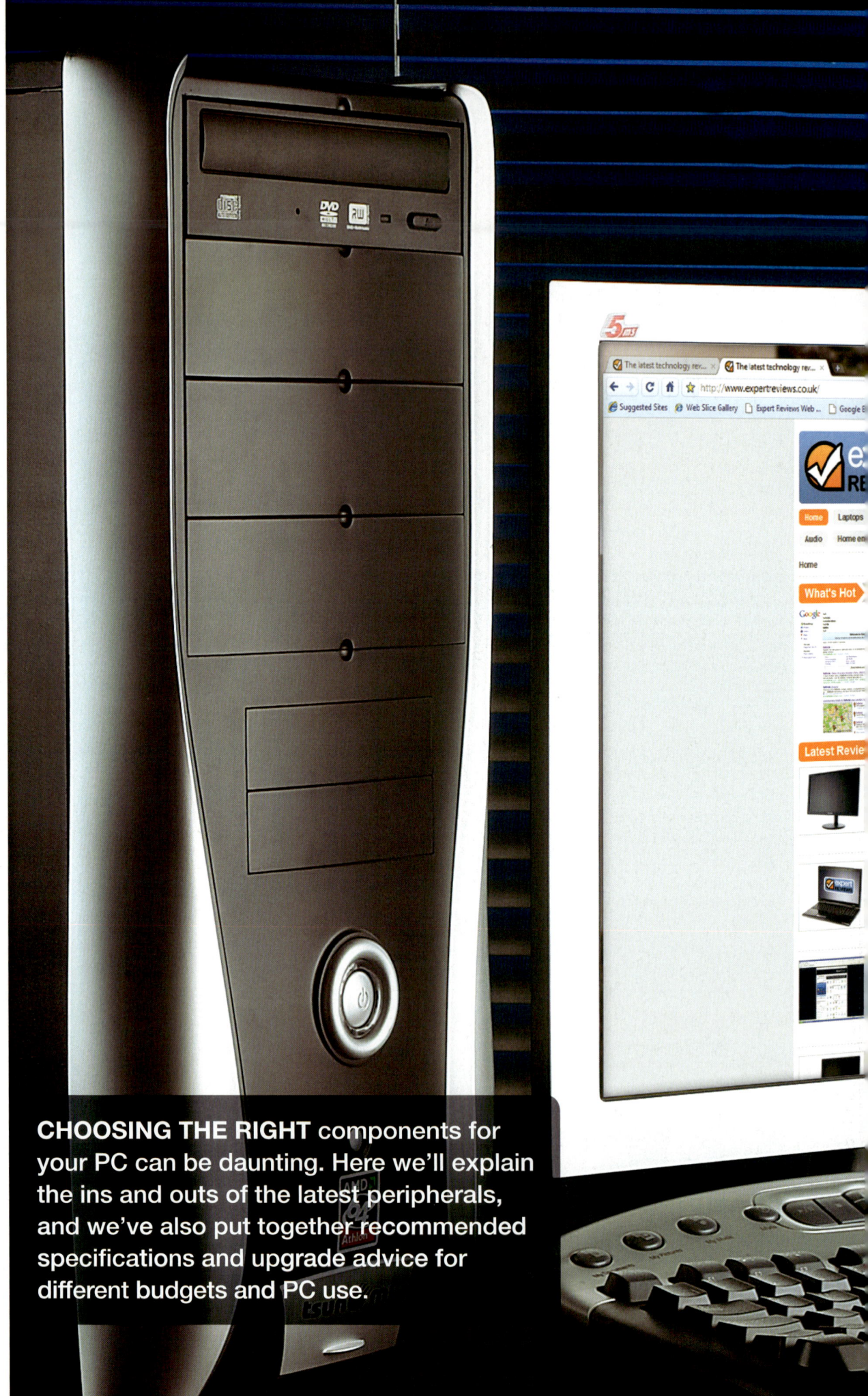

CHAPTER 3
CHOOSING YOUR HARDWARE

CHOOSING THE RIGHT components for your PC can be daunting. Here we'll explain the ins and outs of the latest peripherals, and we've also put together recommended specifications and upgrade advice for different budgets and PC use.

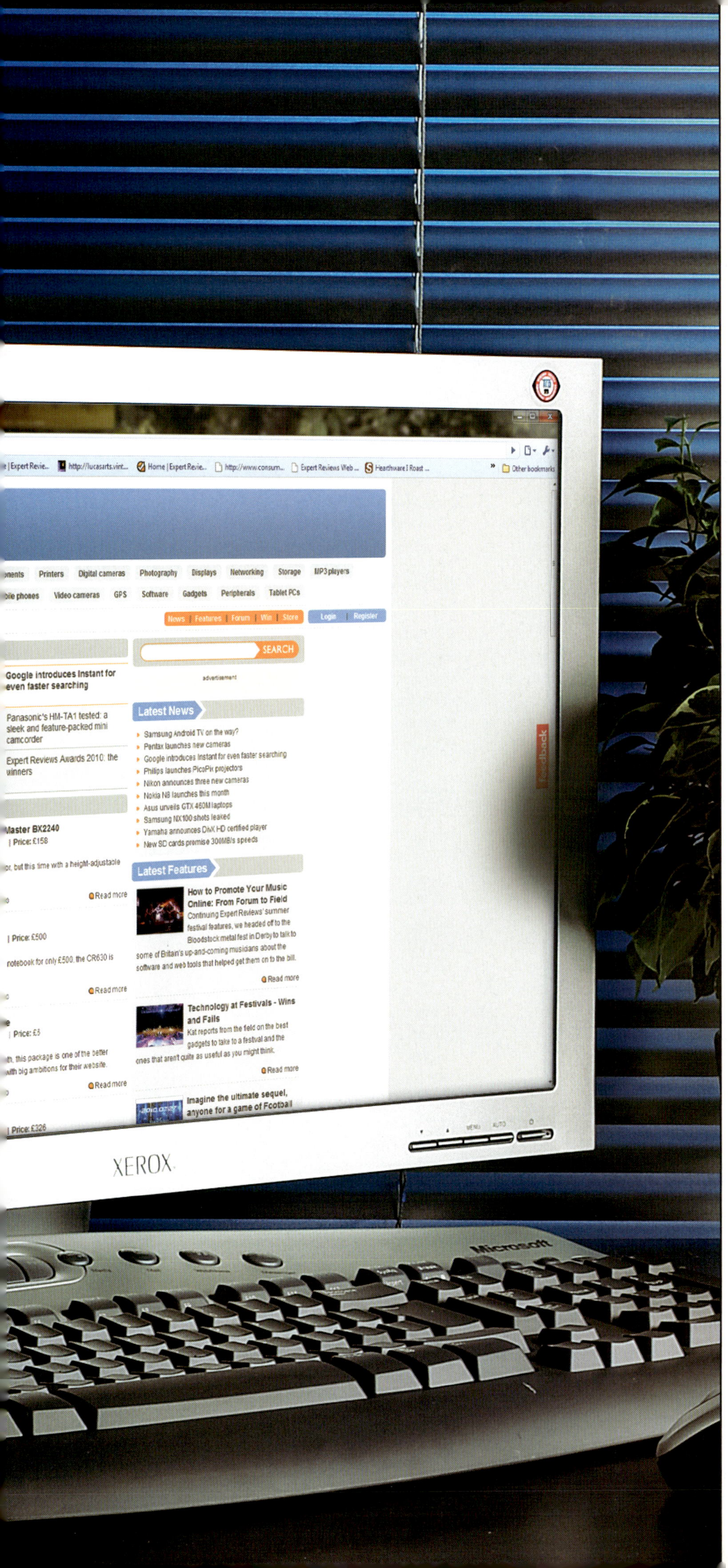

IN THIS CHAPTER

Choosing an AMD processor

AMD'S PROCESSORS CAN'T match Intel's processors for speed at the high end, but for normal computers they strike a great balance between performance and price. Its processors are easier to understand and upgrade, as there are two main types of processor socket to choose from: socket AM2+ and socket AM3.

First, we need to explain processors cores. A core is essentially a processor on a single chip. All modern processors have at least two cores (known as dual-core), so each processor really acts like two processors. This is brilliant for running multiple applications or for applications written to use multiple cores, such as video-editing suites. High-end processors have four cores (quad-core) and are even faster in video-editing applications and at running multiple programs. AMD also has some processors with three cores (tri-core).

SOCKET AM2+
Socket AM2+ processors are common AMD processors, but have mostly been replace by AM3 processors. There's still a vast range from which to choose and all will work in any AM2+ motherboard. They'll also work in older AM2 motherboards, but won't run at full speed because AM2 boards only

support a slower HyperTransport speed (the bus the processor uses to communicate to system devices such as the graphics card). Unfortunately, they won't work in AM3 motherboards because of a new pin configuration of that socket.

They're good value, but choice is limited to the Phenom and Phenom II ranges, which comes in tri- and quad-core models. Currently, the best choice is the Phenom X4 9950 Black Edition (around £92). This processor is incredibly fast and its Black Edition moniker means that it's easy to overclock if you want a free speed boost. If you want lots of power, the Phenom II X4 940 quad-core processor (around £126 including VAT) is a brilliant choice.

SOCKET AM3
Socket AM3 processors give you the widest range of options. These processors can be used in older AM2+ motherboards, which are currently quite cheap, and newer AM3 motherboards. If you buy an AM3 motherboard, you'll also need to buy DDR3 memory, which is a little more expensive than DDR2 memory (see page 31 for more information on different memory types).

The AM3 processor range includes the Phenom II range and Athlon II X2 (which are essentially Phenom processors with two cores) ranges. For a budget computer, we recommend an Athlon II X2 240 (around £44). If you want a bit more power, the Phenom II X2 550 Black Edition (around £80) is hard to beat, and this dual-core processor can also be easily overclocked.

For the best performance going, the Phenom II X4 955 Black Edition processor (around £146 including VAT) is a good choice, but the six-core Phenom II X6 1090T (around £225) is even quicker. This is a great processor for intensive tasks, such as video editing, but may be a bit excessive for a standard desktop computer.

LOW POWER
AMD currently doesn't have any Atom-equivalent processors, so if you want to build a low-power entry-level computer or network storage device, unfortunately you're out of luck.

↘ AMD's quad-core Phenom II X4 processor offers masses of power for around £126 including VAT

Choosing an Intel processor

YOUR CHOICE OF Intel processors is defined by your motherboard's socket type (see page 28 for more information on choosing a motherboard). Choosing the processor is fairly straightforward, and there are three types of socket available: LGA775, LGA1366 and LGA1156. We'll explain each socket type in turn.

Again, it's important to understand processor cores. A core is essentially a processor on a single chip. All modern processors have at least two cores (known as dual-core), so each processor really acts like two processors. This is brilliant for running multiple applications or for applications written to use multiple cores, such as video-editing suites. High-end processors have four cores (quad-core) and are even faster in video-editing applications and at running multiple programs.

LGA775 PROCESSORS

LGA775 processors are slowly being phased out, although they make a good budget choice for some people. Processors that fit into these sockets include the Core 2 Duo, Core 2 Quad, Pentium Dual-Core and Celeron Dual-Core chips.

The most important thing that you need to be aware of is that you'll require a motherboard that supports your processor's external bus speed. Depending on your choice of processor, this will be either 200MHz, 266MHz, 333MHz or, rarely, 400MHz. Confusion can arise because this number is often multiplied by four to give the front-side bus speed (which is used by the processor to communicate with every other component in your PC). You may see motherboards quoted as supporting 800MHz, 1,066MHz, 1,333MHz or 1,600MHz FSB speeds instead.

For a budget computer, we recommend the Pentium Dual-Core E5200 processor, which costs around £46 including VAT. It's powerful, and great value. If you want a bit more power, the Core 2 Duo E7500 processor costs around £82 including VAT.

LGA1366 PROCESSORS

Older Core i7 processors use the LGA1366 socket. These are all quad-core or six-core processors, but a technology called HyperThreading makes the

processor act like an eight-core or 12-core processor. These are the fastest processors you can buy, but you'll pay a high premium. We therefore don't recommend them for most people.

LGA1156 PROCESSORS

The new Core i3, Core i5 and Core i7 processors are based on the LGA1156 socket and are the best choice for most users. One of the best features of these processors is that they'll all work in the same motherboard, making upgrading a doddle.

The Core i5 and i7 processors support TurboBoost, which increases the processor's speed when it's under load, improving performance. The majority of processors use HyperThreading to virtually double the number of cores, while most processors also have graphics chips built in.

For a budget computer, the Core i3-540M (around £101) is the best choice, as it's very quick. The Core i5-750 is a true quad-core processor and gives incredible performance for around £150, but it doesn't have a built-in grapics chip.

For the ultimate in performance, the Core i7-860 (around £222) is a great choice.

ATOM PROCESSORS

Finally, Intel's Atom processors are low-powered models and perfect for entry-level computers or for network storage. The Intel Desktop Board D945GCLF2 (around £55 including VAT) is the best choice as it's a motherboard and dual-core Atom 330 processor in one.

↖ The Core i3, i5 and i7 processors provide the ultimate in power

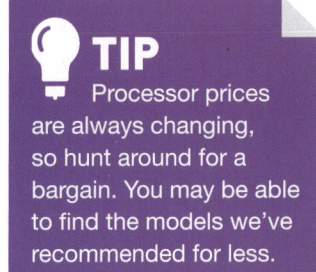

TIP
Processor prices are always changing, so hunt around for a bargain. You may be able to find the models we've recommended for less.

Choosing a Motherboard

THE MOTHERBOARD IS arguably the most important part of your computer, as it defines which processor, memory, graphics card and other components you can install.

SOCKET TO 'EM
The first choice is the socket type, as this defines which processors you can fit. For Intel Pentium Dual-Core, Celeron Dual-Core and Core 2 processors, you need a motherboard with an LGA775 socket. Motherboards with Intel's P43 or P45 chipset are a good choice, and there are also 'G' variants that have onboard graphics.

For the Core i3, Core i5 and Core i7 processors, you need a motherboard with the LGA1156 socket. Currently Intel's H55 chipset is the best, as it supports these processors' on-board graphics. For older Core i7 chips, you need an LGA1366 socket. Intel's X58 chipset is currently the best choice.

For AMD processors an AM2+ motherboard can take every current AM2+ or AM3 processor. However, some will require a BIOS update to work with the latest processors. This can be tricky, as you'll need a processor that will work with the motherboard to perform the upgrade. Our advice is to check the manufacturer's website to see if a BIOS upgrade is necessary to install your chosen processor; if it is, you can either choose a different model or ask your supplier to upgrade it for you.

AMD's AM3 motherboards can only take AM3 processors, but will have the maximum upgrade potential in the long run and are the best choice. The only downside to these boards is that they require DDR3 memory, which is a little more expensive than DDR2. For either motherboard, AMD's 790 or 785 chipsets are great choices.

SIZE MATTERS
Motherboards come in two common sizes: ATX and microATX. ATX motherboards measure a maximum of 305x244mm and will fit in ATX cases only. MicroATX motherboards measure a maximum of 244x244mm and will fit in ATX and microATX cases. The main difference between the two types is that microATX motherboards have fewer expansion ports. Mini-ITX motherboards are designed for tiny cases, although the

⬆ Make sure your chosen motherboard has enough spare ports

motherboards will also fit in most standard cases. Intel's destop Atom processors typically use Mini-ITX motherboards.

EXPANDING OPTIONS
Make sure that the motherboard you choose has enough SATA ports for hard disks, IDE ports for optical drives, and PCI and PCI-E slots for any additional expansion cards that you want to install, such as a TV tuner.

Look for onboard graphics if you want to save money and aren't interested in playing games. If you want to play games and want the best-quality output for Blu-ray movies, then you should buy a dedicated graphics card. You'll need a PCI-E x16 slot to fit a dedicated card.

You can also buy motherboards with multiple graphics slots, which are certified for Nvidia's SLI or ATI's CrossFire technologies.

RECOMMENDED CHOICES
If you want an AM2+ motherboard, Gigabyte's GA-M720-US3 (around £56 including VAT) is a good ATX board; Asus's M4A78-HTPC/RC (around £64 including VAT) is a decent AM2+ microATX board. If you want an AM3 motherboard, we recommend Gigabyte's GA-MA785GMT-UD2H (around £69 including VAT).

For Intel systems, Asus's P5QL/EPU (around £54 including VAT) is a good choice for LGA775 processors. For LGA1366, Biostar's TPower i55 (around £110 including VAT) is a great choice. For MicroATX, look at the MSI P55M-GD45 (around £85 incuding VAT).

💡 **TIP**

After choosing your motherboard check the manufacturer's website to see if it needs a BIOS update before you can use your chosen processor; if it does, pick a different motherboard instead, as you may have trouble turning your computer on to perform the update if your processor is not recognised.

THE POWER SUPPLY.

THE POWER SUPPLY OF THE GOLD CLASS.

Modu87+ and Pro87+ are the ideal choice for the most popular 500 to 900 wattage PSU range: The bar-raising DHT topology allows for a peak efficiency of 93%, giving 80 PLUS® Gold certification. Up to four massive 12V rails for maximum safety and most stable voltage. Thanks to the innovative RPM control SpeedGuard and the patented Twister bearing, Modu87+ and Pro87+ are virtually silent during operation.

With 5 year manufacturer warranty

Website **www.the-power-supply.com** • E-Mail **support@enermax.de**

Supplier **awd-it.com** • **scan.co.uk** • **specialtech.co.uk** • **yoyotech.co.uk**

Because you can never have too much
performance.

WD® high-performance hard drives put you ahead of the game.

Our ultra-fast internal hard drives can certainly handle the demands of today's fast-paced graphic-intensive PC games. WD Caviar® Black™ offers PC enthusiasts cutting-edge performance, 7200 RPM spin speeds and best-in-class benchmarks. For gamers on the go, WD Scorpio® Black™ mobile drives deliver 7200 RPM performance critical for high-end gaming—without compromising battery life—in a smaller 2.5-inch form factor. And for the ultimate in gaming performance, there's the 10,000 RPM WD VelociRaptor®, the fastest SATA hard drive on the planet.

PUT YOUR LIFE ON IT®

Choosing Memory

MEMORY IS one of the most important components in your computer. The more you have, the better Windows will run, as it can keep all its data and applications in system memory; when Windows starts to run out of physical memory it begins using the hard disk as virtual memory, which is incredibly slow.

It's not quite as easy as buying the right type of memory and plugging it in, though, as you need to consider how much RAM you want and the configuration of it. Here, we'll explain your options.

MEMORY TYPE

The first thing you need to know is the type of memory that your computer needs, which will be dictated by the slots in your motherboard. Memory will be either DDR2 or DDR3: the types aren't interchangeable, so you need to make sure you buy the right one. You motherboard's manual and its manufacturer's website will let you know which memory you need to install.

A further clue is that Intel Core I3, i5 and i7 and AMD AM3 motherboards all require DDR3 memory. Intel Core 2, Pentium Dual-Core and Celeron Dual-Core, and AMD AM2 motherboards all require DDR2 memory.

SPEED DEMONS

It's not just a simple case of buying the right type of memory, but also getting the right speed. We'll look at DDR2 memory first. This comes in speeds of PC2-6400 (800MHz) and PC2-8500 (1,066MHz). For Intel systems, you need to buy the memory that is the closest match to the processor's front side bus (FSB) speed. You can fit PC2-8500 RAM in a system with an 800MHz FSB, but it will simply run a bit slower. For AMD systems that require DDR2 memory, you can fit PC2-8500 memory. You can expect to pay around £25 including VAT for 2GB of PC2-8500 RAM.

For computers that require DDR3 memory, there's a choice of PC3-6400 (800MHz), PC3-8500 (1,066MHz), PC3-10600 (1,333MHz) and PC3-12800 (1,600MHz). PC3-10600 memory is currently the best value and will work with all DDR3

processors. You can expect to pay around £37 including VAT for 2GB of this memory.

MEMORY BANK

Once you know which type of memory you need, you can choose how much RAM you want to install. We recommend a minimum of 2GB, but you should get more for better performance. Remember, there's a limit on the memory you can install. This is both set by the motherboard (check its specifications carefully) and by Windows.

If you have a 32-bit edition of Windows, it can only access around 3.5GB of memory (fit 4GB maximum); 64-bit versions of Windows have no practical limit, so you can fit more. That said, 4GB should be enough for most people.

CONFIGURATION

All modern motherboards and processors support at least dual-channel memory. This works by sending memory data over two channels, and thus increases performance. For this to work, you have to install memory in even numbers of modules: so, for a dual channel system with 2GB, you'd need two 1GB modules.

LGA1366 Core i7 processors use triple-channel memory, so you need to install memory in multiples of three. Most memory manufacturers will sell packs of memory with the required number of modules.

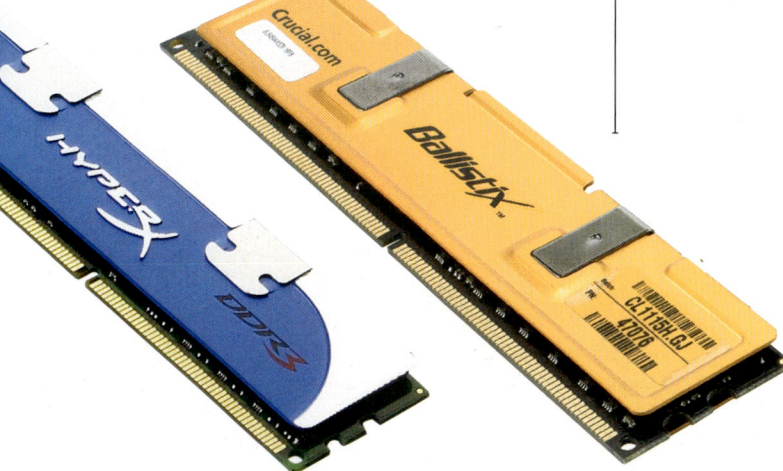

↑ Make sure you get the right memory for your chosen motherboard

Choosing a
Graphics card

MANY MOTHERBOARDS HAVE built-in graphics, but these deliver only basic games performance. For something a little more, you need a dedicated graphics card.

SIZE AND FEATURES

If you're building a media centre PC, a graphics card can be used to decode Blu-ray movies, leaving the processor free for other jobs. The chances are that you'll have a tiny case that accepts only a low-profile graphics card. There aren't many of these available; Sapphire's Radeon HD 5450 (around £32 including VAT) is the best choice.

The other factor you'll need to consider is how many slots a card takes up. The most powerful cards take up two expansion slots, so you can only fit them in large cases.

All modern graphics cards support HDCP, so you can plug them into an HD TV and watch Blu-ray movies. To do this you'll probably need a DVI-to-HDMI adaptor. For ATI cards you need to use the official ATI adaptor, or sound won't be transmitted over the connection. To make sure you get the necessary adaptor and cables, buy the full version of any card you want, not the OEM editions.

All modern graphics cards (ATI 5000 series and Nvidia 400 series) support PAP, so you can send Full HD Blu-ray sound to a compatible amplifier.

Finally, the most powerful modern graphics cards require an eight-pin PCI Express connector on your power supply.

↑ For the best games performance, you'll need a dedicated graphics card

RECOMMENDED CHOICES

For general high-performance gaming, the Sapphire Radeon HD 5770 (around £131 including VAT), is the best choice. For the next step up, the Zotac GeForce GTX 460 768MB card is a great choice at around £158. It's relatively short and cool for a modern graphics card, making it good for a smaller case.If you want no-holds-barred performance, Sapphire's Radeon HD 5850 (around £225 including VAT) is a fantastic choice.

Choosing a
Power supply

YOUR POWER SUPPLY brings your PC to life and ensures that there's enough power going to each component. Cheap power supplies are available, but in our experience they're unreliable, can break easily and often deliver unstable voltages that can crash a computer. Pick branded, more expensive models and it will save you money in the long run.

POWER UP

Your main choice when picking a power supply is getting one with the right power output, which is measured in Watts. For a basic entry-level PC, look for a 500W supply; for a mid-range or high-end PC, you'll need a 650W supply. For very powerful computers with lots of hard disks and powerful graphics cards, you should buy an 800W supply or higher.

The other thing to consider with power supplies is the number of power connectors that they have. Make sure that the supply you choose has enough SATA and Molex connectors for your computer.

Check that the supply supports your chosen graphics card; powerful modern graphics cards have eight-pin PCI Express connectors, and your power supply must have the matching connector for this to work. If you want to use ATI's CrossFire or Nvidia's SLI, look for a supply with multiple six- and eight-pin PCI Express connectors.

RECOMMENDED CHOICES

OCZ's ModXstream Pro 500W (around £52 including VAT) is a good entry-level

↑ Make sure your power supply has the right connectors for your PC

power supply. For a more powerful computer, try Be Quiet!'s 650W DarkPower Pro (around £104 including VAT). For very powerful computers, FSP's 1,200W Everest Pro (around £207 including VAT) is a great choice.

Choosing a
Hard disk

YOUR HARD DISK stores your operating system, applications and all your data. Getting the right model is therefore incredibly important. The choice should be fairly simple, but here we'll explain what features to look out for.

FULL CAPACITY
All modern hard disks and computers use SATA interfaces. This makes your choice infinitely easier. Your primary consideration when buying a hard disk is to get a drive with the highest capacity that you can afford. However, small and extremely large hard disks usually cost more per gigabyte, so aren't especially good value. Unless you're on a particularly tight budget, it's worth

spending a few pounds more to get a larger, better-value disk.

Finally, if you're planning to use RAID – where you use multiple hard disks to create one virtual disk with better performance, data protection or both – you should buy identical drives.

RECOMMENDED CHOICES
Hard disks have fallen a lot in price recently, so large disks are comparatively cheap. The smallest hard disk we would recommend is Seagate's 500GB Barracuda 7200.12, which costs around £37 including VAT; a 160GB hard disk will cost only a few pounds less and isn't worth it. For more capacity, Samsung's

↑ When choosing a hard disk, look for the highest capacity you can afford

750GB F1 DT (around £54 including VAT) or Seagate's 1TB Barracuda 7200.12 (around £60 including VAT) are good value.

If you think you'll need lots of storage space, Seagate's 1.5TB Barracuda 7200.11 (around £90 including VAT) is an excellent choice.

Choosing a
Case

YOUR CASE DEFINES what your computer looks like, how many components you can fit inside and even the size of motherboard and type of graphics card that you can fit. Making the right choice is therefore incredibly important. Here's what to look out for.

SIZE OF THE PRIZE
The most important factor is the size of motherboard that you can fit. Most cases can take a full-sized ATX motherboard (see page 28 for more information). However, some cases can accept only microATX motherboards, while some specialist cases are designed for tiny Mini-ITX motherboards.

Larger cases can take smaller types of motherboard, but not the other way round, so make sure that you buy a case big enough for your motherboard.

COMPONENTS
Another thing you'll need to consider when choosing a case is the number of components that you can fit inside. Look for a case that has enough 3½in drive bays for hard disks and enough 5¼in drive bays for optical drives.

The size of the case can also play an important part in deciding which expansion cards you can fit: media centre cases often have only enough room for low-profile graphics cards, which aren't very common.

RECOMMENDED CHOICES
More expensive cases are generally quieter, better looking and also easier to build. Choose a decent-quality case and you'll be happy, but pick a cheap and nasty model and it could ruin your new build.

↑ Good-quality cases are quieter and better-looking than cheap models

Akasa's Zen AK0ZEN-01 BK (around £35 including VAT) is a good choice for a budget computer. For something a bit sturdier, Antec's mini P180 (around £65 including VAT) is a great choice. For a high-end computer, Antec's P182 (around £104 including VAT) is excellent. For a media centre PC, try ThermalsTake's Xaser Bach (around £120 including VAT).

BUDGET PC

This budget computer will be good enough for basic computing tasks, such as photo editing and surfing the web. You can add a faster processor, install Windows 7 and add a better graphics card if you want a better PC.

SHOPPING LIST
Recommended minimum specifications

PROCESSOR
| Intel Pentium Dual-Core E5200 | £46 |
| (AMD Athlon II X2 240 | £44) |

MOTHERBOARD
| Intel: Gigabyte GA-G31M-ES2L | £35 |
| (AMD: Asus M2N68-AM Plus | £36) |

CASE
| Akasa Zen AK-ZEN-01 BK | £40 |

HARD DISK
| 500GB Seagate Barracuda 7200.12 | £30 |

MEMORY
| 2GB Corsair Value Select DDR2 PC2-5300 | £35 |

OPTICAL DRIVE
| Samsung Super-WriteMaster SH-S202J | £14 |

OPERATING SYSTEM
| Ubuntu Linux 9.04 | Free |

POWER SUPPLY
| OCZ ModXStream Pro 500W | £60 |

- -
| **TOTAL** | **£260** |

SHOPPING LIST
Recommended minimum specifications

PROCESSOR
| Intel Core i3 540 | £101 |
| (AMD Phenom II X2 550 Black Edition | £80) |

MOTHERBOARD
| Intel: Biostar TPower i55 | £110 |
| (AMD: Gigabyte GA-MA785GMT-UD2H | £69) |

CASE
| Antec Mini P180 | £58 |

HARD DISK
| 750GB Samsung F1 DT | £42 |

MEMORY
| 4GB Corsair TwinX XMS3 DDR3 PC3-10666 | £83 |

OPTICAL DRIVE
| Samsung Super-WriteMaster SH-S202J | £14 |

OPERATING SYSTEM
| Windows 7 Home Premium | £70 |

GRAPHICS CARD
| Sapphire Radeon HD 5770 | £131 |

POWER SUPPLY
| Be Quiet! DarkPower Pro 750W | £128 |

- -
| **TOTAL** | **£737** |

MID-RANGE PC

This powerful computer will be able to cope with any application and its dedicated graphics card means that it can also play games. Look for a bigger hard disk and quad-core processor if you want more from your PC.

HIGH-END PC

This is a stunning PC that will be more than good enough for any job. There's little need to upgrade here, but a larger hard disk and faster graphics card could boost performance.

SHOPPING LIST
Recommended minimum specifications

PROCESSOR	
Intel Core i5 750	£150
(AMD Phenom II X4 955 Black Edition	£146)
MOTHERBOARD	
Intel: Biostar TPower i55	£110
(AMD: Gigabyte GA-MA785GMT-UD2H	£69)
CASE	
Antec P183	£105
HARD DISK	
1TB Seagate Barracuda 7200.12	£48
MEMORY	
4GB Corsair TwinX XMS3 DDR3 PC3-10666	£83
OPTICAL DRIVE	
LG GGC H20L	£76
OPERATING SYSTEM	
Windows 7 Home Premium	£70
GRAPHICS CARD	
Sapphire Radeon HD 5850	£225
POWER SUPPLY	
Be Quiet! DarkPower Pro 750W	£128
TOTAL	**£756**

EXTREME PC

This PC is incredibly fast, but you're paying a lot of money for it. The graphics card will deliver the best games performance. If you want an even faster computer, look to buy an Intel Core i7 Extreme Edition processor.

SHOPPING LIST
Recommended minimum specifications

PROCESSOR	
Intel Core i7 860	£220
(AMD Phenom II X4 955 Black Edition	£146)
MOTHERBOARD	
Intel: Biostar TPower i55	£110
(AMD: Gigabyte GA-MA785GMT-UD2H	£69)
CASE	
Antec P193	£126
HARD DISK	
1.5TB Seagate Barracuda 7200.12	£70
MEMORY	
4GB Corsair TwinX XMS3 DDR3 PC3-10666	£83
OPTICAL DRIVE	
LG GGW H20L	£140
OPERATING SYSTEM	
Windows 7 Ultimate	£120
GRAPHICS CARD	
Sapphire Radeon HD 5870	£320
POWER SUPPLY	
FSP Everest Pro 1200W	£173
TOTAL	**£1,362**

MEDIA CENTRE PC

This system will give you plenty of disk space for digital TV recording, and the optical drive is capable of playing Blu-ray films. Arcsoft's TotalMedia Theatre 3 Blu-ray playback software costs around £70.

SHOPPING LIST
Recommended minimum specifications

PROCESSOR	
Intel Pentium Dual-Core E5200	£46
(AMD Phenom II X2 550 Black Edition	£80)
MOTHERBOARD	
Intel: Gigabyte GA-G31M-ES2L	£35
(AMD: Asus M2N68-AM Plus	£36)
CASE	
ThermalTake Bach Media Lab	£120
HARD DISK	
1.5TB Seagate Barracuda 7200.11	£140
MEMORY	
4GB Corsair TwinX DDR2 XMS2 PC2-8500	£115
OPTICAL DRIVE	
LG GGC H20L	£76
OPERATING SYSTEM	
Windows 7 Home Premium	£70
OTHER	
Hauppauge WinTV Nova TD500 dual digital tuner	£55
GRAPHICS CARD	
Sapphire Radeon HD 5450	£32
POWER SUPPLY	
OCZ ModXStream Pro 500W	£60
TOTAL	**£749**

MINI PC

This small PC won't take up much room on your desk, but it'll be powerful enough for most tasks. The PCI-E x16 slot is quite short, so you may find that it's hard to fit a dedicated graphics card for games.

SHOPPING LIST
Recommended minimum specifications

PROCESSOR	
Intel Core i3 540	£101
(AMD Phenom II X2 550 Black Edition	£80)
MOTHERBOARD	
Intel: Biostar TPower i55	£110
(AMD: Gigabyte GA-MA785GMT-UD2H	£69)
CASE	
Antec Minuet 350 (includes 350W PSU)	£80
HARD DISK	
500GB Seagate Barracuda 7200.12	£30
MEMORY	
4GB Corsair TwinX XMS3 DDR3 PC3-10666	£83
OPTICAL DRIVE	
Samsung Super-WriteMaster SH-S202J	£14
OPERATING SYSTEM	
Windows 7 Home Premium	£70
TOTAL	**£488**

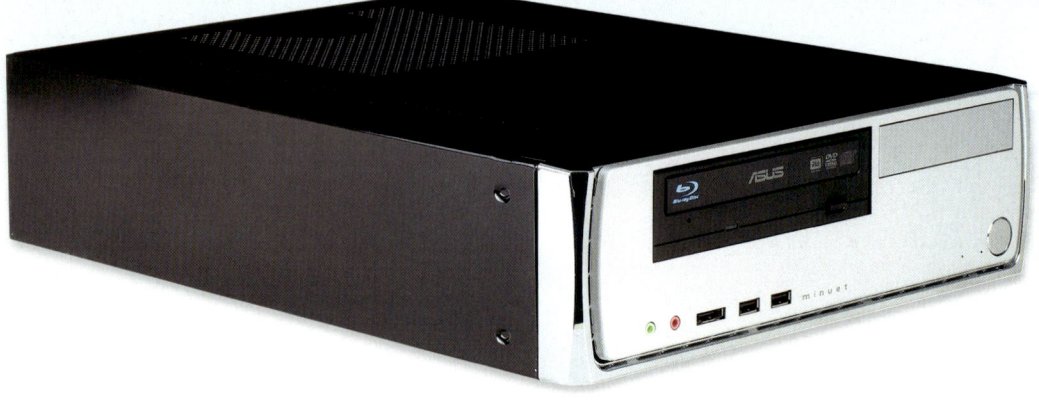

LOW-POWER PC

This tiny and cheap computer is absolutely great value. It'll cope with everyday tasks well and its low-power processor and integrated graphics chip means it'll cost very little to run. Look at one of the other PCs here for better performance.

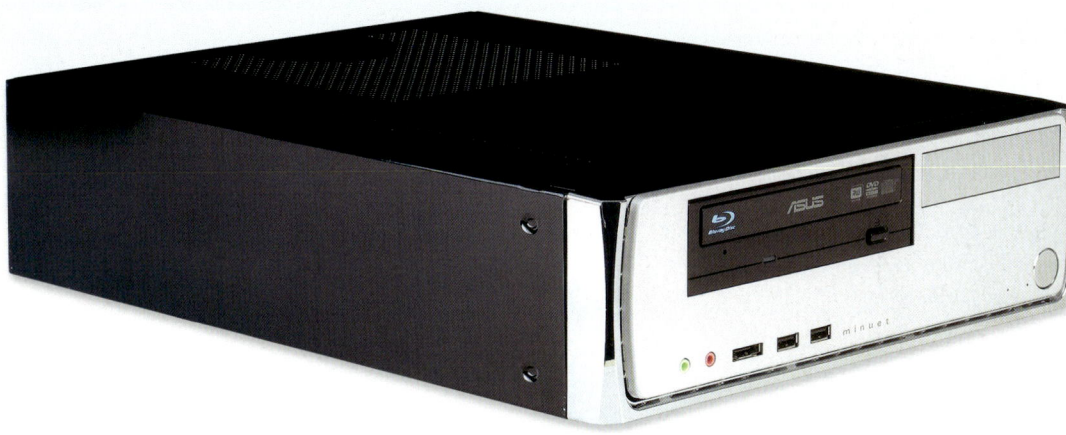

SHOPPING LIST
Recommended minimum specifications

MOTHERBOARD	
Intel Desktop Board D945GCLF2 (includes Atom 330 processor)	£65
CASE	
Antec Minuet 350 (includes 350W PSU)	£80
HARD DISK	
500GB Seagate Barracuda 7200.12	£30
MEMORY	
2GB Corsair Value Select DDR2 PC2-5300	£35
OPTICAL DRIVE	
Samsung Super-WriteMaster SH-S202J	£14
OPERATING SYSTEM	
Linux	Free
TOTAL	**£224**

HOME STORAGE

SHOPPING LIST
Recommended minimum specifications

MOTHERBOARD	
Intel Desktop Board D945GCLF2 (includes Atom 330 processor)	£65
CASE	
Akasa Zen AK-ZEN-01 BK	£40
HARD DISK	
2x 1.5TB Seagate Barracuda 7200.11	£140
MEMORY	
2GB Corsair Value Select DDR2 PC2-5300	£35
OPTICAL DRIVE	
Samsung Super-WriteMaster SH-S202J	£14
OPERATING SYSTEM	
FreeNAS	Free
POWER SUPPLY	
OCZ ModXStream Pro 500W	£60
TOTAL	**£354**

The case may not be as small as a NAS, but this low-power computer will be perfect for sharing files over your network. The motherboard has only two SATA ports, so you'll need to add a SATA card if you want more hard disks.

Essential peripherals

ALTHOUGH GETTING THE base specifications for your PC and choosing the right operating system is incredibly important, you should also start thinking about the other peripherals you want to use. If you're sitting in front of your computer all day, buying a decent monitor and a comfortable keyboard and mouse is incredibly important. Don't scrimp and save on the extra peripherals, as you'll end up not enjoying using your new PC. Here, we'll talk you through the options that are available to you.

MONITORS

The monitor is your window into your computer. When you use your PC, it's this display that you'll be staring at all the time. Getting one that produces a decent image and fits your needs is, therefore, incredibly important.

If you haven't bought a monitor for a while, you'll be surprised at the increased choice available. For starters, regular 'square' monitors are pretty much a thing of the past, and have been replaced by widescreen monitors. These make watching films more pleasant and make working with things such as large spreadsheets much easier. With wider resolutions than standard monitors, things such as Windows Vista's Sidebar fit more comfortably on the screen and still leave plenty of rooms for documents.

Widescreen monitors, like standard displays before them, come in a range of different sizes and resolutions. At the bottom of the pile are budget 17in and 19in models, which have a 1,440x900 resolution. These typically start at less than £100. However, in our eyes they're not worth it. Instead, 22in monitors, such as BenQ's G2220HD, are larger and easier on the eye than 19in models and cost only a little more from around £130. The main benefit, however, is that most models have a resolution of 1,920x1,280, so you get a lot more information onscreen, and can watch Full HD video. If you'd like something a little bigger, 24in models such as Samsung's 2494HM have the same resolution and cost around £200.

If you want to take the next step up, you'll need a 26in monitor, such as LG's W2600H-PE. These have a resolution of 1,920x1,200, so are capable of displaying full 1080p HD video. For standard Windows use, this large desktop is a pleasure to use.

↗ A 22in widescreen monitor is a great choice for a new PC, and can be picked up relatively cheaply

If money's no object, you can opt for an even bigger screen with an even larger resolution. Dell's 3008WFP is a massive 30in monitor with an incredible 2,560x1,600 resolution, although at £1,033 it's also incredibly expensive.

When choosing a suitable monitor, it's worth being able to decipher the specifications to make sure you get one suitable for your needs. The viewing angles (horizontal and vertical) describe how far from straight on you can get before the picture deteriorates. Higher viewing angles are better, particularly if you want to use your monitor to show films to more than one person.

The brightness of a monitor is measured in candela per square metre (cd/m^2). The higher the number, the brighter the picture, so the easier your monitor will be to see. Brightness levels from $300cd/m^2$ should be chosen.

The contrast ratio of a monitor tells you the difference between the darkest shade (black) and the lightest shade (white) that the monitor can produce. Many modern monitors use dynamic contrast ratios, where the backlight is dimmed to increase the range of shades that can be produced. Typically, a monitor with a contrast ratio of 1,000:1 or higher should be able to produce dark blacks and bright whites.

The final specification that you'll come across is the response time. This measures how long it

TIP
If your PC has two graphics outputs – most graphics cards do – you can run two monitors together and split the Windows desktop over both.

takes the monitor to change a pixel from black to white and back to black, although some manufacturers 'cheat' and quote a grey-to-grey time. High response times imply that the picture will take a long time to change, so fast-moving action, as in games, could end up with ghosting and smearing. In our extensive tests we've noticed that as long as a monitor has a response time of 25ms or lower, you won't get any problems. Don't get drawn into paying more money for a monitor just because it has an incredibly quick advertised response time.

The only other option to consider is the type of inputs you want on your monitor. If the PC you're building has a digital DVI output, look for a monitor with a matching input. This will give you the best-quality picture. If you want to watch HD movies, then look for a monitor with an HDMI connection or HDCP support on its DVI input. If your PC only has an analogue D-sub output, you'll need a monitor with one of these. Most monitors that support DVI also have an D-sub input, too. If you want to connect a games console or regular DVD player, you'll need a monitor with SCART, S-video, composite or S-video inputs. These are a lot rarer, though.

↖ The Desktop Wave's curved keyboard fits perfectly under your hands and makes typing easier

KEYBOARDS AND MICE

The keyboard and mouse remain the main way that we interact with our computers. Buying the right set is crucial if you want to make your computer easy to use. The most cost-effective way to buy a new keyboard and mouse is to get a set that includes both.

Most sets will include wireless peripherals. These are reliable and generally have long battery lives. With no cables to clutter up your desk, we highly recommend these products. The main choice you'll have to make is whether you want a regular keyboard or an ergonomic model.

Regular keyboards, such as Logitech's Cordless Desktop LX710 Laser (around £27 including VAT), are easiest for most people to use, as they place the keys in a straight line. For touch-typists, ergonomic keyboards can be better, as the keys are placed more naturally for the typing position. However, we've never got on very well with the full-on ergonomic models with the 'split' in

↑ A 24in monitor has a high resolution, which is perfect for Windows applications and movies

the middle of the board. We've found that Logitech's Cordless Desktop Wave (around £42 including VAT) provides a decent balance between comfort and ergonomic design. It has a slight 'smile' to it and each key is at a slightly different height to match the differences in finger length. It's a great keyboard if you're going to be doing a lot of typing.

Although wireless mice are fine for using Windows, if you play a lot of games a wired mouse is a much better option. This is because they don't have as much lag in them, so each mouse movement is replicated instantly in your game – essential if you want to get that accurate head shot. In this case, we'd recommend buying a dedicated gaming mouse, such as Razer's Death Adder (£40 including VAT).

If you love playing the latest games, you should think about buying a mouse mat, rather than using the surface of your desk. With the right mat, such as the ICEmat 2nd Edition (around £30), you'll get a low-friction surface, so your mouse will glide around effortlessly.

SPEAKERS

To get the best out of your computer, you need to invest in a decent set of speakers. Don't rely on

↗ These surround-sound speakers can connect to your DVD player as well as your PC, making them ideal for use in a home-entertainment setup

those built into your monitor, as they'll never be able to produce the clean balanced sounds of a dedicated set. Fortunately, buying speakers doesn't have to be expensive.

First, work out what kinds of speakers you want. Standard 2.1 sets have two stereo speakers and a sub-woofer, which produces rich, thumping bass. If you primarily use your computer for music or games, then these kinds of speakers will suit your computer. The best set we've reviewed, Logitech's Z-323, costs only £36. For this, you'll get incredibly rich and detailed sound.

Next, you have the choice of surround-sound speakers. These are ideal if you want immersive sound around you when you're watching films and want to enjoy the full soundtrack, for example. Surround-sound speakers typically come in 5.1 or 7.1 speaker configurations, where the .1 is the bass sub-woofer and the 5 and 7 refer to the number of satellite speakers. To be honest, 7.1 sets aren't worth it unless you'll be using your computer in a massive room. Besides, the extra two speakers and cables mean that you're just adding clutter to your home. A 5.1 set will suit most people.

Again, there's a choice of sets to consider. Standard 5.1 PC speakers, such as Logitech's X-540 (around £52), use analogue mini-jack plugs that connect to the sound card's outputs at the

↑ A decent set of 2.1 speakers will produce rich sounds in games and music

rear of your PC. To enjoy surround sound on your DVDs and HD movies, you'll need software capable of decoding the sound to analogue outputs. Windows Media Center will decode Dolby Digital soundtracks, but not DTS; CyberLink's PowerDVD will do all formats, but you'll need to upgrade to the full version from any 'lite' version that came bundled with your optical drive.

Alternatively, buying 5.1 speakers with a built-in decoder, such as Logitech's Z-5500 Digital (around £200), means that you can connect your computer digitally to the speakers and let them do the hard work of decoding. For this to work, you'll need to have an S/PDIF output from your PC. The Z-5500 speakers have optical and coaxial S/PDIF inputs and can decode Dolby Digital and DTS soundtracks. They also have 5.1 channel analogue inputs, so you could still let your PC do the audio decoding. The benefit of this system is that you can also connect your regular DVD player to the speakers, so you can use them for your home cinema setup, too.

TV TUNERS

With Media Center now built into Vista Home Premium and Windows 7, turning your PC into a fully fledged hard disk recorder simply requires you to add a TV tuner. With Media Center's excellent free programme guide, you'll find a PC the easiest hard disk recorder to use. When you make your choice, there are a few things to consider.

First, it's not worth buying an analogue-only tuner. The analogue TV service is being turned off over the next few years, leaving only digital TV. That said, if you can't get a very good reception for digital TV, look to get a hybrid tuner with both digital and analogue capabilities; this way you can use the best signal but still switch over to digital when the time comes.

The best choice for most people is a digital tuner. As Media Center can handle two tuners at once, allowing you to record one channel while watching another, it makes sense to buy a TV card with dual tuners. This doesn't have to be expensive, as Terratec's Cinergy DT USB XS Diversity (£60) shows. This USB tuner plugs into a spare USB port, but you can also get internal tuners that plug into a spare PCI or PCI Express slot for similar money. The Diversity tag means that

the card can use both tuners to improve the quality of your TV reception. However, using it in Diversity mode means you can only watch a single channel, as with a single-receiver TV tuner.

Finally, Freesat now means that you can get HD TV for free, and some cards give you this ability on your PC. To use the service, you'll need a satellite dish, such as those provided by Sky. The downside to Freesat at the moment is that Vista Media Center doesn't currently support the service, so you'll have to use the software bundled with the card. Fortunately, Windows 7 supports it, so use this OS if you want Freesat.

↑ A dual tuner allows you to watch one TV channel while recording another

CHAPTER 4

BUILDING YOUR PC

THE MAIN TASK you have when building a PC is making sure that you put all the components together correctly so that your new computer works first time. Our detailed step-by-step advice will help you put any PC together from start to finish.

Taking the case apart

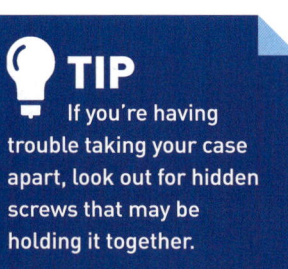
REMOVE THE FRONT Many cases require you to remove the front panel. Some simply lift off, but check for screws and clips inside.

SCREWS Most cases are held together by screws that need to be removed. Thumbscrews such as these can be undone without a screwdriver.

HOW TO...
Take the case apart

1 REMOVE THE SIDES
Start by taking off the side panels to get inside the case. As noted on the diagram opposite, you may need to take the front panel off first to get at the screws to remove the side panels. Some cases, like the one pictured, have thumbscrews, so you don't even need a screwdriver. If your case has a second panel, make sure that you remove this, too, so that you can work on both sides of the case when you're inside it.

2 TAKE OUT INNARDS
Once you're inside your case, you need to check it for accessories. It's common for manufacturers to put spare screws, proprietary drive rails and instruction manuals inside. Take out everything that isn't screwed into place. Look for silica gel taped to the side as well. Remove any packaging so that you're left with a bare interior.

3 REMOVE OPTICAL DRIVE BLANKING PLATES
In order to fit your optical drive later, you may need to remove some plastic and metal blanking plates. At this point, if you haven't had to already, it's probably helpful to take the front of the case off. Your case's manual will tell you how to do this, but most cases simply unclip from the inside.

Look for the 5¼in drive bay into which you'll fit your optical drive. Match this up to the front panel. On some cases this will be the top one, which will have a flap to hide the optical drive from view, so you don't have to get a drive the same colour as your case. On other cases, you'll have a plastic blanking plate on the front panel that should unclip.

Inside the case, you'll find a metal blanking plate that you'll need to remove. By gently rocking it backwards and forwards, you should be able to break the connection. Be careful not to cut yourself doing this.

4 REMOVE FLOPPY DRIVE BLANKING PLATES
If you're planning to fit a memory card reader or floppy disk drive, you'll need to follow the same steps you did for the optical drive. Find the 3½in drive bay you want to use and break off the metal blanking plate. Next, pop out the corresponding plastic blanking plate on the front panel.

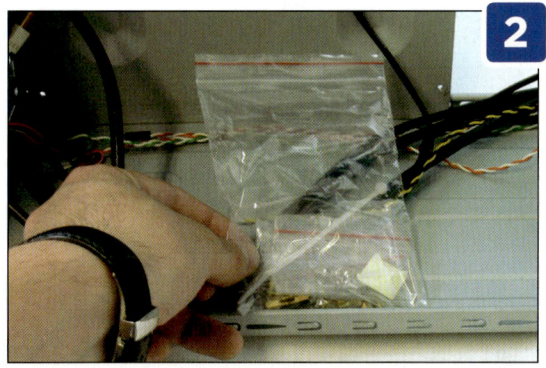

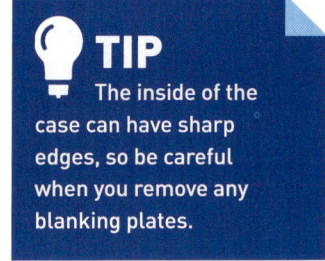

TIP
The inside of the case can have sharp edges, so be careful when you remove any blanking plates.

Installing the power supply

The ATX connector provides power to your motherboard

The SATA connector is for hard disks and optical drives

A standard PCI Express graphics card connector

The newer 8-pin PCI-E power connector

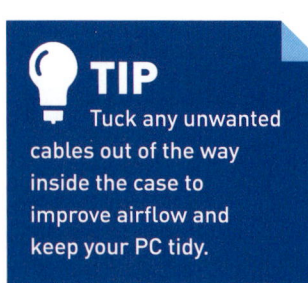

TIP
Tuck any unwanted cables out of the way inside the case to improve airflow and keep your PC tidy.

The secondary motherboard power connector

A connector for floppy disks and memory card readers

The Molex connector is for hard disks

HOW TO...
Install the power supply

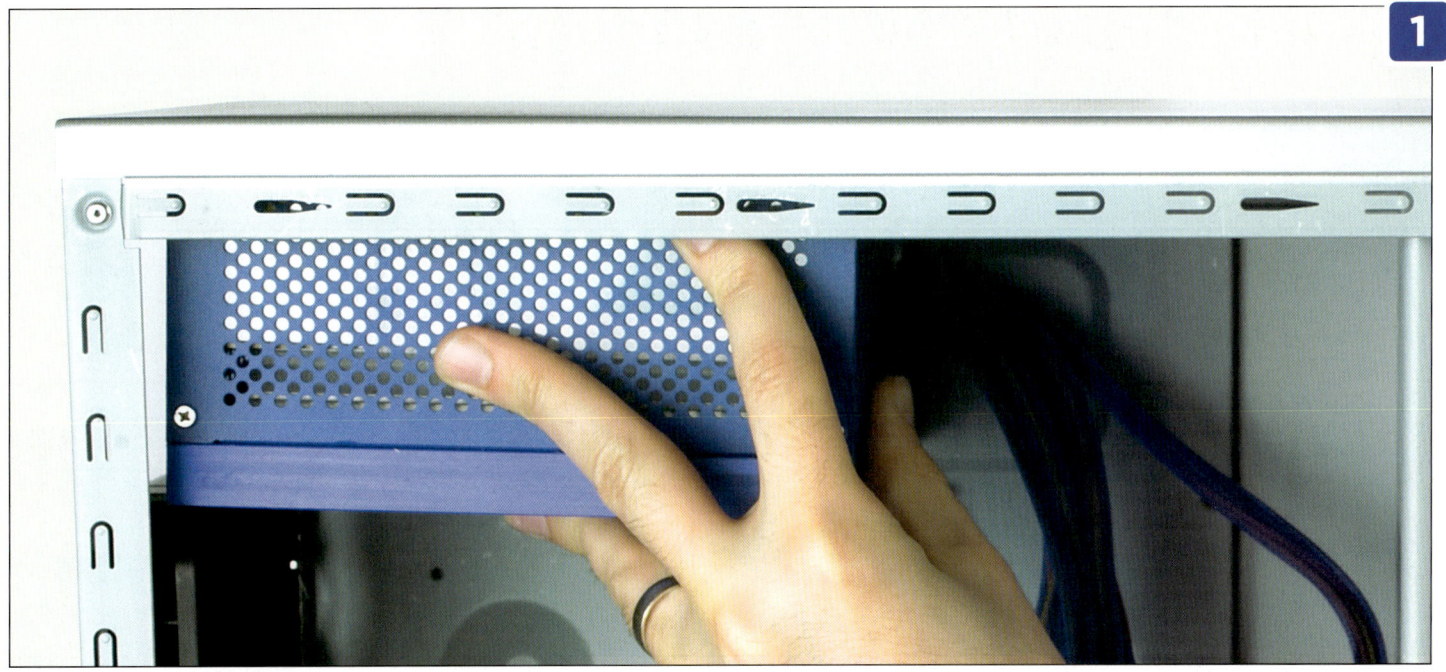

1

1 FIT SUPPLY ON TO SHELF
If your power supply fits at the top of your case (some cases have space at the bottom), you'll see a small shelf for it to rest on. Slide the power supply on to this shelf and push it backwards until it makes contact with the back of the case.

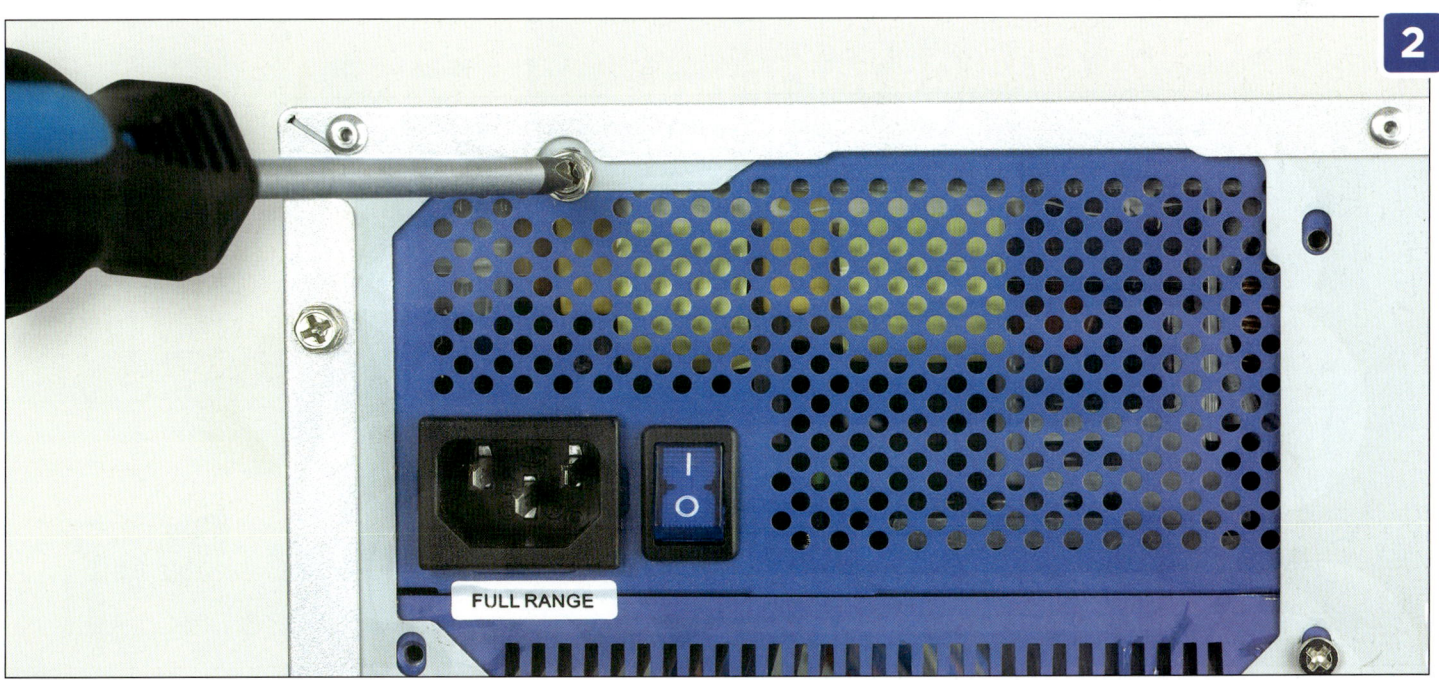

2

FULL RANGE

2 SCREW IN SUPPLY
If your power supply is the correct way round, its screw holes will match up with those in the back of the case. If they don't, remove the supply and rotate it 180°. Use four screws to attach the power supply securely to the case.

No.1 USB 3.0 Motherboard

[A Story about Quality Ⅲ]

GIGABYTE Helps You Quick Charge Your iPhone / iPad / iPod Touch

There's no denying that the Apple iPhone, iPad and iPod Touch have been a huge success and many of you may own one. However, both devices suffer from one small problem, they don't charge very fast when connected to your PC. Wouldn't it be great if your iPhone charged just as quickly from your computer as it does from the charger?

GIGABYTE's latest motherboards are equipped with ON/OFF Charge technology which allows you not only to charge your iPhone, iPad or iPod Touch, but it allows you to Quick Charge it. As an added bonus, it can even be charged when your PC is turned off, so even if you forget to plug it into your charger after you've synced up your music, it will be fully charged when you need it.

Quick Charge	PC Power	Working	Standby	Suspend to RAM	Suspend to DISK	Shutdown	Charge time (Lower is Better)	
		(S0)	(S1)	(S3)	(S4)	(S5)		
GIGABYTE ON/OFF Charge		Yes	Yes	Yes	Yes*	Yes*		Up to 40% Faster
Traditional Design		No	No	No	No	No		

* Due to certain mobile phone limitations, users may need to connect the mobile phone to their PC before the PC enters S4/S5 mode to enable a quick charge from non ON/OFF Charge USB ports. Charging results may vary by model.

GIGABYTE Ultra Durable 3 Motherboard

X58A-UD3R

890FXA-UD5

870A-UD3

Based on GIGABYTE's unparalleled 3x USB power boost design, plus an entirely new hardware design, GIGABYTE ON/OFF Charge Technology provides a set of white and red colored USB pin headers that can easily be connected to your system's front USB 2.0 ports, that not only act as a normal USB port, but also double as a quick charge ports for your mobile device. It doesn't matter if your iPhone, iPad or iPod Touch is plugged into the quick charge USB port while the system is turned on, in sleep/standby mode, or even turned off, as it always enables you to charge your iPhone, iPad or iPod Touch.

Quick Charge will also cut the charging time by up to 40 percent thanks to yet another innovative GIGABYTE design. The reduced charging time means it only takes about two hours to fully charge your iPhone, iPad or iPod Touch, something that would take in excess of three hours using a standard USB port.

Delivers **Maximum** CPU Power

GIGABYTE Unlocked Power

CPU performance will never be the same since the launch of the new Intel 6 Core CPUs including the Intel Core™ i7-980X, which offers performance levels that have far exceeded the expectations of even the most critical hardware reviewers and enthusiasts. In order to offer the best power delivery for these powerhouse CPUs and future 1366 socket processors, GIGABYTE engineers have completely redesigned the traditional PWM power design of the motherboard to deliver first class system performance and stability.

Introducing the all new GIGABYTE Unlocked Power, with completely reengineered 24 phase power design able to deliver more unadulterated power to the CPU than any existing desktop motherboard.

Delivers Maximum CPU Power

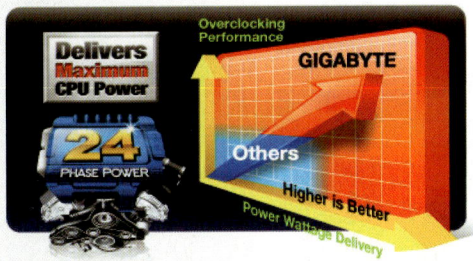

GIGABYTE was the first motherboard manufacturer to realize the importance of using only the highest quality components for this highly critical area of the motherboard with their Ultra Durable™ 3 design. In addition to using smaller-sized name brand Japanese solid capacitors, GIGABYTE Unlocked Power features an all new 24 phase design which utilizes low core energy loss Ferrite Core Chokes, as well as Low RDS(on) Driver-MOSFETs which are able to handle a higher current load, and at the same time, offer better power efficiency and lower operating temperatures.

Dual Power Switching

GIGABYTE Unlocked Power also delivers better durability and longer component lifespan due to the industry's first Dual Power Switching* design. When Dual Power Switching is activated, 2 sets of 12 power phases operate in tandem, automatically turning on one set of 12 phases and powering down the other 12, allowing the non active set to rest. Unlike a traditional power design where some of the same power phases are always in operation which can cause them to wear out and fail prematurely, GIGABYTE Dual Power Switching ensures that each set of phases share the power workload, effectively doubling the lifespan of the phases.

*For Power Switching functionality, DES must be active.

Auto Failure Protection

Another unique feature of GIGABYTE's Dual Power Switching is that if one of the power phases for whatever reason is damaged or fails, the motherboard will automatically disable its group of 12 phases, allowing the motherboard to operate using the other set of twelve. Of course with a traditional motherboard, if one power phase fails, the board is unable to operate.

GIGABYTE Ultra Durable 3 Motherboard

X58A-UD9

Power Phase Boost with Multi-Gear Switching

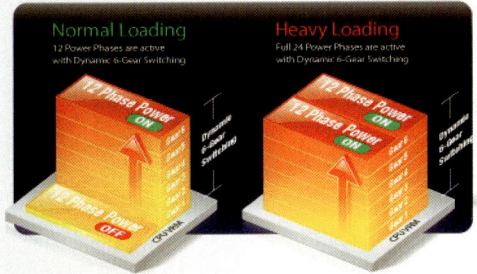

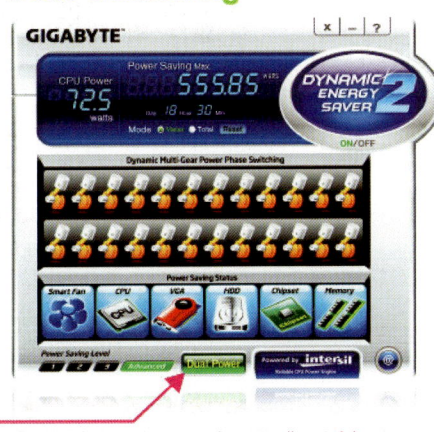

When Dual Power Switching is activated, 2 sets of 12 power phases operate in tandem, automatically turning on one set of 12 phases and powering down the other 12*.

*Dual Power Switching automatically switches power phases during each system boot up. Users can also manually switch between sets of power phases by turning off and then on the Dual Power button in the DES utility.

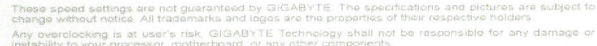

Installing the motherboard

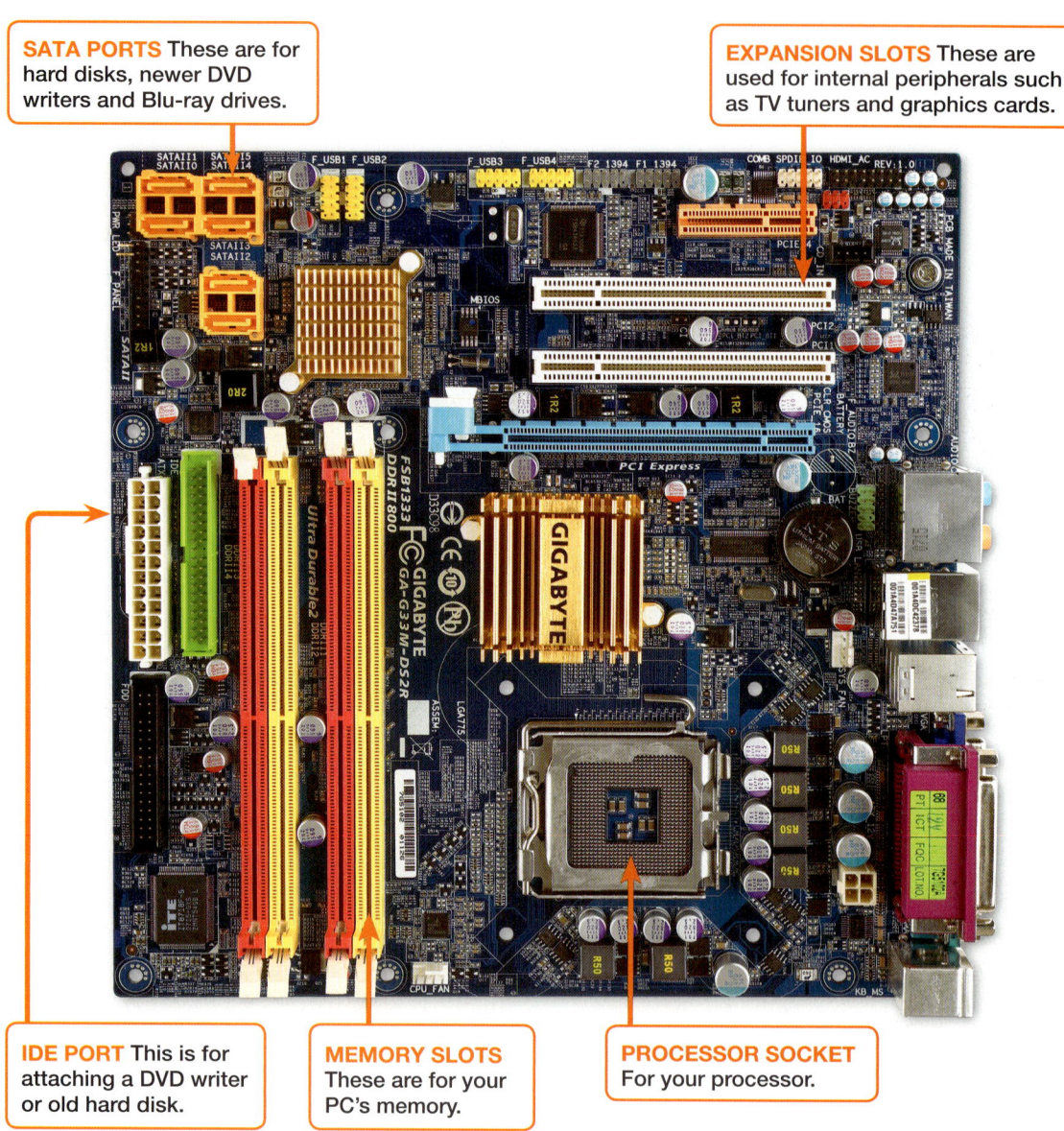

SATA PORTS These are for hard disks, newer DVD writers and Blu-ray drives.

EXPANSION SLOTS These are used for internal peripherals such as TV tuners and graphics cards.

IDE PORT This is for attaching a DVD writer or old hard disk.

MEMORY SLOTS These are for your PC's memory.

PROCESSOR SOCKET For your processor.

TIP
Blanking plates can be difficult to fit. Push them in until they click, but don't worry if they're not entirely level around the sides.

REAR PANEL CONNECTORS These ports are fixed on your motherboard.

HOW TO...
Install the motherboard

1 UNPACK THE BOARD
Open your motherboard's box. You'll see lots of cables, a driver CD, a metal blanking plate with holes cut out and a manual. Take these components out and put them to one side, as you'll need them later on.

The motherboard will be inside an anti-static bag and resting on top of anti-static foam. Slide the motherboard out of the bag, but leave it attached to the foam for now. Place the motherboard and foam on top of the anti-static bag, and take out the metal blanking plate.

2 MEASURE BLANKING PLATE
The blanking plate fits into the case, and gives you access only to the ports that your motherboard has. However, some motherboard manufacturers use generic blanking plates that fit their entire range of boards. With these, you may need to remove some metal covers to give access to your motherboard's ports.

The easiest way to see is to hold the blanking plate up to the motherboard until the cutouts match the ports on your board. The blanking plate should be pushed against the motherboard with the ridge pointing out, so any text is readable. It will only fit one way, so manoeuvre it until it's the right way. Make a note of any ports that are covered.

3 REMOVE UNNECESSARY BITS
If you need to remove any parts of the blanking plate, you should do that now. You'll have two options for doing this. First, you may have to remove a bit of metal, in a similar way to the metal blanking plates on your case. These should be rocked gently out until the metal snaps.

Second, some ports may be covered by a flap. In this case, the flap should be bent inwards (towards where the motherboard will be). Make sure that you bend it far enough for the motherboard's port to be given enough clearance to pass underneath.

4 INSTALL THE BLANKING PLATE
From the inside of the case, you need to take the blanking plate and push it into the gap at

TIP
Motherboards can require a bit of force to be inserted. Push from the sides of the board; don't force any components, as this could cause damage.

the rear of the case. Remember to align it so that it's the same way up as when you measured it against your motherboard.

The ridge round the outside of the plate should clip into the hole. Be warned that this can be really fiddly and the blanking plates don't always fit perfectly. It should, however, clip into place and remain stable without any support.

5 MEASURE WHERE THE MOTHERBOARD GOES

Next, you need to see where the screw holes for the motherboard will go. Lie the case flat on the desk and make sure that all the internal cables are out of the way. When you've got a clear case, take the motherboard off its foam backing and slide it gently into the case. Make sure that its rear ports are pushed up against the blanking plate correctly. Take a note of where the screw holes in the motherboard go, and remove the board. Place it back on its foam.

6 FIT THE RISERS

You need to fit risers where you noted the screw holes. These will be included with the case and look like tall copper screws. Their job is to hold the motherboard off the bottom of the case, so it isn't shorted out when its contacts touch the metal. The risers simply screw into the pre-drilled holes in

the case. Use as many risers as there are screw holes in the motherboard, making sure that you screw them tightly into position with your fingers.

7 SLIDE THE MOTHERBOARD INTO PLACE

Put the motherboard back in the case, making sure that all its screw holes have risers underneath. If some are missing, check to make sure that you haven't screwed the risers into the wrong place. You'll probably notice that the motherboard has a tendency to be slightly off from the risers. This is normal, and is caused by pressure from the backplate pushing against the motherboard. Simply line up the motherboard's ports with the backplate and push the motherboard towards it until the screw holes line up. This will take a bit of gentle force.

8 SCREW THE MOTHERBOARD DOWN

With the motherboard in place, you can start to screw it in. Start with the corners, holding the motherboard firmly, so that its screw holes line up with the risers that you put in.

When screwing the screws in, don't use too much pressure as you don't want to break the motherboard. Ideally, you want the screws tight enough for the board to be secure, but not so tight that it feels as though the board is going to start cracking.

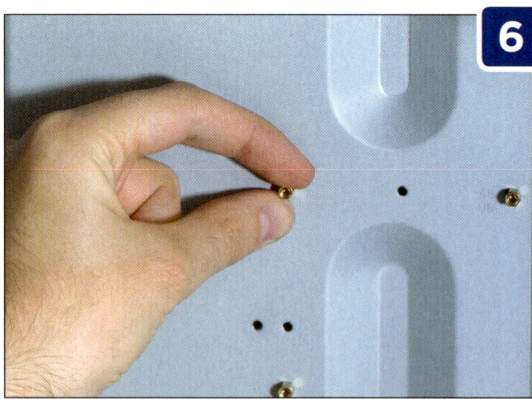

Once you've done the corners, you can put screws in the other holes. How many you put in is up to you, but you shouldn't need to do all of them to make the motherboard secure. Keep going until the motherboard is firmly in place.

9 IDENTIFY ATX CONNECTORS

With the motherboard in place, you're ready to connect it to the power supply. There are two connectors that you'll need to plug in. The first is the ATX connector. On modern motherboards, you need a 24-pin connector. There's only one of these on the power supply. However, as older motherboards only required a 20-pin connector, there's usually a four-pin connector that can be detached. Make sure that this is connected and that you have an unbroken 24-pin connector.

10 PLUG IN ATX CONNECTOR

You need to plug this 24-pin connector into the matching connector on the motherboard. This should be easy to find, but it's usually located by the IDE ports on the right-hand side of the motherboard.

The ATX connector will only plug in one way, so you can't get it wrong. Once it's lined up, the connector should plug in smoothly. There's a clip on it to hold it in place. This will require gentle pressure to get it to clip in, but no more. If you're

having to force the cable, then the chances are that you've got the connector the wrong way round. Once the cable is in place, give it a gentle tug to make sure that it's secure.

11 IDENTIFY SECONDARY CONNECTOR

Modern motherboards also have a secondary power connector. On most boards this is a single four-pin connector, but some require eight-pin connectors. Check to see what your power supply has, as you may need to buy an adaptor.

In a similar way to the 24-pin connector, the eight-pin connector on power supplies can be split into two. If your motherboard has only a four-pin connector, you'll have to split it into two halves. Only one of these will plug into the motherboard.

12 CONNECT SECONDARY CONNECTOR

Locate the secondary motherboard power connector. Your board's manual will tell you exactly where it's located, but on most motherboards it's near the processor socket. Next, plug the power supply's secondary connector into it. This plug will only go in one way, so there's no chance of getting it wrong. The connector should slide gently into the plug. You'll need to apply a bit of force in order to get the clip to lock into place, and you should hear it click when it's in properly.

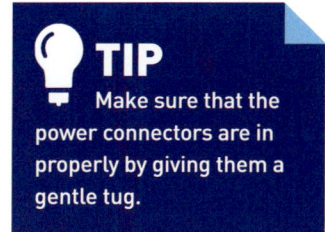

TIP
Make sure that the power connectors are in properly by giving them a gentle tug.

HOW TO...
Install an Intel processor

1 LIFT THE PROCESSOR CAGE
Intel's processor sockets are covered by a cage. A new motherboard will also have a plastic cover on top. First, remove this cover. It should easily unclip. To access the socket, unclip the handle that runs down the side of the socket and lift it up. This releases the retaining clip for the main cage.

Lift the main cage up and out of the way to expose the socket. Be careful not to touch any of the pins inside the socket, as bending them will stop the processor from working correctly.

2 INSTALL THE PROCESSOR
The processor has two cut-out notches in its sides, which line up with the ridges in the socket. This prevents the processor from being put in the wrong way round. You'll also notice an arrow on the processor. This should line up with the corner of the socket that has its pins arranged diagonally.

Line the processor up and sit it gently in the place. If it doesn't sit properly, then you've got it the wrong way round. Once you're happy with the processor's position, close the drive cage and pull the retaining handle down. This should take a bit of force, but if it feels like there's too much resistance, check that the processor is seated properly.

3 THERMAL PASTE
Thermal paste fills in micro-cracks in the surface of the processor and the surface of the cooler, ensuring that there's efficient heat transfer between the two. Some fans come pre-coated with thermal paste, in which case you can skip this step.

If it doesn't, you'll need to apply your own. This is easy to do. First, squeeze a tiny blob of thermal paste into the middle of the processor. Take a thin bit of card and use this to spread it, so that the surface of the processor is coated. Don't spread it over the side of the cage, and add more thermal paste if you don't have enough.

4 ATTACH THE FAN
Most Intel coolers clip into the four round holes on the outside of the processor socket. If you're not using an Intel reference cooler bundled with your processor, check the cooler's instructions; some need a backplate screwed to the motherboard.

For all other coolers, you'll see four feet. Make sure that all the feet are rotated away from the direction of the arrow. Line up the cooler so that

the four feet touch the holes in the motherboard. It's best to try to get the power cable pointing towards the header on the motherboard marked CPU (we'll cover this later).

Starting at diagonally opposite sides, push the four feet into the place. You'll need some force, and the feet should click into position. When done, check the cooler is seated properly and that it isn't wobbly. If it is, make sure the feet are properly in position.

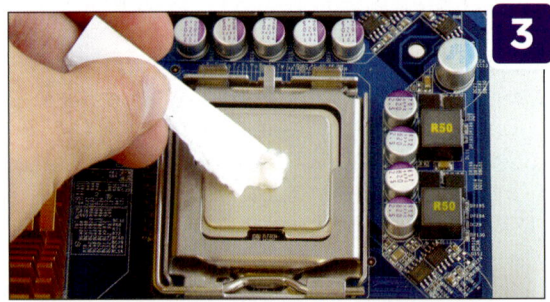

TIP
The plastic clips on Intel coolers can be annoying to fit. Make sure the black plastic clips are raised before fitting the cooler, and push diagonally opposite clips in together.

HOW TO...
Install an AMD processor

1 OPEN THE SOCKET LEVER
AMD's processors fit into AM2, AM2+ or AM3 sockets. The sockets are very similar, so the installation instructions are the same.

To fit the processor in the socket, first lift the lever. This unclips to one side and rises vertically above the board. This will move the socket very slightly, aligning the holes in the plastic socket with the connectors beneath. The processor should drop into place with no force, hence the socket's type: zero insertion force (ZIF).

2 FIT THE PROCESSOR
The processor can fit only one way into the socket. Make sure the arrow on top of the processor is aligned with the arrow on the processor socket. Gently push the processor into place. You should feel it click into position when it's all the way in. If it feels like you have to use too much force, stop and check that the processor is correctly aligned.

Once the processor is all the way in, check round it to make sure that it's sitting flush against the plastic socket. If it's not, push gently down on the sections that aren't flush. Push the lever down and clip it back into place to secure the processor.

3 THERMAL PASTE
Thermal paste fills in micro-cracks in the surface of the processor and the surface of the

cooler, ensuring that there's efficient heat transfer between the two. You may find that your fan comes pre-coated with thermal paste, in which case you can skip this step.

If it doesn't, you'll need to apply your own. This is simple to do. First, squeeze a tiny blob of thermal paste into the middle of the processor. Take a thin bit of card and use this to spread it, so that the surface of the processor is coated. Don't spread it over the side of the processor, and add more thermal paste if necessary.

4 FIT THE COOLER
If you're using a third-party cooler, check its instructions for how to fit it. If you're using an AMD cooler that came with your processor, fitting it is simple. Around the processor socket is a plastic cooler mount, with two nodules sticking out. These are designed to hold your cooler's clips.

Take your cooler and open its handle. Fit the metal clip without the handle on it over one nodule and push it snugly against the mount. Place the cooler flat across the top of the processor. Push the cooler's remaining metal clip over the second nodule and close the handle. This will require a bit of force to get the handle all the way down. We'll cover connecting the fan's power connector later.

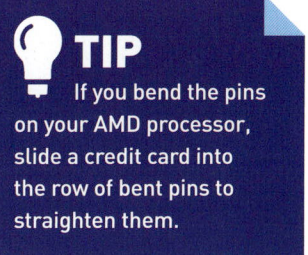

TIP
If you bend the pins on your AMD processor, slide a credit card into the row of bent pins to straighten them.

Installing memory

DUAL MEMORY Motherboards have dual memory channels. Installing two memory modules – one in each channel – can increase performance. The slots to use are usually the same colour, but check your motherboard's manual first.

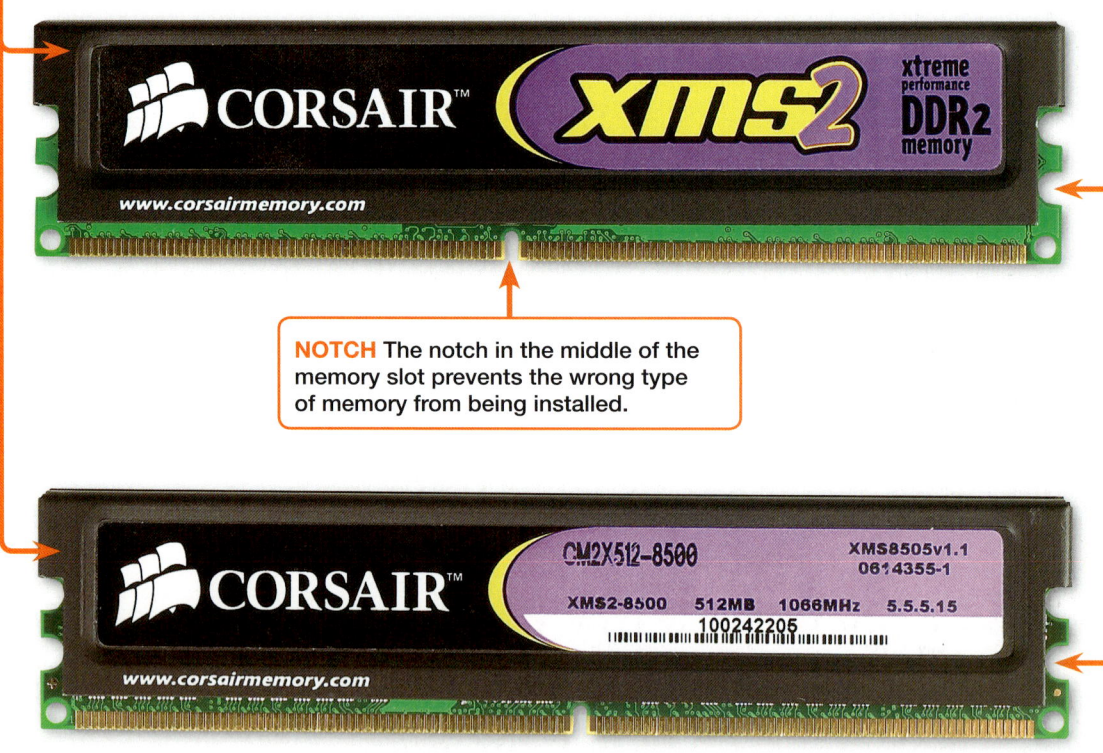

NOTCH The notch in the middle of the memory slot prevents the wrong type of memory from being installed.

CLIPS The clips at the side of the memory slot hold the RAM in place. You open them to install memory, and they close automatically when the RAM is installed.

TIP
Make sure your memory is lined up properly before you insert it to prevent damage.

HOW TO...
Install memory

1 IDENTIFY WHICH SLOTS TO USE
Presuming that you've bought memory in a kit with two sticks of RAM, you should now identify the slots in which you're going to install the memory. As noted opposite, the slots to use are usually the same colour, but you should check your motherboard's manual carefully to make sure that you're using the right ones.

To be doubly safe, the slots will also be numbered to make it easier to follow the motherboard manual's instructions.

2 OPEN THE RETAINING CLIPS
To install your memory, you need to open the clips on either end of the slot into which you're going to insert your memory stick. Pick the first slot and push open these clips; they should open gently without any force, clicking as they open. The clips should open to around 45°, but don't force them further open when you feel resistance.

3 LINE THE MEMORY UP
To fit the memory, you need to slide it into the slot. Make sure that the notch in the memory lines up with the ridge in the socket. If it doesn't, then you've got the memory the wrong way round.

If the memory still doesn't fit, then you're using the wrong type of memory. Check the memory's instructions and motherboard's manual to see what type you need.

4 CLIP THE MEMORY INTO PLACE
Once the memory module is lined up, press firmly on both sides to push it into place. The clips should spring back and click into position. Check the clips are in place and nestled against the notches in the side of the memory module. If they're not, try pushing the memory down a bit further. You can also push the clips up to help them lock into place.

Once your first module is in place, repeat these steps for any remaining modules.

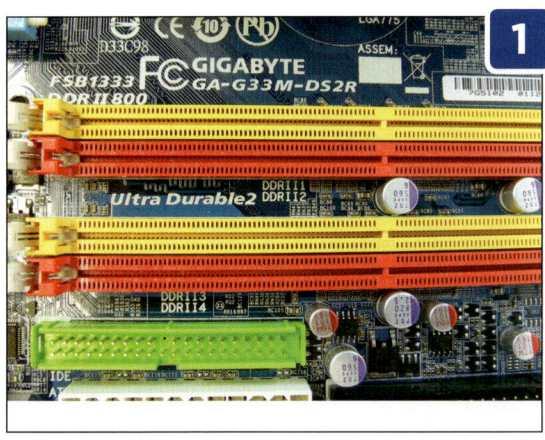

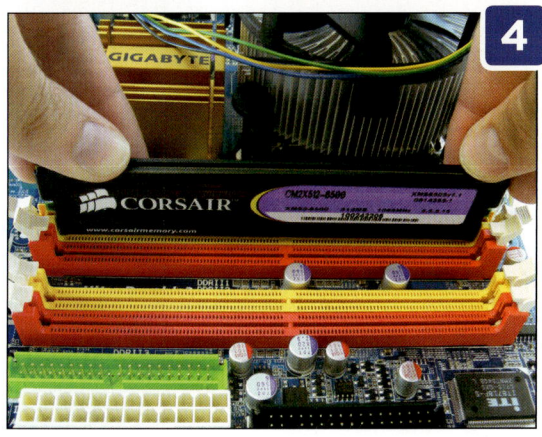

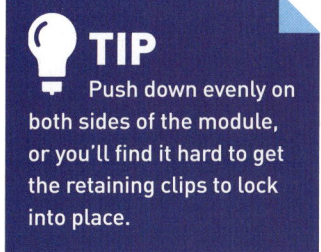

TIP
Push down evenly on both sides of the module, or you'll find it hard to get the retaining clips to lock into place.

HOW TO...
Fit the internal cables

1 POWER

To get your PC to turn on when you push the power button, you need to connect the power switch to the motherboard. Among the loose cables in your case, you'll find a two-pin connector. This will usually be marked PWR SW, but check the case's manual if you're not sure.

This needs to be connected to the power jumpers on the motherboard. Typically, these will be located on the bottom-right of the motherboard and will be marked, although you should double-check your motherboard's manual to make sure. The connector will just plug over the two pins and should connect easily.

2 RESET

If your case has a reset switch – not all do – then there will be a similar connector to the power switch, with RESET SW written on it. Connecting this to your motherboard lets you restart your PC after a major crash, as it resets the hardware and forces your computer to reboot.

To connect it, you need to find the reset jumpers on the motherboard. These will be near the power switch, but you should read your motherboard's manual for an exact location. Simply push the connector over the two pins

to connect the switch. It doesn't matter which way round this connector goes.

3 POWER AND HDD LEDS

The HDD connector connects to an LED on the front of the case and lights up when the hard disk is in operation. This is useful, as you can see whether your PC's working or if it's crashed.

As this connects to an LED, it must be connected correctly. The cable should be marked as positive and negative (this is usually written on the plug). The motherboard HDD jumper will also have a positive and negative port. Check your motherboard's manual carefully to make sure you get this right, and then connect the cable.

Do the same thing for the power LED, which will have a similar connector. This must be connected the right way round, so make sure you get the positive and negative connectors aligned.

4 USB

If your case has front-mounted USB ports or a card reader, you'll need to connect these to spare headers on your motherboard. In all likelihood, the cable in the case will be marked USB.

Your motherboard will probably have spare connectors marked USB, but the manual can tell

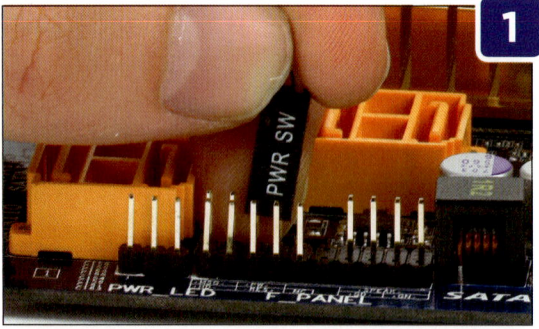

you exactly where these are. USB connectors take power, so you need to plug the cable in the right way round. Fortunately, the USB ports on most cases have a single plug that can only be connected to the motherboard in one way. If it doesn't, you'll need to check the case's and motherboard's manuals carefully to make sure that you install the connectors correctly.

Assuming you're using a block connector, plug it into a spare USB header on the motherboard. We'd recommend using the closest header to the cable to avoid draping cables everywhere.

5 FIREWIRE

Front-mounted FireWire cables plug in much the same way as USB cables. Again, look for a spare FireWire header on the motherboard (the manual will explain where these are), and then connect the FireWire cable to it. The cable may be marked as 1394, as FireWire is also known as i1394.

6 AUDIO

Front-mounted audio ports also need to be connected to the motherboard if you want to be able to plug in your headphones and a microphone. Fortunately, most motherboards and cases have a single block connector that plugs into the front audio connector on the motherboard.

Your motherboard's manual will have full details of where this is connected, but it's usually located by its back panel. Again, there's only one way to connect this cable, so just slide it gently into place. If your case has a Speaker header, plug this into

the appropriate connector on the motherboard. This is used to give warning beeps.

7 FANS

It's common for modern cases to have extra fans pre-fitted. These help increase airflow through the case and keep your PC cool. While fans can be connected directly to the power supply, it's better to connect them to spare fan headers on the motherboard. This way, the motherboard can automatically control the fan speed and keep your PC running as quietly as possible.

If your fans end in three- or four-pin connectors, you can plug them into your motherboard. Look at the manual to find a spare fan connector and then plug in the fan's power connector. Three-pin connectors can plug into four-pin ports and vice versa. The cables can also plug in only one way, so it's easy to get it right.

8 CPU FAN

The processor fan, which we installed earlier, can now be connected to the motherboard. In the same way as system fans, the processor's fan speed is controlled by the motherboard based on the processor's temperature. This keeps your computer as quiet as possible.

There's a special connector for the processor fan on the motherboard, which is often called CPU FAN. Check your motherboard's manual for its location. This is likely to be a four-pin connector, but three-pin processor fans can also plug in. The connector can go in only one way, so just plug it in.

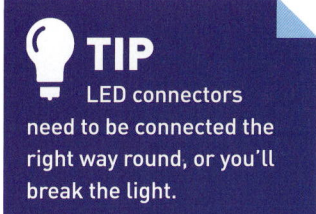

TIP
LED connectors need to be connected the right way round, or you'll break the light.

Installing a hard disk

SATA POWER Plug the hard disk's power in here.

SATA DATA Plug one end of the data cable in here and the other end into a SATA port on the motherboard.

SATA PORTS These are for hard disks, newer DVD writers and Blu-ray drives.

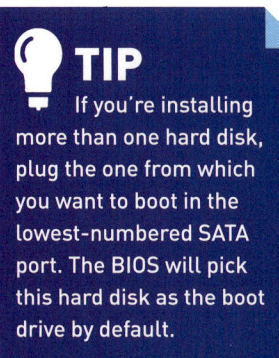

TIP

If you're installing more than one hard disk, plug the one from which you want to boot in the lowest-numbered SATA port. The BIOS will pick this hard disk as the boot drive by default.

HOW TO...
Install a hard disk

1 FIT HARD DISK INTO A BAY

To fit a hard disk, you need to find a 3½in drive bay. Be careful not to use one of the external bays, which have a cutout on the front of the case, as these are designed for memory card readers and floppy disk drives.

If your case has drive rails or screwless fittings, you'll need to read the case's manual for instructions on how to fit these drives. For other cases, slide the hard disk into a spare drive bay until the screw holes in the side of the drive line up with the holes in the drive bay. The disk should then be secured with four screws: two either side of the case. Suitable screws should have been provided with the hard disk or case. Screw these up tightly to prevent the drive wobbling.

2 PLUG IN SATA POWER

In the main picture opposite, you can see the SATA power connector on the hard disk and on the power supply. Locate the correct connector from your power supply and plug it into the back of your hard disk. It goes in only one way and clicks when it's connected. Be extremely careful when plugging it in, as downwards pressure can break the clip surrounding the power connector. If you do this, the power plug won't stay in place.

3 PLUG IN SATA DATA CABLE

Unlike IDE, SATA uses a simple and thin connector to carry data. Your motherboard will ship with several SATA cables, so take one of these from the box. Plug it gently into the rear of the hard disk. It will plug in only one way and will click when it's properly connected.

Be careful when you plug it in, as downwards pressure can break the connector and prevent the SATA cable plugging in.

4 PLUG SATA DATA CABLE INTO MOTHERBOARD

Next, you need to find a spare SATA port on your motherboard. These are usually located at the bottom-right of the board and are numbered. The lower the number, the higher up the boot chain your hard disk is. If you're installing more than one hard disk, therefore, make sure the drive from which you're going to boot is plugged into the lowest-numbered port. Check the motherboard's manual to ensure that all the ports do the same thing; some boards have ports reserved for RAID.

Connecting the SATA cable is easy, as it will plug in only one way. It will click when the cable is connected properly.

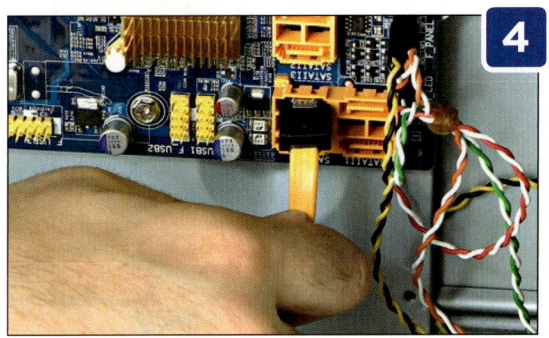

TIP
SATA connectors on hard disks can be broken easily, so be careful when inserting and moving cables.

Installing an optical drive

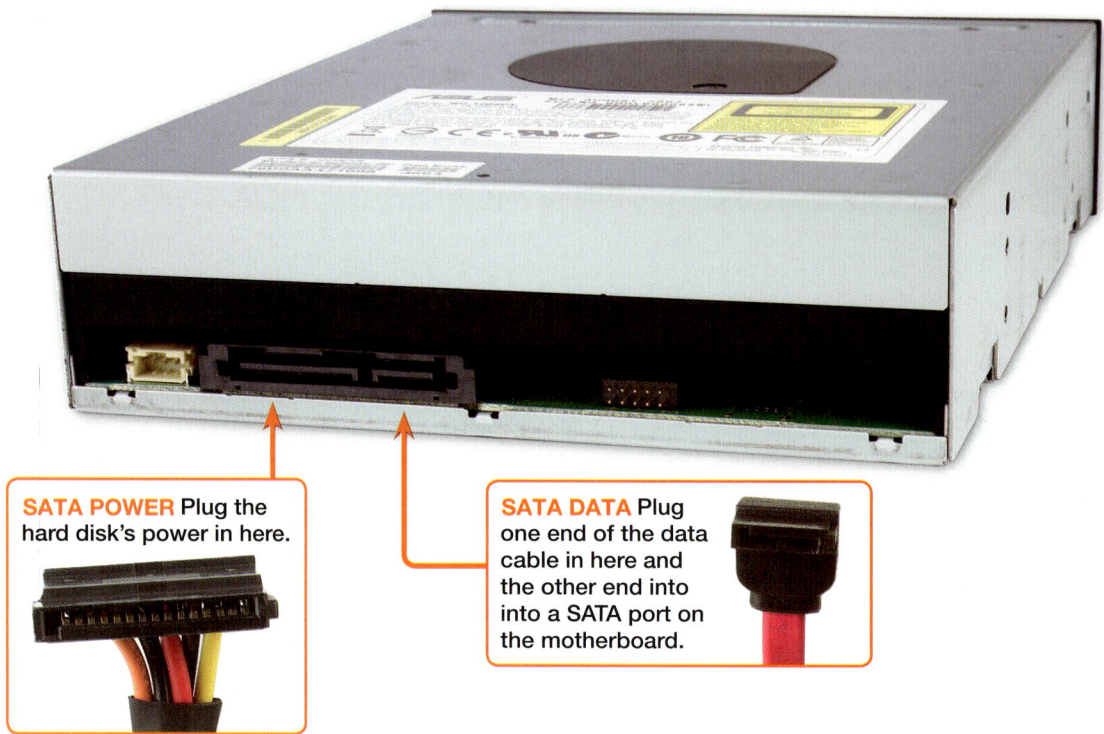

SATA POWER Plug the hard disk's power in here.

SATA DATA Plug one end of the data cable in here and the other end into into a SATA port on the motherboard.

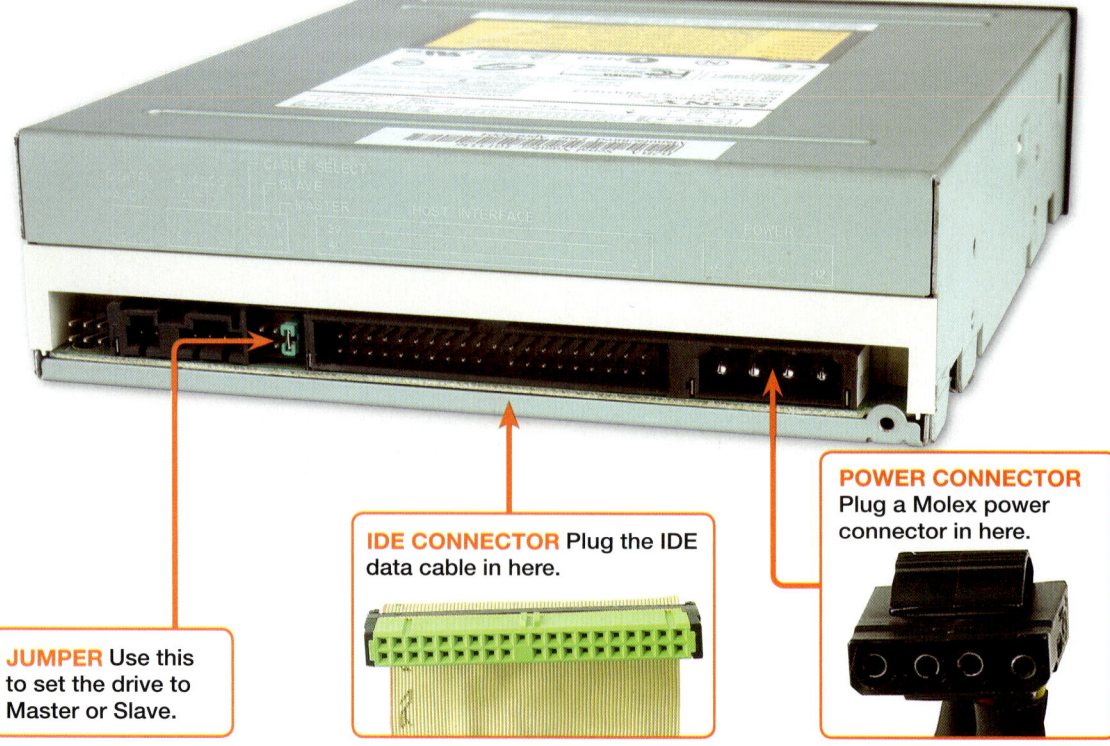

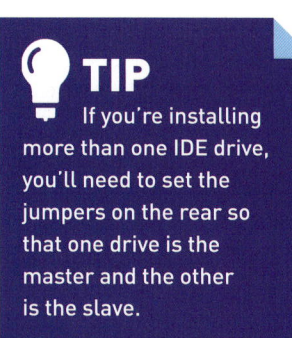

TIP
If you're installing more than one IDE drive, you'll need to set the jumpers on the rear so that one drive is the master and the other is the slave.

JUMPER Use this to set the drive to Master or Slave.

IDE CONNECTOR Plug the IDE data cable in here.

POWER CONNECTOR Plug a Molex power connector in here.

HOW TO...
Connect an optical drive

1 FIT THE DRIVE

First, fit the optical drive into a spare 5¼in drive bay in the case. Some cases have flaps at the front to hide the optical drive from view. If you have a screwless case or your drives need to be fitted on runners, consult your case's manual for full instructions.

Other cases require you to screw the drive into place. The optical drive needs to be slid into the case from the front. This often means that you need to have the front of the case removed, if you haven't done that yet. Slide the drive into the bay. The front of it needs to be flush with the case where there's no flap, and slightly further back if your case has a drive flap.

To tell where the drive should be, push it in until the screw holes in its side match up with the round screw holes inside the case. Now use the four screws (provided with the optical drive or case) – two either side – to hold the drive in place.

2 FIT THE IDE CABLE

Most optical drives use the older IDE data connector. If yours uses SATA, follow the instructions for fitting a hard disk (page 60). An IDE cable is a wide ribbon cable. It's harder to plug in than a SATA cable, but shouldn't cause any problems if you know what to look out for. First, the cable can plug in only one way due to a blocked-off connector in the cable. Second, the coloured cable (red or white depending on the cable provided with your motherboard) goes to the right of the connector closest to the power connector. Plug the cable in gently and as straight as possible so as not to bend any pins on the drive.

3 FIT THE POWER CABLE

Optical drives tend to use a Molex power connector. This is the large four-pin connector on your power supply. Locate a free one and push it into the drive's power connector. Use a bit of force to get it to connect properly. Once you think it's in, give it a gentle tug to make sure it's secure.

4 FIT THE IDE CABLE INTO THE MOTHERBOARD

Now you're ready to plug the cable into the motherboard. Don't get the connector confused with the floppy disk connector; check your motherboard's manual for its location. The IDE connector can plug in only one way, thanks to a notch in the motherboard's connector. Plug in the cable gently as straight as possible to avoid bending any pins.

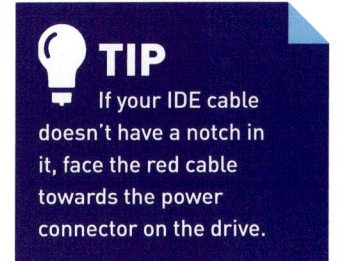

TIP

If your IDE cable doesn't have a notch in it, face the red cable towards the power connector on the drive.

Installing a graphics card

CROSSFIRE CONNECTOR This is used when you install two ATI graphics cards. Nvidia cards have a similar SLI connector.

PCI EXPRESS x16 CONNECTOR This plugs into the corresponding slot on the motherboard.

PCI EXPRESS POWER CONNECTOR Connect your power supply's graphics power connector in here.

TIP
PCI Express x16 slots typically have retaining clips. You'll need to use this clip if you have to remove a graphics card later.

HOW TO...
Install a graphics card

1 REMOVE BLANKING PLATE
To fit a graphics card, you'll need to locate the PCI Express x16 slot and remove the associated blanking plate. If you're going to fit a double-height card, then you'll need to remove the blanking plate for the next expansion slot as well.

The steps will differ according to your case, so check its manual for full details. Typically, blanking plates are either screwed in place individually, or a single retaining bar holds them all in place. Remove whatever's holding the blanking plates in place. Some blanking plates just lift out, while others are attached to the case and need to be rocked backwards and forwards to snap them out.

2 PLUG CARD INTO SLOT
With the blanking plates free, you can put your card into the case. This is easy to do: simply line up the graphics card's connector with the slot in the case. The card should look like it's upside down, with the fan pointing towards the bottom of the case.

Pressure on both sides of the card should be enough to make sure that it ends up seated in the expansion card slot properly. You should check the card when you think it's in place to ensure that you've made proper contact. If you can still see some of the card's slot sticking out, then push the offending side in a bit further.

3 SCREW CARD IN PLACE
How you remove the blanking plate will depend on how you attach your card securely, so check the case's manual for full details. In most instances, you'll need to screw the card into place. Line up the top of its connector with the screw hole in the case and screw it into place so that the card can't move in its slot.

4 CONNECT POWER ADAPTOR
Most modern graphics cards require a secondary power source to run. These will need a dedicated PCI Express six-pin power connector. This is on most modern power supplies, but if yours doesn't have one, a Molex-to-PCI Express adaptor is often bundled with graphics cards. The PCI Express power connector can plug in only one way and can be pushed easily into place.

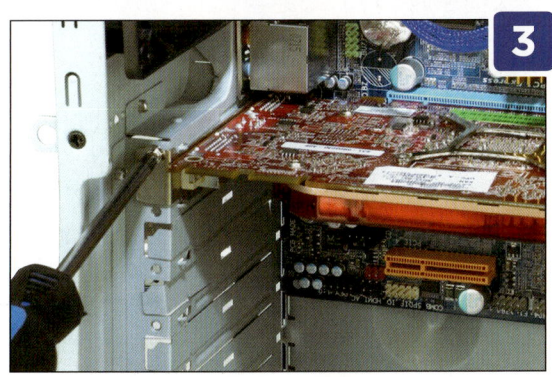

TIP
Don't forget to plug in the PCI Express power connector (if required), or your PC may not turn on.

Installing expansion cards

PCI SLOTS An older type of expansion slot, but there are plenty of cards that will fit them.

PCI EXPRESS x1 SLOT The newest type of expansion slot. Also look out for x4 slots, which look similar but are longer.

PCI EXPRESS x16 SLOT If you don't install a dedicated graphics card, this slot can be used for expansion cards.

TIP
PCI Express cards can fit in a higher socket type, so an x1 card can fit in an x4 slot and so on.

HOW TO...
Plug in expansion cards

1 LOCATE SPARE SLOT
Before you start, carefully read the instructions that came with your expansion card as some require you to install software first. If yours does, you'll need to finish building the PC and install the operating system and necessary software before fitting the expansion card.

When you're ready, find a spare slot (PCI or PCI Express) on your motherboard. Ideally, leave a gap between other expansion cards, such as your graphics card, to increase airflow and keep your PC running cool.

2 REMOVE BLANKING PLATE
To fit an expansion card, you'll need to remove the expansion slot's blanking plate. The steps will differ according to your case, so carefully check its manual for full details. Typically, blanking plates are either individually screwed in place or held in place by a single retaining bar. Remove whatever's holding the blanking plates in place. Some plates just lift out, while others are attached to the case and need to be rocked backwards and forwards to snap them out.

3 FIT THE CARD
PCI and PCI Express cards are fitted in the same way. Line up the connector on the bottom of the card with the slot in which you want to put it. Slots have notches part of the way along, which you need to line up with the gap in the card's connector. When you've done this, push the card into place. It will take a bit of force to get the card to slide home properly. If the card doesn't feel like it's going to go into the slot, remove it and make sure it's lined up and that you're trying to install it into the correct slot. When the card is in place, check round it to make sure the connector is firmly in the slot. If the card doesn't look level, apply pressure to the part of the card sticking up until it clicks into place.

4 SCREW IT IN
When your card is firmly in place, you need to secure it in its slot. As some cases use proprietary fixing methods, check your case's manual for instructions on how to do this. If you need to use a screw, line up the screw hole in the card's blanking plate with the screw hole in the case. Tighten the screw up to the point where the card feels firm and doesn't wobble in the slot.

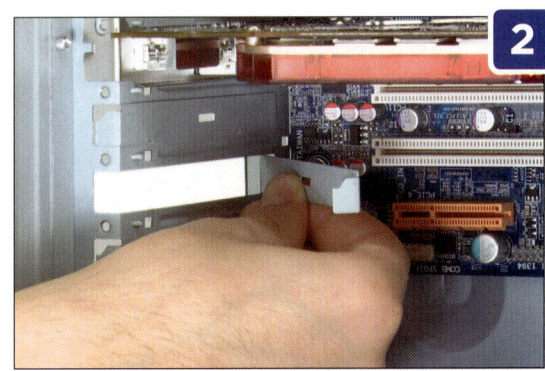

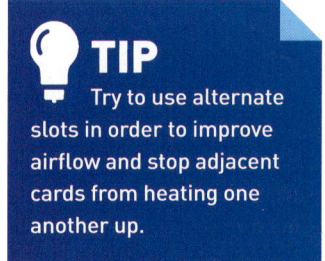

TIP
Try to use alternate slots in order to improve airflow and stop adjacent cards from heating one another up.

HOW TO...
Put the case back together

1 CABLE TIDY

If the inside of your computer is neat and tidy, you'll get better airflow and keep it cooler. A neat PC is also easier to work on should you need to install an upgrade later on.

One way to keep your case tidy is to fit cable ties. Simply locate loose cables that are running in the same direction and loop a cable tie around the bunch. Slide the strap through the buckle and pull it tight. The ratchet should click into place and stop the cable becoming undone. If it doesn't, you've inserted the strap the wrong way into the buckle. You can clip the long strap off when you're done. For extra neatness, loop the strap through drive bays in the case. This will anchor your cables out of the way.

2 KEEP CABLES OUT OF FANS

It's worth double-checking that none of your power cables is in the way of the fans inside your PC. If they are, you run the risk of severing your cables when you turn your PC on for the first time. Pull any loose cables out of the way of fans and secure them with cable ties if necessary. The processor fan (particularly on Intel's designs) is often the worse culprit for snagging cables, so check this one carefully.

3 ATTACH FRONT

Check your case's manual for the exact fitting instructions. If you removed its front, now is the time to fit it again. Line its clips up with the holes in the case and push firmly to reattach it. If you find that your optical drive sticks out too far, you've probably fitted it incorrectly. Undo its screws (or fixings if your case is screwless) and slide it further into the case. Screw it back in and fit the front of the case.

4 ATTACH SIDES

Check your case's manual carefully for full fitting instructions. For most cases, fitting the side panels is a matter of lining up their clips with the grooves on the inside of the case. Take each panel in turn, slide it into place and attach it firmly with a screw.

5 CONNECT NETWORK CABLE

If you want to connect your PC to a broadband router via an Ethernet cable, now's the time to plug it in. Vista's and Windows 7's installations can use a the internet to search for updated drivers, to make your installation smoother. Even if you're not using Windows 7 or Vista, being able to connect straight to the internet after installing an operating system is really useful.

6 CONNECT KEYBOARD AND MOUSE

To install an operating system, you'll need to connect a mouse and keyboard. Most motherboards support older PS2 keyboards and mice as well as newer USB models. PS2 keyboards plug into the purple port and mice into the green one. Simply line up the notch in the plug with the one in the port in the back of your computer and push.

For USB keyboards and mice, plug the connector into a free USB port; it will go only one way. For other USB devices, check their manuals before plugging them in. Many devices require you to install drivers first, so you'll have to install an operating system before you can plug them in.

7 CONNECT SPEAKERS

You can connect your speakers to your PC now. This is useful, as after installing an operating system you'll be able to check instantly whether the sound is working properly. How you connect your speakers will depend on how many you're plugging in. Generally speaking, surround-sound speakers have colour-coded cables, so you just need to match the cable with the same-coloured port on the back of your PC. For stereo speakers, plug a 3½mm jack into the green port on the back of the PC. Headphones generally connect to the green port on the front of the case.

8 PLUG IN MONITOR

Finally, you need to connect your computer to a monitor. This is simple. If your screen has a DVI input and your graphics card has a DVI output (pictured), you need a DVI-to-DVI cable. These are D-shaped, so they will plug in only one way. Line up the cable with the graphics card's connector and push the cable straight in. Screw it in place using the thumbscrews on either side of the connector. Repeat this on job on the monitor.

If your monitor has a blue analogue D-sub connector, you have two options. For graphics cards with DVI outputs, you'll have to plug in a DVI-to-D-sub connector first. You can then plug the D-sub cable into this and the monitor. If you're using onboard graphics with a D-sub output, plug the cable directly into this and the monitor. Just like DVI connectors, D-sub connectors are D-shaped, so they'll plug in only one way.

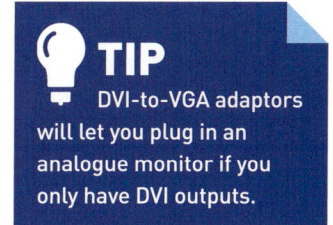

TIP
DVI-to-VGA adaptors will let you plug in an analogue monitor if you only have DVI outputs.

CHAPTER 5

POWER ON

BEFORE YOU CAN install an operating system on your newly assembled PC, you'll need to change a few settings in the BIOS. The BIOS is where you can configure the speed of your processor and memory, make settings such as a system password and choose the time at which the PC boots up every day. In this chapter, we'll show you how to access the BIOS and make the appropriate changes.

Into the BIOS

THE BIOS IS the part of your motherboard that detects and controls all your PC's hardware. It's arguably one of the most important parts of your computer. In the first part of our look at the BIOS, this month's Advanced Projects will show you around the settings so you can make sure that your computer is correctly configured.

Your BIOS makes sure that all your hardware is working correctly before your operating system starts. Getting it configured correctly will make your PC run more smoothly and reduce the number of errors you see. It's important to check the BIOS settings when you buy a new motherboard, perform an upgrade, or have to replace the onboard battery. The BIOS can be a confusing place to visit, so in this chapter we'll show you how to configure it.

ENTERING THE BIOS

The first thing you have to do is get into the BIOS. You do this by pressing a hotkey when you first turn on your PC. Typically, you need to press the Delete key when you first see something on your computer's display. However, we've seen some BIOSes that use F1, F2 or F10. Look out for an onscreen message that tells you which key to press. If you press the key too late, press Ctrl-Alt-Del to restart your computer.

Once you're inside the BIOS, you'll see a set of menus. The screenshot below shows you what

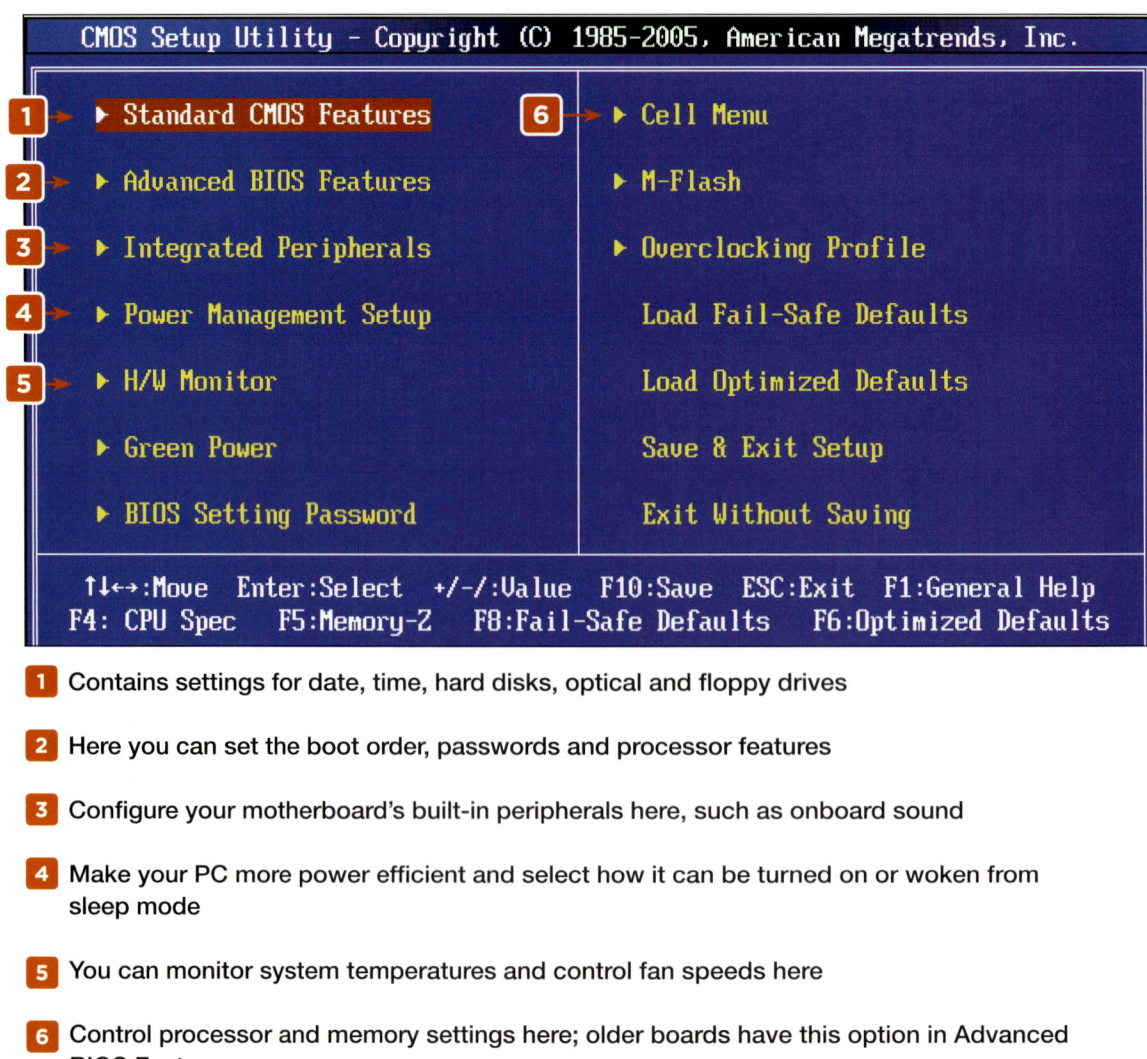

1 Contains settings for date, time, hard disks, optical and floppy drives

2 Here you can set the boot order, passwords and processor features

3 Configure your motherboard's built-in peripherals here, such as onboard sound

4 Make your PC more power efficient and select how it can be turned on or woken from sleep mode

5 You can monitor system temperatures and control fan speeds here

6 Control processor and memory settings here; older boards have this option in Advanced BIOS Features

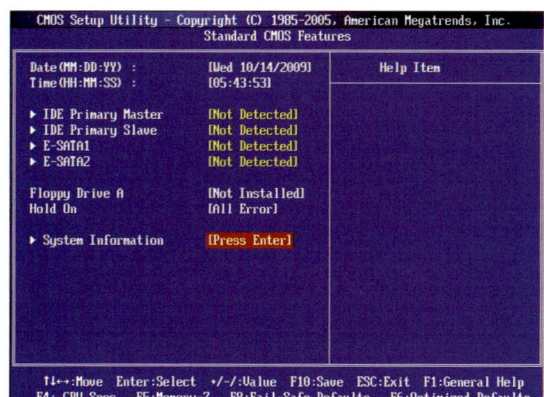

↑ The Standard CMOS Features page lets you set your PC's date and time

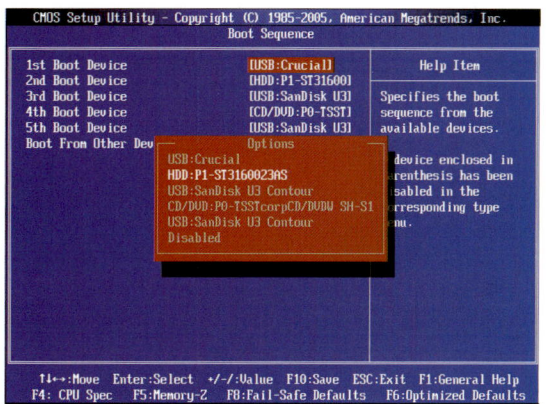

↑ You need to tell your BIOS which device you want to boot from first

each option is for. Be aware that your computer's BIOS may not look exactly like this, as each one is slightly different. However, this screenshot is representative of most BIOSes and the options we'll tell you to change will be available on the vast majority of computers, although you may need to hunt for them a bit.

One word of warning: changing settings that you don't understand can damage your PC. We recommend following our instructions carefully; you should make changes to other settings only if you're confident of what you're doing. We'll walk you through the settings that you should check in your BIOS in order. Navigate through the BIOS using your computer's cursor keys and select a menu option by pressing Enter. You can press Escape to move back a menu.

SETTING THE DATE AND TIME

First, select the Standard CMOS Features menu. The next screen will show you your computer's date and time. Set them correctly, as a wrong date and time can prevent things such as secure websites from working properly, as your PC can think that a website's identification certificate is out of date. If your time was set correctly but keeps resetting itself, you'll need to replace your motherboard's CMOS battery.

To set the date and time, select the day, month and year individually, pressing '+' or '-' to increase or decrease the value. This screen may also display your hard disks and optical drives, depending on your computer's storage configuration. At the very least, it will display all IDE devices connected to your computer, but not necessarily SATA devices.

The final options let you select whether you have a floppy disk drive and how to handle errors. If you don't have a floppy drive, select Not Installed from the menu. It's best to set the computer to

Hold On All Errors: if you have a problem, it will stop your computer from starting Windows, potentially causing bigger problems.

ADVANCED STORAGE SETTINGS

Press Esc to go back to the main menu and then select Integrated Peripherals. Look for a menu called On-Chip ATA Devices or similar. There may be an option for SATA devices in the Integrate Peripherals menu. Here you should find an option to change the SATA mode (it may also be called RAID mode). Select it and you'll have a choice of options: IDE, RAID and AHCI. IDE makes your SATA hard disks act like older IDE hard disks. RAID lets you use multiple hard disks to create one logical drive with either built-in protection or faster performance; however, RAID can cause problems, and if your motherboard breaks, recovering your data can be very difficult, so we don't recommend using it here.

AHCI is SATA's native mode and supports advanced features such as Native Command Queuing (NCQ), which intelligently queues all reads and writes to a hard disk to boost performance. This is the best choice if you have SATA hard disks. If AHCI is selected, your hard disks will no longer appear in the Standard CMOS Features menu. Instead, you'll either have a menu called AHCI Configuration (or similar), which will let you view your attached hard disk, or you'll see a different screen when you first turn on your PC that lists your SATA devices.

A word of warning about AHCI, though: if you already have an operating system installed, changing the SATA mode to AHCI from IDE will cause your computer to crash. If you're planning to reinstall your operating system from scratch, however, AHCI is a good option. The only caveat is that some older motherboards don't support DVD drives when using AHCI, so you may need

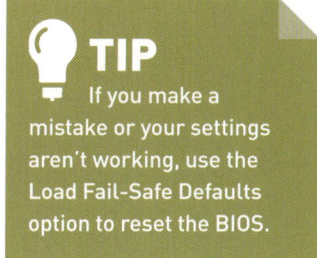

TIP
If you make a mistake or your settings aren't working, use the Load Fail-Safe Defaults option to reset the BIOS.

an IDE optical drive. If you're in any doubt at all, leave the SATA mode as IDE.

SETTING THE BOOT ORDER

To configure how you want your computer to boot, you need to edit the Boot Sequence Order in the Advanced BIOS Features menu. This will be a separate menu option or simply part of the Advanced BIOS Feature menu. Editing these options will let you select which device you want to boot from first. For installing a new operating system and running bootable discs, it makes sense to set the first boot device as your optical drive. Press Enter on 1st Boot Device and make sure that CD/DVD (or similar) is selected.

The second boot device should be your hard disk. Depending on your BIOS, there are two ways to do this. First, you'll either be able to select the physical hard disk from which you want to boot (you may need to take your disk out and look at the model number to make sure you have the right one), or you'll only be able to select Hard Disk. For the latter option, look for a Hard Disk Boot Priority menu. This will let you select the boot order of all the hard disks in your computer. This can be a useful tool: if you're running multiple operating systems installed on different hard disks, for example, you can simply select which one you want to boot from in the BIOS without having to mess around with boot managers or other complex software.

Finally, you can set your BIOS to boot from compatible USB drives. This can be complex, however, and the procedure depends on your computer. Modern BIOSes will detect USB keys as hard disks, so that you can simply select your USB key as the first device to boot from. Older motherboards don't have such good support, and you may find that your USB key is not supported. You may also find that older USB keys often can't be detected by a BIOS correctly.

You'll need to take booting from USB devices on a case-by-case basis.

OTHER DEVICES

The BIOS lets you configure which other devices on your motherboard are currently in use. The settings for these will be in the Integrated Peripherals menu. Here you'll see options for things such as the HD Audio Controller. You should disable devices that you won't use.

If you've added a dedicated sound card, for example, select HD Audio Controller, Disabled from the menu. You shouldn't need to disable too many devices, but look for outdated devices that you're unlikely to need, such as COM ports (also called serial ports and used to connect to older peripherals, such as PDAs, before USB), and parallel ports (used for old printers).

If you're not using these ports, you can disable them, as they otherwise waste system resources. Simply select a port, such as COM Port 1 (this may be in a separate I/O devices menu) and select Disabled. Repeat for the other ports that you're not using.

If you're using a USB keyboard, look for an option to enable it. If you don't, you'll find that your keyboard won't work after the BIOS has done its Power On Self Test (POST) and before Windows starts, such as when you're running the Windows installer.

READY TO BOOT

With these basic settings configured, you're ready to boot from your PC. Before you do, we'll show you how to save your BIOS settings. Go back to the BIOS's main menu and you'll see an option called Save & Exit Setup. Select this and choose OK on the next menu to apply your changes. Your computer will reset and start booting. Alternatively, if you've made a change you didn't want to, you can simply select Exit Without Saving instead.

⬆ Disable any legacy ports you don't need to use

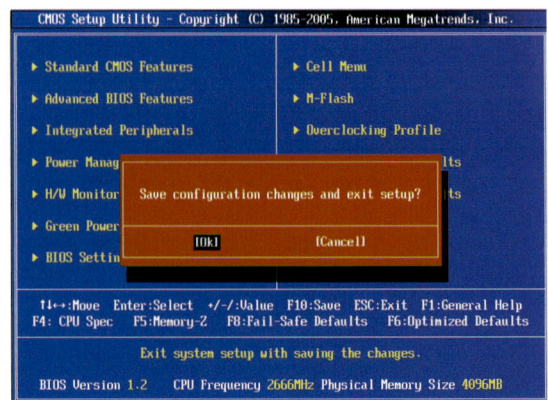

⬆ Keep any changes before you boot your PC

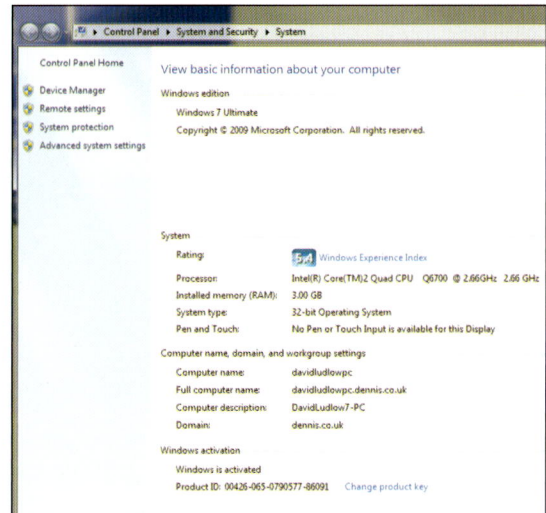

↑ You can check your processor's rated speed in Windows' Control Panel

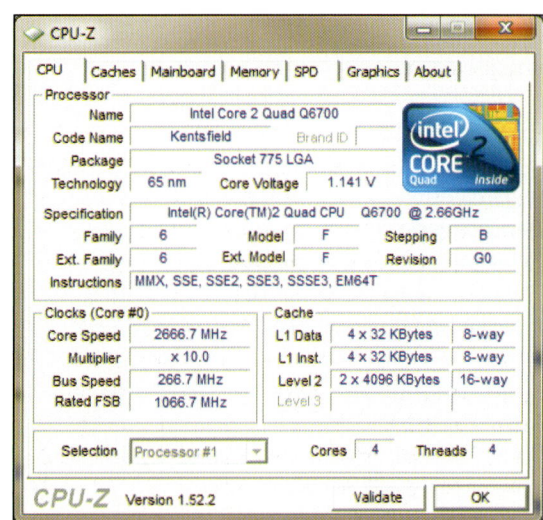

↑ The freely downloadable CPU-Z utility enables you to check your processor's current settings

If the settings you've made have stopped your computer from booting or you're experiencing other problems, you can go back into the menu and select Load Fail-Safe Defaults or Load Optimized Defaults instead. The former selects simple settings that should work with all hardware; the latter option sets slightly more powerful options. In both cases, you'll need to configure your BIOS from scratch.

ADVANCED BIOS CONFIGURATION

Perhaps the most important job that your BIOS does is to tell your PC how fast the processor and memory should run. If these settings are incorrect, you may find that your computer either runs more slowly than it should, or it will run faster but could crash intermittently. It's therefore important to make sure that your BIOS is configured correctly.

PROCESSOR SPEED

To check your processor's speed, you first need to find the correct setting. This may be in a dedicated menu, such as Cell Menu, or listed under Advanced BIOS Features. Whether you're running an Intel or AMD processor, its overall speed is based on two settings: an external bus speed and a multiplier (often called the processor ratio in the BIOS).

The external bus speed multiplied by the multiplier gives you your processor's speed. For example, a Core 2 Duo E8500 has a clock speed of 3.16GHz. This is made up of an external bus speed of 333MHz multiplied by a x9 multiplier (9 x 333MHz = 3.16GHz).

If either of these settings is incorrect, your PC won't run at its designated speed. In addition, if the external bus speed is incorrect, it will have a

knock-on effect on your memory's speed. It's important to make sure that this setting is correct. First, you'll need to know how fast your processor should run. The easiest way to do this is to start Windows. Right-click Computer from the Start menu and select Properties. You should see a screen that lists your processor model name followed by '@ xxxGHz'. This is your processor's rated speed in gigahertz. We'll show you how to check processor speeds for all processors below.

For AMD processors, working out the processor speed is simple, as the external bus speed (probably called HyperTransport speed in the BIOS) should be set to 200MHz. You can then set the multiplier. This can be done if you know your processor's rated speed in megahertz (multiply its gigahertz rating by 1,000). If you don't know your processor's rated speed, you can find a list of AMD processors at *http://tinyurl.com/amdprocessors*. Typing the model name into Google will also bring up help. Simply divide your processor's rating in megahertz by 200 to get its multiplier.

For Intel Core i3, Core i5 and Core i7 processors, the external bus (probably called base clock or base frequency) should be set to 133MHz. As with AMD's processors above, all you have to do to find out the multiplier is divide your processor's rated speed in megahertz by 133. You can find a list of Intel processor speeds at *http://tinyurl.com/intelprocessors*.

To make things even more confusing, older Intel processors often have their frontside bus (FSB) speed quoted. This is quad-pumped, so is four times faster than the external bus speed. To find out your processor's external bus speed, first find out its FSB speed at *http://tinyurl.com/ intelprocessors*. Divide the listed FSB speed by

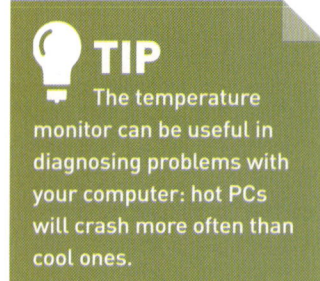

TIP The temperature monitor can be useful in diagnosing problems with your computer: hot PCs will crash more often than cool ones.

four to get the external bus speed, and divide your processor's speed in megahertz by the external bus speed to get the multiplier.

In your BIOS, find the options for CPU Ratio (or multiplier) and, depending on your processor, the base frequency, FSB or Hyper-Transport speed. Use the plus and minus keys on your keyboard to adjust these settings.

CHECKING YOUR SETTINGS

Your BIOS may display your processor's speed based on the settings that you've changed. This can help you make sure that you've configured it properly. If not, don't panic as it can be checked in Windows. To do this, save your settings and reboot your computer.

Install CPU-Z (*www.cpuid.com*) if you don't already have it, and run the application. Click on the CPU tab and at the bottom you'll see your processor's current bus speed and multiplier. The multiplier may be lower than expected as modern processors reduce it when your PC isn't busy in order to save power and reduce heat.

To boost the processor to its maximum speed, download Hot CPU Tester (*www.7byte.com*). Install the software and run it, ignoring any messages about buying the full version. Click Burn-in and Run CPU Burn-in. Select CPU-Z and the multiplier will be at its maximum (it may be sluggish to switch to CPU-Z, but don't worry).

Next, check that the Core Speed is set to your processor's correct rating. If it's not and the bus speed is set correctly, you'll need to go back to your BIOS and adjust the processor's multiplier. If the bus speed is incorrect, you'll need to

CPU-Z — SPD				
Memory Slot Selection	Slot #4	DDR2		
Module Size	512 MBytes		Correction	None
Max Bandwidth	PC2-6400 (400 MHz)		Registered	
Manufacturer	Corsair		Buffered	
Part Number	CM2X512-8500		SPD Ext.	EPP 1.0
Serial Number			Week/Year	23 / 06

Timings Table	JEDEC #1	JEDEC #2	EPP #1
Frequency	270 MHz	400 MHz	533 MHz
CAS# Latency	4.0	5.0	
RAS# to CAS#	4	5	6
RAS# Precharge	4	5	6
tRAS	13	18	15
tRC	15	22	30
Command Rate			2T
Voltage	1.8 V	1.8 V	2.200 V

↑ You can use the free CPU-Z application to make a note of your memory's supported speeds

adjust this. You can now click Stop CPU Burn-in on Hot CPU Tester.

MEMORY SETTINGS

Before we go back to the BIOS, it's best to check your memory's correct speed and settings by going back to CPU-Z and clicking on SPD. This reads the configuration from your memory to get the optimal settings. Look at the Max Bandwidth section and note down the megahertz rating (this may be half the speed you're expecting as memory runs at twice its stated bus speed, so DDR2 800MHz actually has a 400MHz clock speed). Look at the timings table and find the Frequency entry that matches your memory's Max Bandwidth speed. Note down all the information in the table, including CAS# Latency, RAS# to CAS# and so on.

Once you have this information, restart your computer and go into the BIOS and the menu you used to configure your processor. Your memory's speed is defined by the processor's external bus speed multiplied by a multiplier called the memory ratio. Change the memory ratio until your memory is set to the correct speed. For example, on a Core 2 Duo E8500 (333MHz), DDR2 800MHz memory should be set to a memory ratio of 1.2 (1.2x333=400MHz). Your BIOS should then display the correct full memory speed; in other words, it will show 800MHz for DDR2 800MHz RAM, not the 'true' speed of 400MHz.

Some BIOSes don't have a memory ratio setting, but rather have a menu option that lets you select your memory's full speed, such as

↑ Select the correct CPU Base Frequency to get the right processor speed

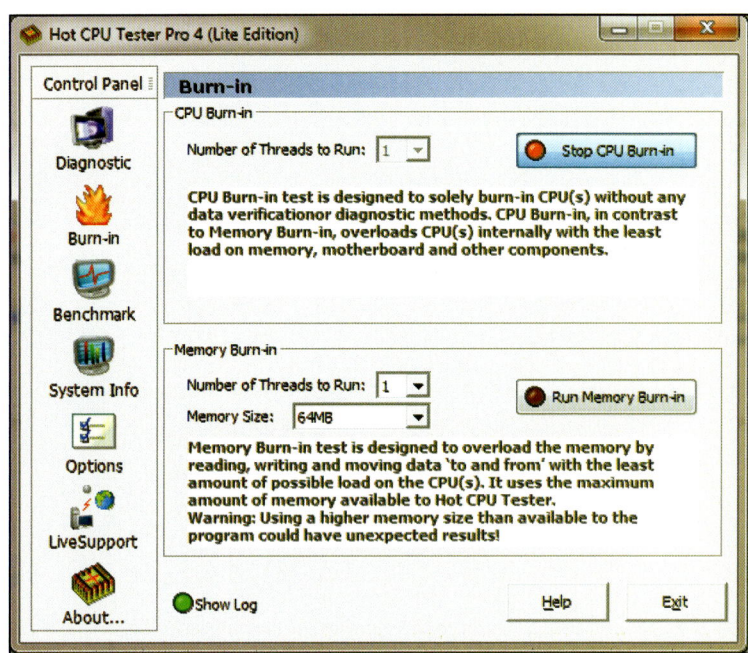

↑ You can use the free application Hot CPU Tester to push your processor to its rated speed

800MHz. Simply select the correct speed from the drop-down list.

Next you'll need to adjust the DRAM Timing Mode. This should be set automatically, but some memory defaults to a slower speed to ensure your PC boots up. The memory timings will be the second set of figures you noted down when you were using CPU-Z.

The headings in the BIOS may not match those taken from CPU-Z, and there may even be more headings displayed. What's important is that the timings in the BIOS are in the same order as in CPU-Z. CAS Latency (CL) will be clearly marked. Starting here, set each row to the value in the corresponding row that you noted down. When your memory is correctly configured, you can save the settings and continue.

POWER SETTINGS

The final job in the BIOS is to make sure that your PC is correctly configured to save power. To do this, find the Power Management Setup (or similar) menu. Here you can change the Advanced Configuration and Power Interface (ACPI) mode. Look for an ACPI option and set it to S3, rather than S1. This configures your computer so that in Sleep mode it will only supply power to the memory.

This means that your computer will only use a few watts of power; in S1 mode pretty much the entire computer remains on in Sleep mode, which wastes power.

Under this option you'll be able to set the Restore On AC Power Loss feature. This tells your computer what to do after it's lost power – after a power cut, for example. Off will leave your PC off, On will make it turn on when power is restored, and Last State will leave your PC off if it was turned off, but otherwise turn it back on.

WAKE UP EVENTS

You can also set your BIOS to define which devices can bring your PC out of Sleep mode. All BIOSes have slightly different options. New computers will have an option to remove control from the BIOS and put it entirely on Windows. This requires managing your devices through the Device Manager in Windows, using the Power Management options.

Most devices don't have these options, and you can only select which devices can and can't wake the computer. These will typically include USB devices, PS/2 Keyboard and PS/2 Mouse, plus PCI or PCI Express devices.

We recommend leaving all these settings enabled. You can still manually control which devices can wake the computer by viewing a device's properties in Windows' Device Manager and selecting the Power Management tab.

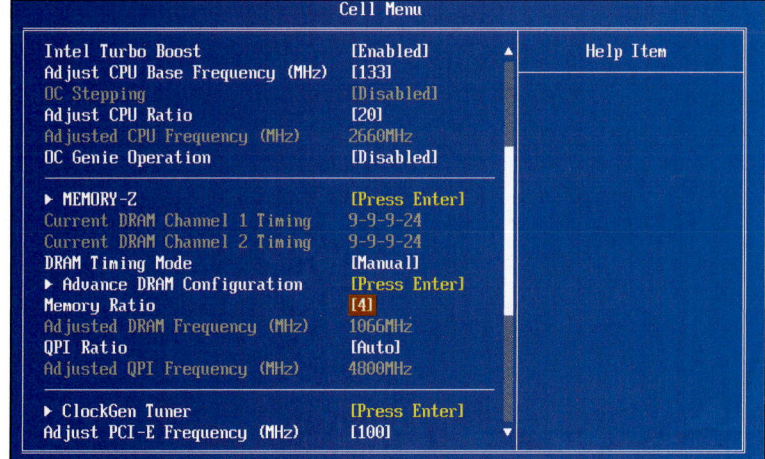

↑ Make sure that you select the correct memory ratio in order to run your RAM at its designated speed

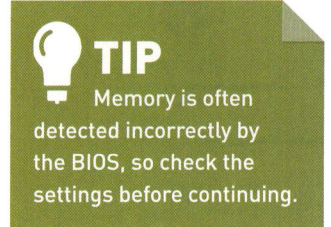

TIP
Memory is often detected incorrectly by the BIOS, so check the settings before continuing.

CHAPTER 6

INSTALLING AN OPERATING SYSTEM

IT'S INCREDIBLY IMPORTANT that you install your PC's operating system and drivers correctly if you want a reliable and stable computer. Whether you've chosen Windows 7 or Linux or you want a Media Center PC for the living room, we'll show you how to install and configure your operating system.

IN THIS CHAPTER

HOW TO...
Install Windows 7

1 START YOUR COMPUTER
Turn on your PC and put the Windows 7 DVD into its optical drive. If you have a new hard disk, the installation routine will load automatically. If you're using an old hard disk with an operating system already on it, you need to press any key when prompted. If you don't, your old operating system will start and you'll have to reset your PC to start the setup wizard. If the new Windows installer doesn't appear, you'll need to access your PC's BIOS. Check the boot options here to make sure your optical drive is listed first.

2 CHOOSE YOUR LANGUAGE OPTIONS
The first screen that appears will ask you which language you want to use. Select English from the drop-down menu. It should change the next drop-down box, but select English (United Kingdom) as the time and currency format if it doesn't. Your keyboard or input method should be set to United Kingdom automatically when you set the language. If it isn't, select United Kingdom from the third drop-down menu. Click Next to continue.

3 INSTALL WINDOWS 7
On the next screen, click 'What to know before installing Windows' if you want additional information about Windows 7. The 'Repair your computer' link starts the repair console, which can fix problems with a current Windows 7 installation. To install Windows 7, click the 'Install now' button.

4 ACCEPT THE LICENCE TERMS
You'll now be prompted to accept the terms. These are long and wordy, but read through them if you want to know what your licence allows. Tick the 'I accept the license terms' box when you're done. Click Next to continue to the next stage.

5 CHOOSE TYPE OF INSTALLATION
On the next screen, you'll be asked which type of installation you want to perform. Upgrade will upgrade your existing version of Windows. It can also be used to repair a damaged Windows 7 installation. However, this option can be run only from inside Windows. For a fresh installation, select Custom (advanced).

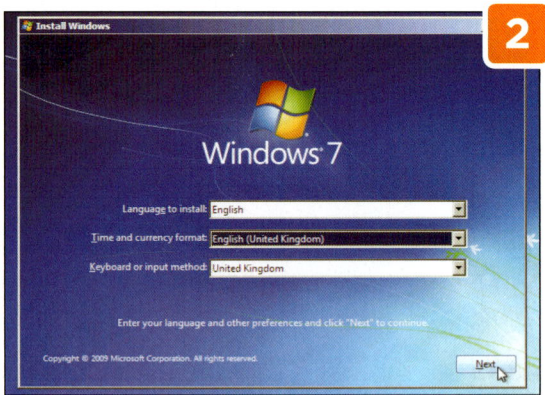

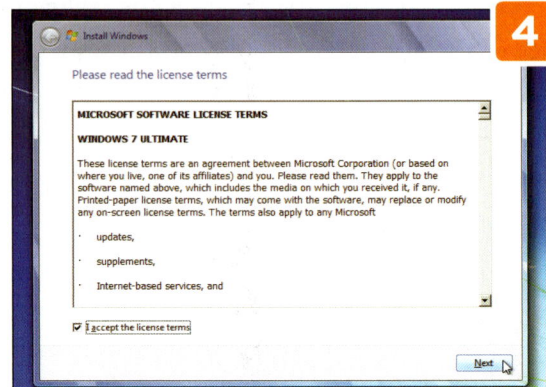

6 **SELECT HARD DISK**

Your hard disk should automatically be detected by Windows 7. If it isn't, click on the Load Driver button and insert the CD, USB key or floppy disk with the relevant driver. You should need to do this only if you're using RAID or you have a new motherboard that Windows doesn't recognise.

If you're using an old hard disk, it's best to start afresh. Select the partition that contains your old operating system, choose Advanced and click Delete. You can also delete any other partitions this way. You're now ready to continue.

For a fresh disk, or an old disk where you've wiped the existing partitions, you can just select Unallocated Space and click Next. Windows will automatically create the necessary disk partitions and perform the installation. We recommend that you have at least two partitions: one for Windows, and a smaller one for storing backups, drivers and other files you want to keep permanently.

Select the Unallocated Space and click Advanced and then New. You have to select the size of the partition in megabytes (where 1,024MB

is equal to 1GB). Generally, we'd recommend leaving at least 40GB (40,960MB) for the second partition. Subtract the size of second partition you want from the figure in the box, and enter this. Then click Apply. Select Disk 0 Unallocated Space, click New and then Apply. You'll get a warning that Windows may create extra partitions, but click OK.

You'll now have two partitions: the one you created, and a 100MB System Reserved partition. Click Disk 0 Unallocated Space, New, and then Apply. You now have all the partitions you need.

7 **FORMAT DISKS**

To make things easier once you've started Windows, you should format your partitions now. Select Partition 2 (the installation will deal with Partition 1 automatically) and click Format. Click OK in the warning box. You'll get a spinning cursor for a few moments while the disk is formatted. Repeat these steps for the second partition and any others you have that you want to wipe (leave all partitions or disks with important data on them alone). When done, click Partition 2 and then Next.

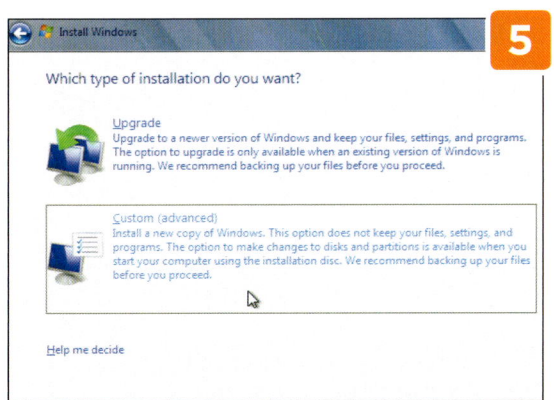

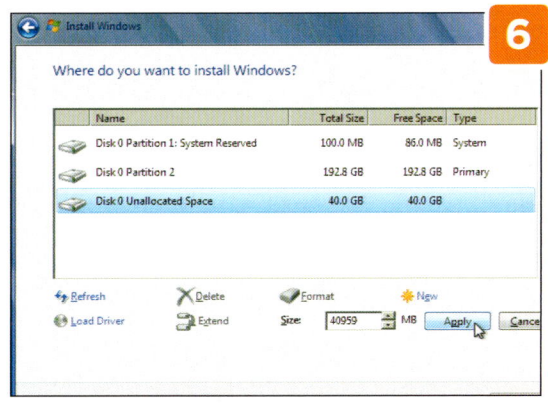

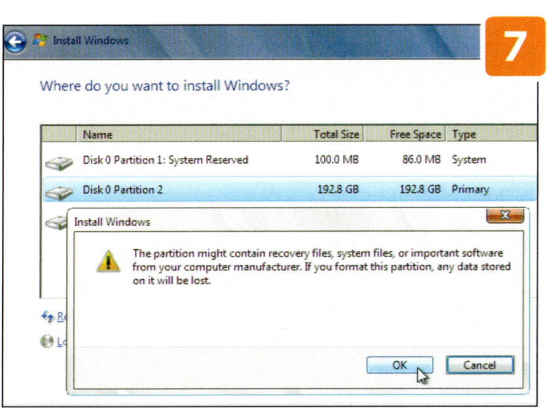

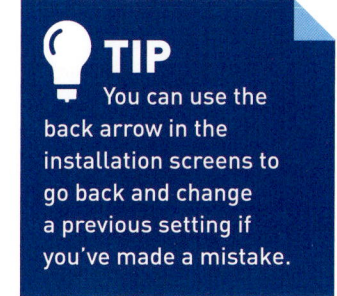

TIP
You can use the back arrow in the installation screens to go back and change a previous setting if you've made a mistake.

8 ### INSTALL WINDOWS FILES
Windows will automatically copy system files and install the necessary drivers to get your PC working on the first partition you created.

9 ### SET UP USERNAME AND PASSWORD
After the installation files have finished copying, you'll be prompted to type in a username for yourself (you can create more for other users later) and a name for your computer. Enter this information and click Next. On the next screen, you're asked to enter a password.

The password is optional, but if you want to protect your files and ensure that only authorised users can access your PC, it's vital that you have one. Finally, enter a hint that will remind you of your password in case you forget it and click Next.

10 ### ENTER PRODUCT KEY
You will now be prompted to type in your product key, which is inside the box in which your copy of Windows came. Leave the 'Automatically activate Windows when I'm online' and click Next.

11 ### TURN ON WINDOWS UPDATES
Windows now asks whether you want to turn on Windows Updates automatically. The best option is to select 'Use recommended settings'. Next, set the date and time of your computer.

If you chose your location as UK in the Windows installation routine, the time will be set to GMT by default. Then click Next. If Windows picked up your network adaptor correctly and found that your computer was connected to a network, you'll be asked to choose the type of network – for most people, this will be Home network. Windows will then start for the first time.

12 ### INSTALL MOTHERBOARD DRIVERS
Although Windows is now working, you still need to install all the relevant drivers to make sure that everything will run smoothly. The trick here is to install any drivers that are for Windows 7; only install Windows Vista drivers if a component isn't working, such as your network adaptor.

Start with your motherboard's drivers. If you downloaded these earlier, insert the USB key or disc to which you saved them. If you couldn't do this, insert the driver disc that came with your motherboard and follow the onscreen instructions. You'll need to download the updated drivers later, and then follow these instructions.

For each driver you downloaded, run the associated file. It's best to start with the chipset driver, but the order afterwards doesn't matter. If Windows displays any warning messages, just click OK. Be careful, as some files you download are just archive files that extract the actual driver

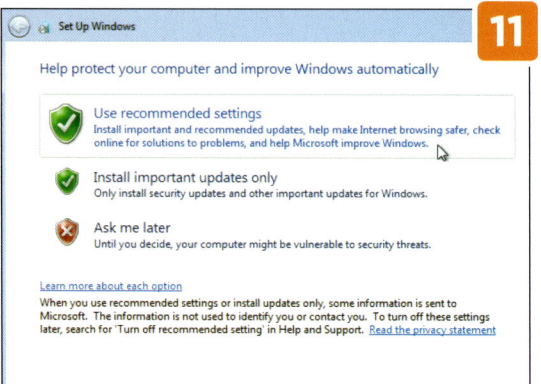

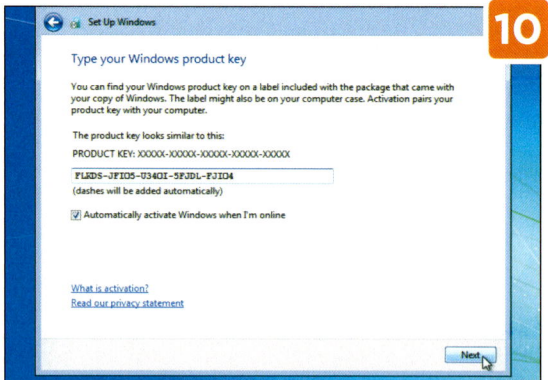

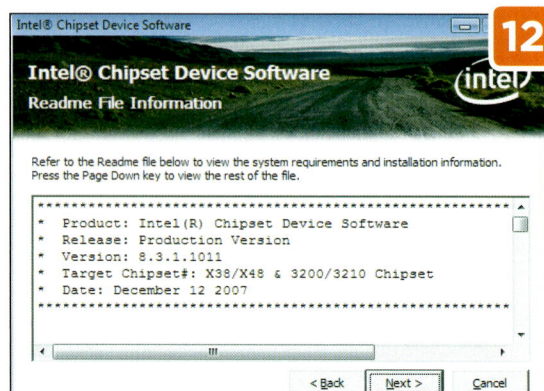

files on to your hard disk. If this is the case, go to the folder to which the files were extracted and run the Setup program. You'll probably need to restart your PC after each driver installation.

13 INSTALL GRAPHICS CARD DRIVERS
Windows will install its own graphics drivers for any onboard or dedicated cards you have. These are fine for running Windows, but you won't be able to play games properly. For this, you'll need to install the graphics drivers.

Both ATI and Nvidia provide a single driver package. Simply run the file you downloaded. If you couldn't download the drivers earlier, you should do it now. (Follow Step 14 if you need to install a wireless adaptor to get online and then come back to this step.) Restart your computer after the graphics drivers have been installed. Right-click on the desktop, select Screen Resolution and adjust the resolution to match your monitor's native resolution.

14 INSTALL OTHER PERIPHERALS
You can now install your other peripherals. Install the relevant driver files for each device that's plugged into your motherboard. For USB devices, install the driver file first and, when prompted, connect the device to a USB port. If you're in any doubt, you should read the manual that came with

your peripheral. If you've installed a wireless adaptor, make sure you connect it to your wireless network and follow the provided instructions.

15 RUN WINDOWS UPDATE
Click on the Start menu, type Windows Update and click the entry that appears. Click the Check for Updates button, and Windows will connect to Microsoft's update server and detect which updates you need.

Click on View available updates and look at the list. Some will have been preselected as important updates, but there are also some optional ones, including even newer drivers for your hardware. Select what you'd like to update, then click install.

When they've finished downloading and installing and your PC has restarted, you'll have a working copy of Windows 7 that's up to date.

16 CREATE A SYSTEM REPAIR DISC
Windows 7 has an option to let you create a disc to repair problems with the operating system. It's worth doing this now while you've got a working PC. To do this, click on the Start menu and type repair, and click on Create a System Repair Disc. Put a blank CD or DVD into your optical drive and click Create disc process. This will take a few minutes. When it's done, take the disc out, label it clearly and put it somewhere safe.

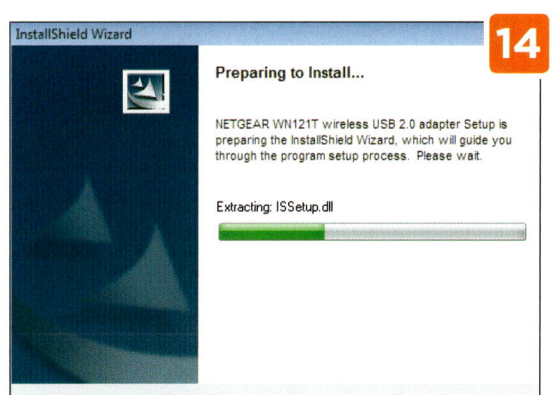

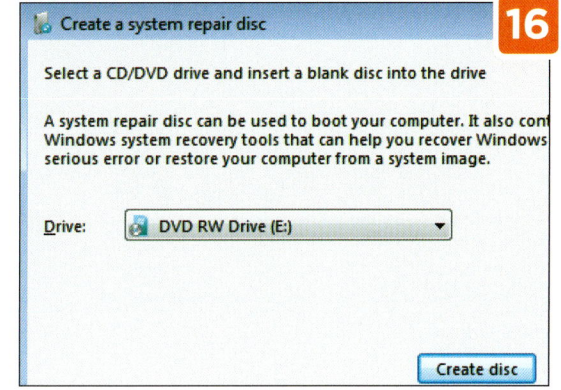

TIP Copying the installation files can take more than an hour, so you'll need to be patient while Windows installs.

Improve Windows Media Center

The default installation of Media Center doesn't let you do much, and you can't play downloaded media such as DivX files very easily. Fortunately, it's easy to tweak – here we show you how

WINDOWS MEDIA CENTER is a brilliant application once you've tweaked it to get rid of all of its minor annoyances and added new features with free software. In this guide we'll show you how to turn Media Center from a useful bit of kit into the best media player you'll ever own.

To make the most of these instructions, you'll need an official Microsoft Media Center Remote (around £30 including VAT from *www.kikatek.com*). We've found that third-party remote controls don't work very well with some of the third-party software we've recommended.

QUICK FIXES

Once you've installed extra software on your computer, we've found that Media Center can often lose screen priority and let the Start menu reappear. Not only is this annoying, but it can actually cause a crash if you're in the middle of watching a video.

This is easy to fix using Media Center. Go to the Tasks section of the main menu and select Media Only and select Yes when prompted. This will force Media Center to run in full-screen mode,

preventing other applications from taking control. To revert to the standard Media Center mode, select the Media Only option again.

If you're using Media Center just for its media capabilities, you should dispense with some of Windows' more irritating automatic features. First, disable automatic updates, otherwise Window may automatically restart your computer. Open Control Panel and select Security (System and Security in Windows 7). Click Turn automatic updating on or off. Select Never check for updates and click OK. You should still update your computer at regular intervals, but use Windows Update in the Start menu manually.

Finally, we recommend disabling the indexing service, which periodically scans your hard disk for Windows Search, but isn't used by Media Center. To do this, right-click on Computer in the Start menu and select Manage. Expand the Services and Applications section on the left-hand panel and click Services. Double-click Windows Search and change the Startup type from Automatic to Disabled and click Apply. Click the Stop button and then click OK.

⬇ Put Media Center into Media Only mode to make sure that it's always the most important application

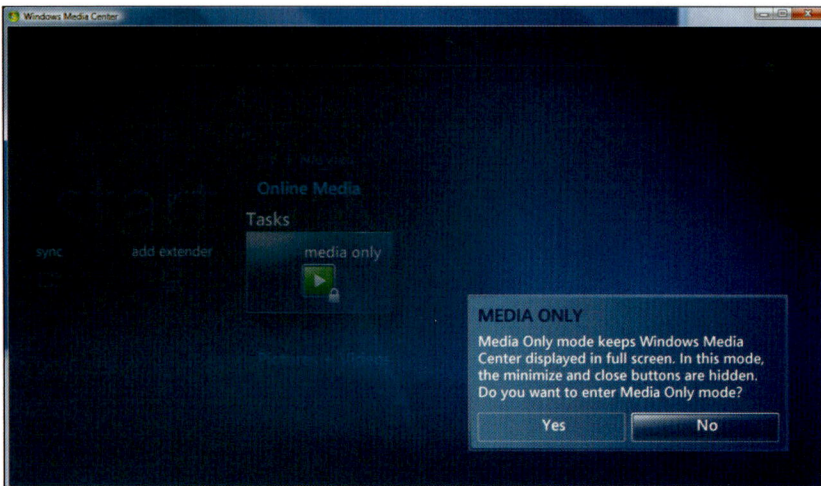

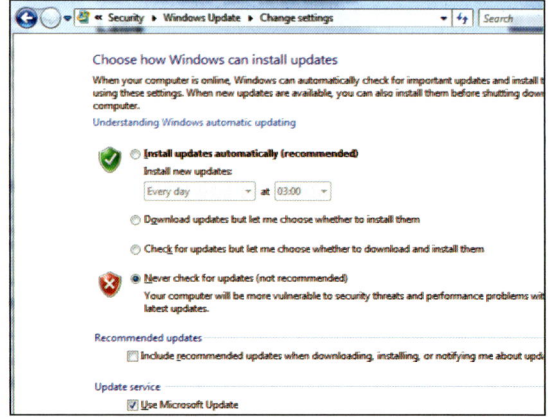

⬆ Turn off automatic updates to prevent Windows from restarting your PC automatically

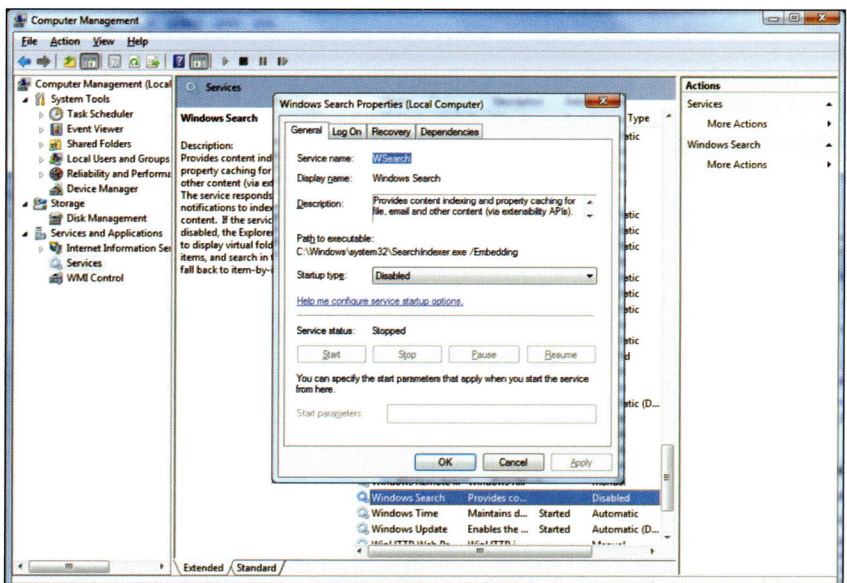

← Disable Windows Search to prevent your computer from thrashing the hard disk

PLAYING ALL MEDIA FILES

Media Center's handling of videos, with the exception of WMV files, is incredibly poor, and you'll find that even if you install the necessary codecs to play other files, you can't even fast-forward them. Fortunately, it doesn't have to be this way, and with some free software you'll be able to do all of these things.

First, uninstall any video codecs that you've already installed, such as QuickTime and DivX, as you won't need them. Then downloaded and install ffdshow tryouts (*http://ffdshow-tryout.sourceforge. net*) using the application's default settings. This is a free audio and video decoder that will handle pretty much any video format you'll throw at it.

It still won't let you fast-forward videos, though, so you also need to download the Media Center Control Plugin version 6 (*http://damienbt.free.fr*). Make sure you get the right version for your operating system (32- or 64-bit). This application lets you fast-forward all videos, add bookmarks and resume from the last point at which you stopped watching.

Before you install it, download and install Microsoft Visual C++ 2008 SP1 (*http://tinyurl.com/ C2008SP1*). Then install Media Center Control Plugin. When the installation has finished, select the option to launch the Media Control Configuration. Click on the Remote control & keyboard tab. There's currently no option to stop a video from fast-forwarding, so click Add command. In the first drop-down menu, select Stop Fast Forward/Rewind. The next two options can be used to set a keyboard short cut for the action, but skip this and select Play from the Remote button drop-down menu. Click Commit changes.

To complete the basic configuration, click on the ffdshow configuration tab. Click on Apply minimal configuration and then OK, then on Apply recommended configuration and then OK. Click Commit changes and OK, then restart your computer to apply the changes.

After your PC has restarted, you'll find that you can play any video format in Media Center, and be able to fast-forward and rewind them. Coming back to a video at a later date will pop up an option that asks if you want to resume the video. Press 'i' on the remote control and select More, then Media Control. You can use the menu options to set Bookmarks for programmes you're watching, so that you can jump to your favourite scenes later.

IMPROVE VIDEO PICTURE QUALITY

The picture quality of many downloaded videos isn't very good, but fortunately, you can fix this. With a DivX video playing take Media Center out of Media Only mode, use your mouse to put the application into windowed mode (the middle icon

↓ You need to configure remote commands in the Media Control window

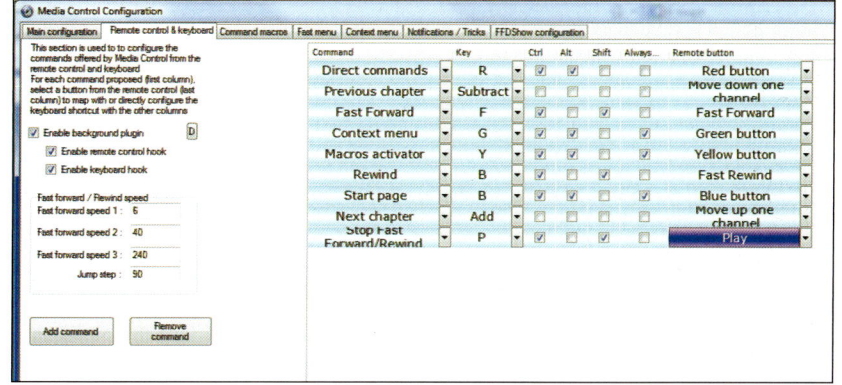

when you move the mouse to the top right). In the Notification Area you'll see two new icons: a blue ffdshow audio decoder and a red ffdshow video decoder. Double-click the audio one first.

First, set the correct audio settings. Put a tick in the Mixer box and then click Mixer. Select the Output speakers configuration from the drop-down menu. For most PCs with surround sound this should be 3/0/2 – 5 channels, but for 7.1 speakers select 3/2/2. If you have surround sound, you also need to tick the LFE box to send the subwoofer its own signal. Next, click Dolby decoder and select Apply Dolby Pro Logic II decoding to all stereo sources. This will upsample stereo soundtracks to use all of your speakers. Click OK.

Double-click the video icon. For every setting that we show you how to adjust, make sure that Process whole image is selected. Put a tick in the Deinterlacing box and select Cubic interpolation from the drop-down menu. This will deinterlace TV shows to match your TV's progressive mode. Put a tick in Postprocessing, and a tick in Picture Processing and adjust the sliders until you're happy with the picture's colour, brightness and contrast. Downloaded video can look harsh, so put a tick in the Blur & NR (Blur and Noise Reduction)

box. We find that setting Soften to 40 or less and Gradual denoise to 40 or less helps reduce noise and produce a better image.

You can bring out the detail in a video by ticking the Sharpen box. Select unsharp mask and adjust the Strength bar until you're happy (around 25 should do it). Now to make sure that the picture looks as good as possible, you can force ffdshow to upscale video to match your TV's resolution.

Put a tick in Resize & aspect, select Specify horizontal and vertical size, and type in the size of your display in the box below, such as 1,920x1,080 for 1080p TVs. By default the video will maintain its aspect ratio, so old TV shows will have black bars down the side of the picture. If you don't like this, select No aspect ratio correction, to fill the screen. Click Apply. You can now maximise Media Center and use it as normal.

There are a couple of problems with Media Control. First, it will also work when you try to play a DVD, prompting you to launch ffdshow. The idea is that ffdshow can take over the picture processing, increasing quality. However, we've yet to get this to work successfully and have found that it stops DVD menus from working. Just wait for the option to disappear.

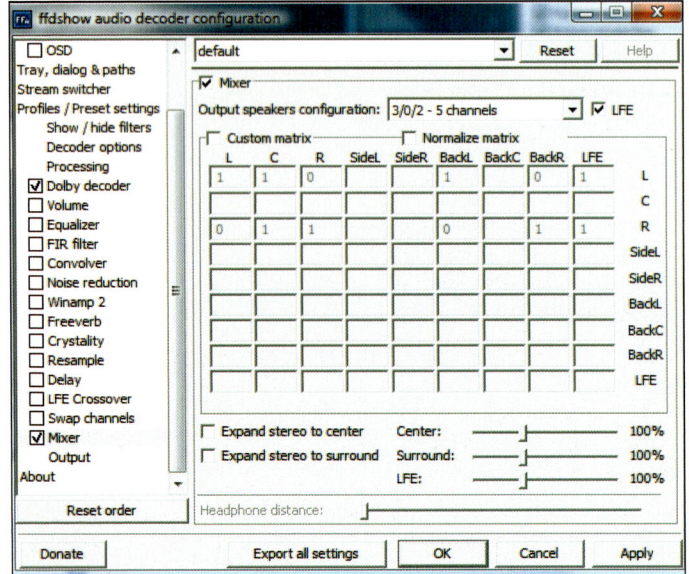

↑ The application ffdshow can turn stereo sound into surround sound

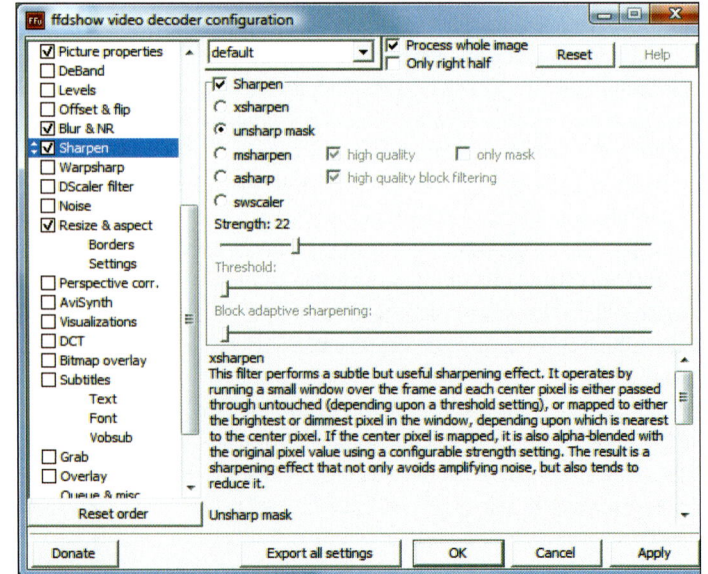

↑ You can also improve the quality of your video with ffdshow

Second, when you stop watching a video, pressing fast-forward later on – when you're watching a DVD, for example – will cause your old video to start playing again. To get round this, when you've stopped watching a video, select Media Control from Media Center's main menu and select Restart Media Center. You'll have to put Media Center back into Media Only mode.

TV EVERYWHERE

Media Center can also be used to catch up with TV shows that you may have missed with the free TunerFree MCE application (*www.milliesoft.co.uk/tunerfree.php*). This provides a single interface for all the major catch-up services, including the BBC's iPlayer and Channel 4's 4oD. Download the application for your operating system (Vista or Windows 7), quit Media Center and install TunerFree using the Typical settings. The process will take several minutes as the database of available programmes is downloaded.

Before you can use the software you need to make sure that your computer has all the necessary codecs to play the files. Visit each service using Internet Explorer (see below) and play a sample video, downloading extra software when prompted.

SERVICE	ADDRESS
BBC	www.bbc.co.uk/iplayer
ITV	www.itv.com/ITVPlayer
Channel 4 On Demand	http://www.channel4.com/4od
Five	http://demand.five.tv

When done, you can start Media Center. TunerFree MCE is installed into the TV + Movies section of the main menu. When you launch the application, you can either browse through the individual channels, or use the options at the top to browse by date or search by keyword.

The default installation also lets you select Hulu, which is a US-only service. To fix this, select Preferences and select Get Hulu so that it has a grey box next to it. Click Save, and then Back. You'll now have access to every TV-on-demand service in the UK.

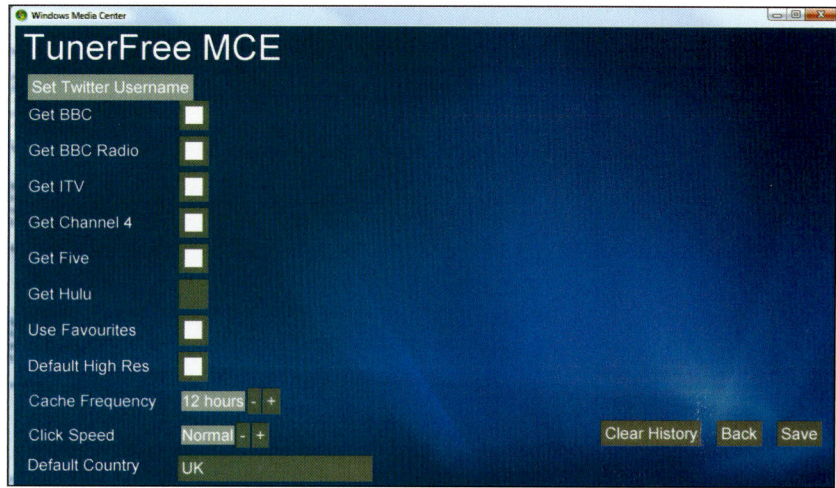

SOUND IMPROVEMENTS

The final adjustment is improving the sound when watching DVDs. Media Center's built-in audio decoder will let you listen to Dolby Digital soundtracks only if you're using analogue outputs, not DTS. This can be fixed easily, however. Download and install AC3Filter (*http://ac3filter.net*). From the Start menu, run AC3Filter Config. Change the output to match your speaker configuration (surround-sound users should select 3/2+SW 5.1 channels).

The other settings, such as the Equalizer and Mixer for adjusting speaker volume, bass and treble, are best adjusted when you're listening to some audio. AC3Filter puts an icon in the Notification Area when compatible audio is playing, which you can double-click to adjust settings on the fly.

To get AC3Filter working in Media Center requires a bit of fiddling. First, you need to find out the CLSID of the software. You can do this by downloading the DirectShow Filter Manager (*www.softella.com/dsfm/index.en.htm*). Run the software and double-click the entry for AC3Filter. Copy the CLSID including the curly brackets.

Run RegEdit and navigate to HKey_Local_Machine\Software\Microsoft\Windows\CurrentVersion\Media Center\Decoder. Double-click PreferredMPEG2AudioDecoderCLSID and paste in the CLSID you copied earlier. Click OK and shut down RegEdit. Now when you watch a DVD, you'll be able to decode DTS soundtracks.

↑ TunerFree MCE lets you watch all of the UK's TV-on-demand services via Media Center

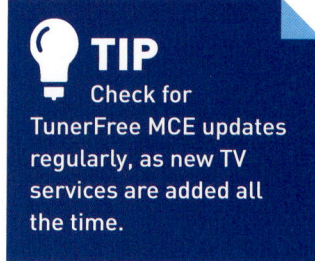

TIP
Check for TunerFree MCE updates regularly, as new TV services are added all the time.

Improve Media Center movies

A default Media Center installation can't play Blu-ray discs or multiregion DVDs. Here we'll show you how to turn your computer into the ultimate playback machine for your movies

BEFORE WE GET into the nitty gritty of improving video playback, we'll talk about sound. Depending on your PC, you'll have a choice of three sound outputs: analogue (the PC decodes surround sound), S/PDIF and HDMI (the sound is sent digitally and not decoded). We recommend using analogue outputs for two reasons: S/PDIF doesn't support HD audio, such as Dolby TrueHD, on Blu-ray discs, and the HDMI outputs on graphics cards downsample HD audio to standard-definition audio, as they lack a technology called PAP.

With analogue you can ensure that you get the best-quality sound, and it will also work better with some of the applications that we're going to talk about here. If you're not happy with the sound from your onboard sound card, upgrade to a PCI Express model, such as Auzentech's X-Fi Forte 7.1 (around £126 including VAT).

MORE FORMATS

Media Center's built-in DVD player is very basic and doesn't support HD formats such as Blu-ray.

↑ To get the best-quality sound, use your PC's analogue outputs

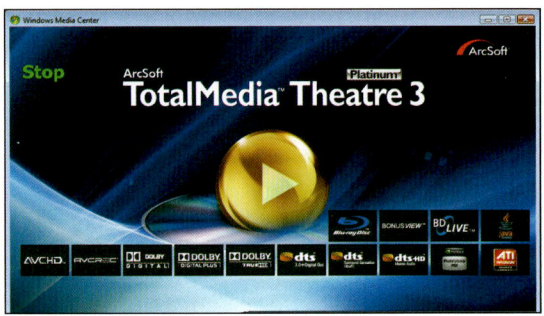

↑ Use TotalMedia Theatre 3 to get the best video playback and support for HD formats

To get better-quality video and HD support, you need a third-party player. We recommend using ArcSoft's TotalMedia Theatre 3 (TMT3) Platinum, which costs $100 (around £63) from *www.arcsoft. com/public/software_title.asp?ProductID=362*.

This software integrates into Media Center. Blu-ray and HD DVD discs will automatically play when you put them in, but DVDs will give you the option of Media Center or TMT3. Always select TMT3 when given the option.

THE MULTIREGION QUESTION

One of the most annoying aspects about using your computer to play discs is that it's hard to make it region-free so it will play movies from any anywhere. With DVD drives, you're allowed to change the region-coding on the drive up to five times. After you've done this, the drive will be locked to a specific region. Getting round this protection, which is known as RPC2, is difficult.

There are programs available that will bypass the region-coding on the disc and drive, but they also bypass the CSS encryption used to protect the discs, which is illegal under UK law.

The only way to get around the problem is to install new firmware on your drive that removes the region lock, turning the drive into an RPC1 model. Before we explain how to do this, you should be

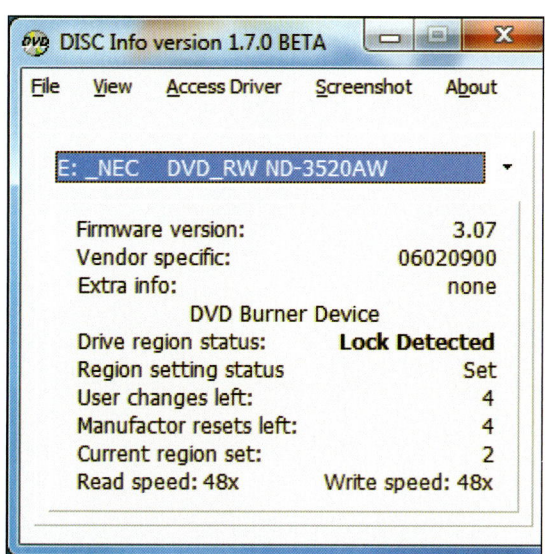

↑ Drive Info tells you the exact model of drive you have and if it currently has a region lock on it

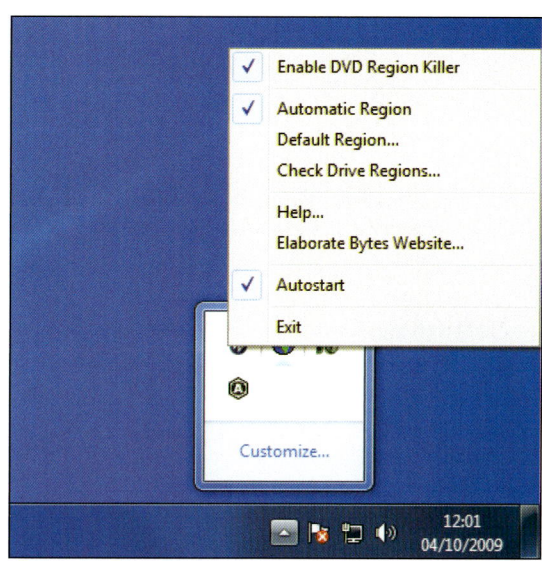

↑ You can use DVD Region Killer to ensure that you can play any DVD on your PC

aware that changing your drive's firmware will invalidate your warranty and, if you get the wrong firmware, can even break the drive. Currently, it's easy to find the right firmware for DVD drives, but firmware for Blu-ray drives is difficult to find.

First, you need to find out your exact drive model by downloading the latest version of DISCInfo (*http://discinfo.rpc1.org*). Run the file – it doesn't need to be installed – and it will tell you the make and model of your drive. You can use this information to find the right firmware. A good place to start is *http://tdb.rpc1.org*, which has tons of firmware for all the most popular drives. If your drive is listed, follow the provided instructions to update its firmware. If you can't find your drive here, you can try searching Google for the name and model of your drive plus "RPC1 firmware".

SOFTWARE UNLOCKING

Once you've unlocked your drive, you'll still have the problem that your DVD playback software also has region-coding built in, which you need to bypass. This can be done easily with DVD Region Killer (*http://tinyurl.com/regionkiller*).

Simply download the software and install it. After rebooting your computer, right-click on its icon in the Notification Area and select 'Enable DVD Region Killer'. You'll now be able to watch a DVD from any region.

BLU-RAY REGION

With Blu-Ray, the region-coding is set in software, but each playback software limits you to five changes. However, this is easy to bypass with the Blu-ray Region Tray Tool (*http://tinyurl.com/*

blurayregion), which lets you make an infinite number of region changes in PowerDVD and TotalMedia Theatre.

Download and run the software (it has to be run each time you start Windows, so save the file to your Startup folder in the Start menu). In the Notification Area you'll see an icon showing you which region (A, B or C) you're currently using. You can either click on the Notification Area icon to change the region or use the keyboard shortcut of Ctrl-Shift-1, -2 or -3 for, respectively, regions A, B or C. You can't have TotalMedia Theatre or PowerDVD running while you change regions.

PLAYING SMOOTH VIDEO

One of the biggest problems with a Windows Media Center PC is getting video to play back smoothly. If you watch carefully you'll notice that the screen will judder and jerk at times. The reason for this is down to the different frame rates of video that exist.

For example, films are all shot at 24fps and shown progressively (one frame at a time). PAL (UK) video is interlaced (each frame is split into two fields, one containing the odd lines and one containing the even lines) and shown at 25fps or 50 fields per second (50Hz refresh rate). NTSC (American) video is interlaced and shown at the bizarre rate of 29.97fps (59.94Hz).

So, the problem is that there are a number of different frame rates and refresh rates that don't match; for example, if you've got a UK PAL TV and a 24fps film, then the two don't match. The solution is to speed up the film to 25fps and interlace it to make the required 50 fields per

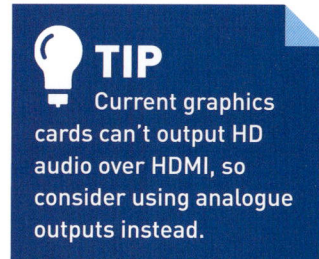

TIP
Current graphics cards can't output HD audio over HDMI, so consider using analogue outputs instead.

second. This is the reason that films on DVD in the UK are four per cent quicker than at the cinema.

However, for NTSC displays this technique doesn't make any sense, as doing the same thing and increasing a film from 24fps to 29.97fps would make it far too quick. Instead, a technique called 3:2 pulldown is used. First the film is slowed down by one per cent to 23.976fps, then for every fourth field of video, one extra field is added to bring the total frame rate up to the required 29.97fps. A good explanation of the technique, and why it's called 3:2 pulldown, can be found at *www.zerocut. com/tech/pulldown.html*.

LCD displays are progressive, not interlaced, so a PAL LCD TV runs at 50fps (a refresh rate of 50Hz). For PAL footage, then, it's a simple case of deinterlacing two fields and sending them as a single frame twice, thereby turning 25fps footage into 50fps footage.

However, put an NTSC disc into your PC's drive when you're running at a refresh rate of 50Hz and you've got a problem: using 3:2 pull down and deinterlacing the footage will get you too many frames (59.94fps), while doubling the disc's native frame rate as you would do for PAL would generate two few frames (47.952fps). In the first case, some frames would have to be dropped; in the second case some frames would have to be repeated more often that others; both create jerky video.

CLOCKING IN

Setting your PC to output the correct refresh rate can help matters, but NTSC discs can still cause problems. PCs can often only output refresh rates of whole numbers, so for NTSC that's 60Hz, even though the format is technically 59.94Hz. The slight difference leaves jerky video.

The wider problem is that PCs don't use the video card's onboard clock to detect the playback rate and make sure that video is being played at the right speed. Fortunately, that's where ReClock comes in.

This application examines the frame rate of a video that's being played and ties its playback into the graphics card's clock. It also checks the refresh rate at which your PC is running and adjusts the frame rate accordingly to make smooth video, so, for example, 23.976fps NTSC video is increased in speed to 25fps for computers running at a refresh rate of 50Hz.

The sound is dynamically adjusted, too, so that speeding up or slowing down video doesn't alter pitch and make it sound strange. It can also run a VBScript to adjust your graphics card's refresh rate, although this is quite complex to set up, and our instructions will leave you with smooth video. Search Google for RunEvent.vbs for more information on how to change your refresh rate to match the source material.

CONFIGURING RECLOCK

First, you need to stop Media Center from changing the refresh rate when it feels like it. Get up a Run command (Windows+R), type Regedit and hit Enter. Navigate to HKey_Local_Machine\Software\Microsoft\Windows\CurrentVersion\Media Center\Settings\DisplayService and change EnableRefreshRateChange to 0.

Next, you need to download ReClock (*http:// forum.slysoft.com/showthread.php?t=19931*) and install it on your PC. Once installed, run ReClock Configuration from the Start menu. You can leave most of the default settings alone, but we had to change 'Audio interface to use for PCM sound' to WaveOut. Also make sure that 'Enable audio timestretching' is selected for both 'When slowing down media' and 'When speeding up media'. This will let ReClock adjust the pitch of audio to make it match the new frame rate.

If you're using an S/PDIF connection – which we don't recommend – then you may have trouble

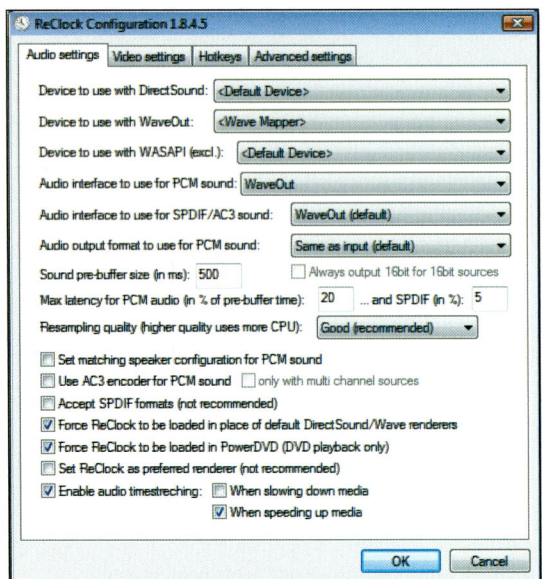

⬆ You need to configure ReClock carefully to get it to work with your hardware

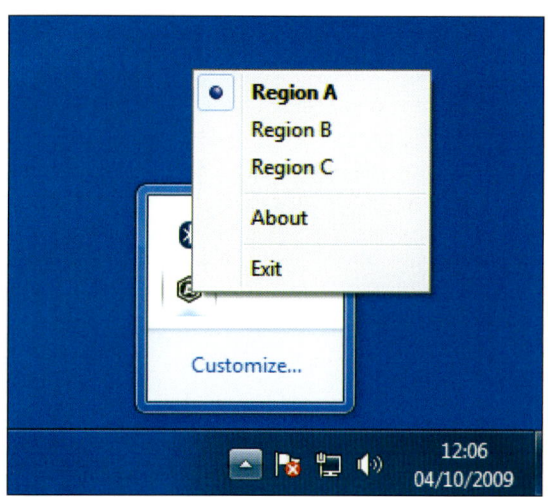

↑ You can change your PC's Blu-ray region easily

making ReClock work, and you may have to select the 'Use AC3 encoder for PCM sound' option.

Next, click on the Video settings tab and change the Hardware access method to DirectDraw. Under 'When frame rate is not found by previous methods, assume' select 24 (fps) for DVDs and 25 (fps) for other files. Click OK to apply the settings.

RUNNING RECLOCK

Now, start Media Center and put in a disc. Choose to play it in Total Media Theatre. When the message pops up asking if you want to use ReClock, select 'Yes, always' and click OK. You'll need to do the same thing with any other video-playing applications that you use and for watching DivX video.

Play a DVD and put Media Center into a Windowed mode. You'll see a clock icon in the Notification Area; double-click this to select some more options. One you may be interested in is 'Enable sound compressor:'. This will make loud sounds such as explosions quieter, which is useful if you're watching a film at night.

The screen will give you details of the sound and frame rate of the video, and will also show you the speed at which it's currently playing your video. Your video will now play correctly, no matter what its frame rate is.

CHANGING THE REFRESH RATE

ReClock doesn't work with all applications, so the next best thing is to change the refresh rate manually. Download SetRR from *www.*

gianlucabove.it/v2/en/setRR and save the file to your hard disk. When you run this file and give it a number as an option it will change your computer's refresh rate to that number.

For LCD TVs, you should make three batch files (text files with .bat file extensions) that will change the resolution to match the three types of movie content (24p.bat for Blu-ray, PAL.bat and NTSC. bat). The files should contain, respectively, the lines setrr.exe 24, setrr.exe 50 and setrr.exe 60 (you can also try 59, if your PC and TV will accept 59.94Hz for NTSC). If your TV doesn't support 24p, don't make the 24p.bat file.

We can use our batch files to change refresh rates manually. First, you need to download the Media Center Launcher Configurator from *http:// tinyurl.com/mclauncherconfig*.

Install the software on your PC then run it as an Administrator by right-clicking on the short cut and selecting Run as Administrator. This software enables you to add your batch files to the Media Center menu. For each one, select the Path to Application (select the batch file), the image to display (search Google for an appropriate picture), the title, description and in which menu you want it to appear. Click Register to apply the settings. For each new program, remember to click the icon next to GUID to generate a new ID for each batch file, or you'll run into problems.

When you start Media Center, your batch files will be available through the main menu. For example, to watch Blu-rays at 24Hz, insert a disc, then select your 24p batch file. Start TMT3 and watch the film. When you're done, run the 50Hz batch file from Media Center's menu.

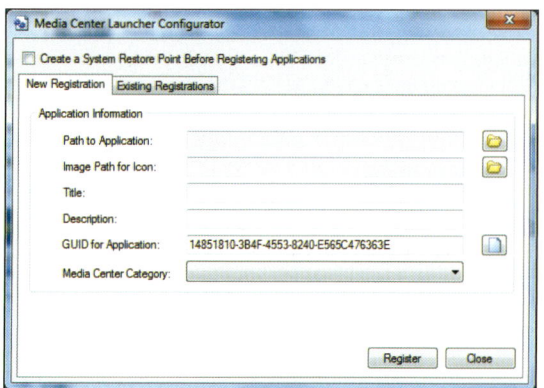

↑ You can add your own applications and batch files to Media Center

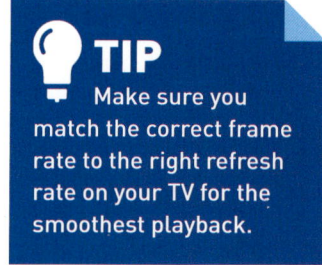

TIP
Make sure you match the correct frame rate to the right refresh rate on your TV for the smoothest playback.

Unbeatable power protection now beats energy costs, too

Back-UPS
Pro 550

APC Legendary Reliability™

Only APC Back-UPS delivers unsurpassed power protection *and* real energy savings

Today's cost-saving Back-UPS

For years you've relied on APC Back-UPS™ to protect your business from expensive downtime caused by power problems. Today, the reinvented Back-UPS does even more. Its highly efficient design noticeably reduces energy use, so you start saving money the minute you plug it in. Only APC Back-UPS guarantees to keep your electronics up and your energy use down!

Unique energy-efficient features

Power-saving outlets automatically shut off power to unused devices when your computer and peripherals are turned off or on standby. Automatic voltage regulation (AVR) adjusts the undervoltages and overvoltages without using the battery. With our patent-pending AVR bypass, the transformer kicks in only when needed and automatically deactivates when power is stable. Plus, APC's highly efficient designs reduce power consumption when power is good and extend runtimes when the lights go out. Together, these power-saving features eliminate wasteful electricity drains, saving you about £25-31 a year. And managing today's Back-UPS couldn't be easier thanks to an integrated LCD that provides diagnostic information at your fingertips.

Trusted insurance for all your business needs

The award-winning Back-UPS provides reliable power protection for a range of applications, from desktops and notebook computers to wired and wireless networks to external storage. The reinvented APC Back-UPS is the trusted insurance you need to stay up and running and reliably protected from both unpredictable power and energy waste!

Keep your electronics up and your energy use down!

Back-UPS models are available with the features and runtime capacity that best suit your application, and many models have been designed with power-saving features to reduce costs.

The high-performance Back-UPS Pro series

High-performance Back-UPS Pro units deliver cost-cutting, energy-efficient features. Power-saving outlets automatically shut off power to unused devices when your computer and peripherals are turned off or on standby, eliminating costly electricity drains. (BR550GI shown above)

The energy-efficient BE700G-UK

The BE700G-UK boasts innovative power-saving outlets, which automatically shut off power to controlled outlets when the computer plugged into the host outlet is deemed asleep, eliminating wasteful electricity drains.
- 8 Outlets • 405 Watts / 700 VA
- 80 Minutes Maximum Runtime
- Telephone/Network Protection

The best-value BE550G-UK

The BE550G-UK uses an ultra-efficient design that consumes less power during normal operation than any other battery backup in its class, saving you money on your electricity bill.
- 8 Outlets • 330 Watts / 550 VA
- 43 Minutes Maximum Runtime
- Telephone/Network Protection

Register today and get a chance to WIN a Canon™ camcorder!

Visit www.apc.com/promo Key Code 79277t • Call 0845 0805034 • Fax 0118 903 7840

APC™
by Schneider Electric

HOW TO...
Perform an Anytime Upgrade

There's no reason to be stuck with the same version of Windows 7. With the help of Anytime Upgrade, you can take advantage of the benefits of other versions as your needs change

WHEN YOU INSTALL Windows 7, you install all the features of every version – it's just that some features are locked. However, with Anytime Upgrade you can upgrade your PC's version of Windows 7 instantly just by buying a new licence key. The Home Premium edition can be upgraded to Professional or Ultimate, while Professional can be upgraded to Ultimate.

The beauty of this type of upgrade is that you don't need to reinstall any software, and your files are left intact on your computer along with your Windows settings. For a full breakdown of the prices, go to *http://emea.microsoftstore.com/uk*.

1 RUN UPGRADE APPLICATION
Click on the Start menu and type Upgrade. Then select Windows Anytime Upgrade from the search results. Selecting 'Go online to choose the edition of Windows 7 that's best for you' lets you buy a new product upgrade key online and upgrades your computer. Meanwhile, selecting 'Enter an upgrade key' lets you type in an upgrade product key, such as the one provided in a retail Windows Anytime Upgrade box; we'll assume this is the choice you've made.

2 ENTER UPGRADE KEY
On the next screen, type in the Upgrade key you were given and click Next. Once the key has been verified, you'll be prompted to accept the licence terms. Click 'I accept'. You'll be presented with a warning telling you that the process takes about 15 minutes and that you should close all open applications and save your work. Click Upgrade and the process will start.

3 INSTALL NEW FEATURES
Your PC checks online to see if any updates are available before upgrading your version of Windows 7. It then begins the main upgrade procedure, which will take a few minutes. Once it's complete, your PC will restart and Windows will reload with the features of the new version unlocked. You'll see a welcome screen with a link to help you find out about the new features.

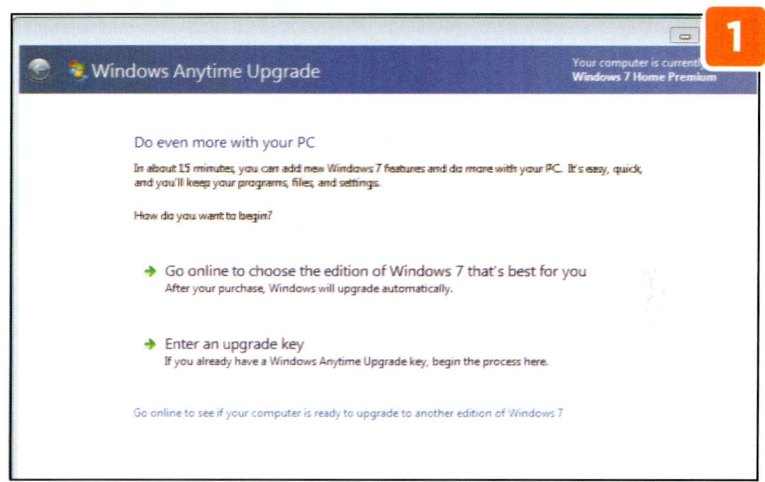

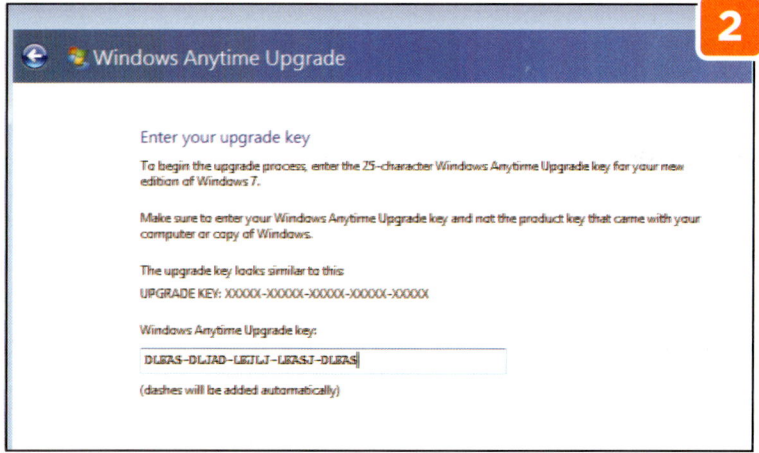

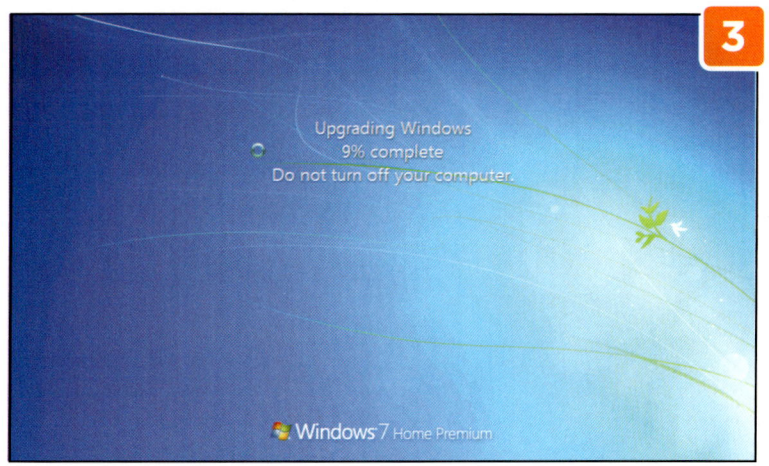

HOW TO...
Install Ubuntu Linux

1 DOWNLOAD UBUNTU
First, download Ubuntu Desktop Edition from *www.ubuntu.com/getubuntu*. The download of Ubuntu 9.04 is 694MB and is an ISO file that needs to be burned to CD before you can use it. Nero Burning Rom and Roxio Creator have built-in tools for letting you do this, but you can also use the free ISO Recorder (available from *http://isorecorder.alexfeinman.com/isorecorder.htm*). Version 2 is for Windows XP and Version 3.1 is for Vista and Windows 7, so make sure that you get the right version for your operating system. Once you've downloaded it, use Explorer to find the ISO file, right-click it and select copy to CD.

Put a blank CD into your optical drive and click Next to copy the file to disc. If you don't have a CD writer, you can ask for a free copy of Ubuntu on CD, but the delivery time may mean that you're better off asking a friend to burn a disc for you.

2 BOOT FROM THE CD
Put the Ubuntu CD that you just created into your new computer's optical drive. Keep an eye out for the 'Press any key to boot from CD' message. If you miss this, you'll have to restart your computer to load the Ubuntu installation routine. The first Ubuntu installation screen should appear very quickly, and here you just need to select the installation language.

3 START INSTALLATION
You're then presented with an installation menu and a handful of options. The default installation option is to try Ubuntu without making any changes to your computer. This simply loads Ubuntu from the CD and doesn't write any files to your hard disk, and is a good way to try out Linux before making any commitments and filling up your hard disk. If you're still not sure about Linux, this is the safest option. To install Ubuntu properly, select the Install Ubuntu option.

The first thing you'll see is the Ubuntu loading screen, which looks a little like that for Windows. It can take a while for Ubuntu to chug through this part of its installation, so don't panic if the orange bar appears to freeze for a spell.

4 SELECT LANGUAGE
Eventually, you'll see the Ubuntu wallpaper and a welcome screen. Hopefully, this is in a

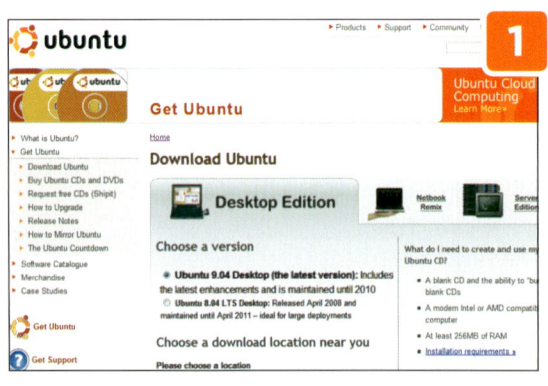

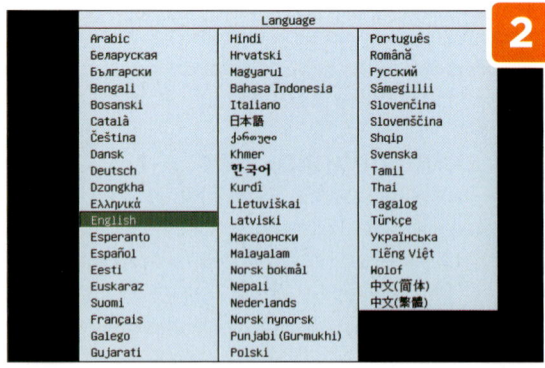

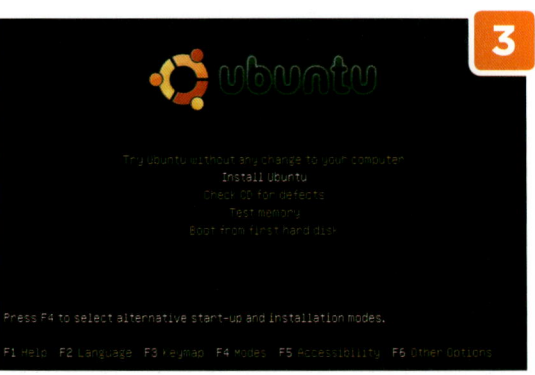

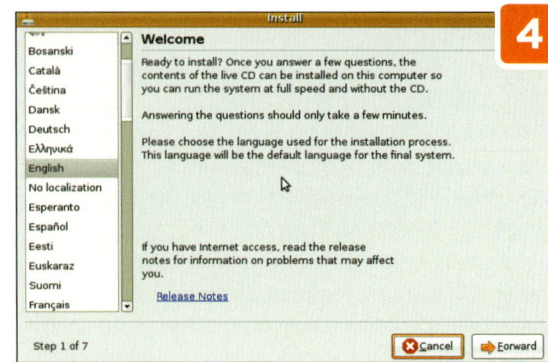

language you can understand; if not, select English from the list on the left.

If your computer is plugged into the internet via a wired connection, you can click the Release Notes link to find out more information on problems that may affect you. When you've finished, click the Forward button to continue.

5 SELECT LOCATION

Now select your location using the drop-down menu. UK cities are grouped under Europe towards the end of the list. Selecting a location in the UK should automatically select the correct time zone. If it doesn't, select the right one using the drop-down menu.

When you've chosen the correct settings, click Forward to continue. Your keyboard layout should be set to United Kingdom; if it's not, select this from the menu and click Forward.

6 SET UP HARD DISKS

By default, Ubuntu uses a simple partitioning system on your PC's hard disk. While perfectly adequate, this is worth tweaking to alter where files are stored. This will let you choose where

your user files (My Documents in Windows) are kept, as well as create separate partitions for program files and virtual memory.

Linux stores user files in the /home folder, and moving this to its own partition is easy. Unfortunately, if you opt to set up one partition manually, you have to set them all up this way, so we'll need to take a slight detour to complete this process. If you just want to stick with Ubuntu's default partition scheme, just leave the Guided option selected, click Forward and move on to step 12.

7 DELETE EXISTING PARTITIONS

Select the Manual option on the Prepare disk space screen and click Forward. The installer will then scan your hard disk and display the disk partitioning tool. The first step is to delete all existing partitions on the hard disk, so select each one in the list and click the Delete partition button.

8 SET BOOT PARTITION

You should now just have free space listed under /dev/sda (Linux's name for the hard disk on the primary IDE channel). Since we're creating

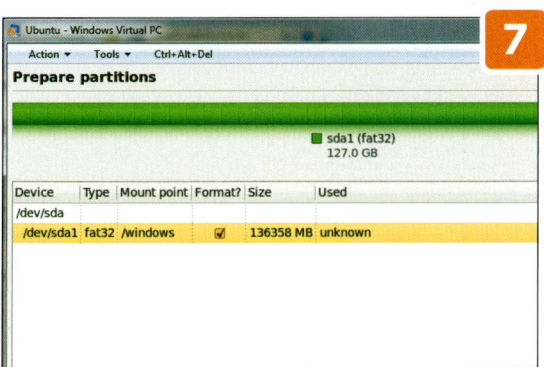

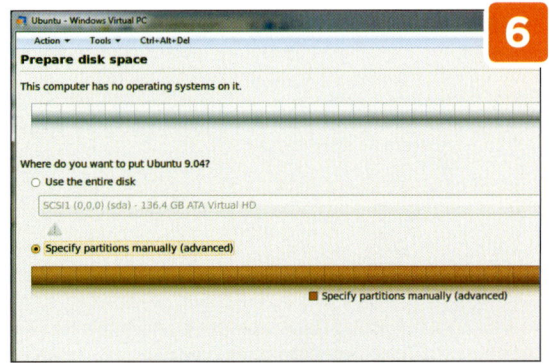

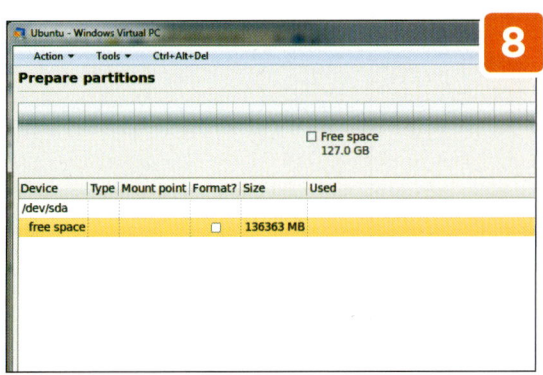

TIP You can try Ubuntu without installing it. Simply boot off the CD and explore the desktop. When you're ready to proceed you just need to run the installer.

partitions by hand, we need to create all the partitions Linux requires, starting with the /boot partition. Select free space in the list of partitions and click New partition. Enter a size of 50 (we're working in megabytes here) and select /boot as the Mount point. Click OK.

9 SET SWAP PARTITION

Linux also needs a /swap partition, which is the equivalent of Windows' swap file used for virtual memory. When your PC's real memory fills up, Ubuntu will swap bits of the memory that aren't currently being used (inactive applications, for example) to the hard disk. This gives the impression that your computer has more memory than it does, so you can run more applications.

Create another new partition in the free space and enter a size equal to the amount of RAM in the computer in megabytes (1GB = 1,024MB). Select Swap area from the Use as drop-down list, leave the other settings at their defaults and then click OK.

10 SET HOME PARTITION

Next is the /home partition, where user files are kept. This is the equivalent of Windows' My Documents folder, but kept on a separate partition.

The advantage of this method is that you can reinstall Linux and your documents won't be overwritten. Make this partition as large as you like, remembering to leave a few gigabytes free for the final /root partition. Select /home as the Mount point before clicking OK.

11 SET ROOT PARTITION

Last is the root or / partition. This is where Ubuntu is installed and it will use all of the remaining space. Set the Mount point as / and click OK.

You can see the final partition structure from the screenshot below, so click Forward when you're ready to continue. That's the end of the custom partitioning.

12 SET A USERNAME AND A PASSWORD

You now need to tell Ubuntu who you are. Type your name into the What is your name? box. This will automatically generate a username for you in the What name do you want to use to log in? box, but you can change this if you like. Type in a password to protect your account and prevent unauthorised users from logging on to your PC.

Finally, your computer will automatically have been given a name based on your name in the

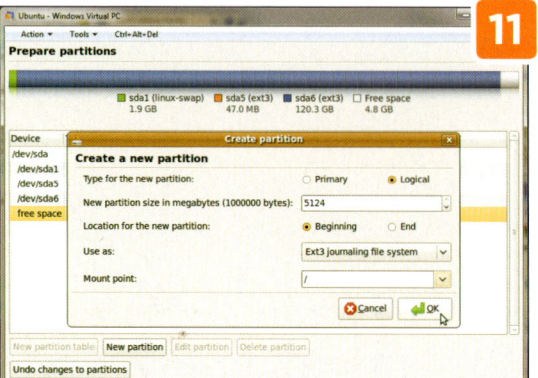

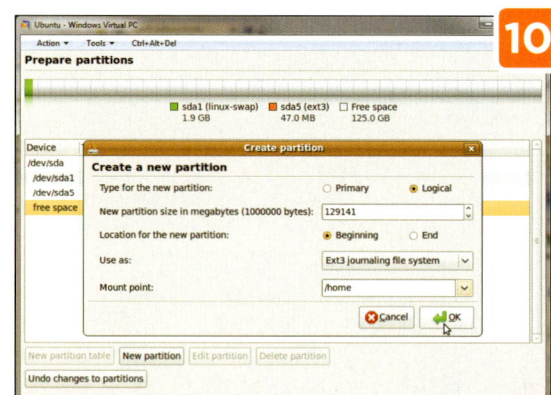

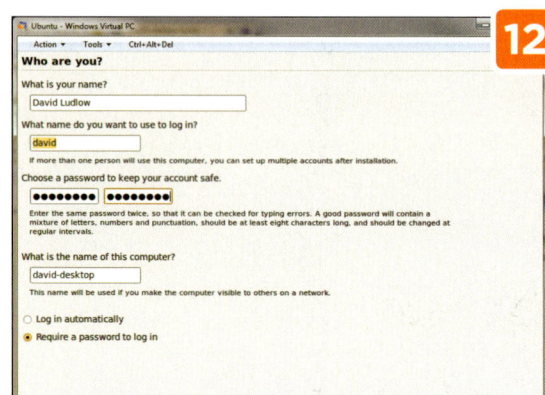

What is the name of this computer? box. You can change this to anything you like, if you prefer. Click Forward when you've finished.

13 INSTALL LINUX

So far, no files have been written to your hard disk, so this is the last chance you've got to back out of the installation. When you're ready to continue, click Install.

Ubuntu will now copy the necessary files to the hard disk partitions you created. This process will take a few minutes, so sit back and let it do its job.

14 START UBUNTU FOR THE FIRST TIME

Once the installation is complete, the Gnome desktop will load. This is very similar to the Windows desktop, and it's where the bulk of your interaction with Linux will take place. You'll find that a whole range of applications have already been installed and you can access them through the Applications menu at the top-left of the screen.

The applications that come bundled with Linux vary, but at the very least you can expect to find an office suite of some description, a web browser and an email client – Ubuntu comes with OpenOffice.org, Firefox and Thunderbird.

Applications can be found in the Applications menu at the top-left of the screen.

15 INSTALL NEW APPLICATIONS

Ubuntu also simplifies the process of finding and installing new programs. Its Add/Remove Applications utility (available in the Applications menu) works in a similar way to its Windows namesake, with the added advantage of offering new applications to install, as well as old ones to remove. New programs are downloaded from the internet and any additional components that are required (known as dependencies) are automatically downloaded, too, which goes a long way to making Linux more user-friendly.

16 INSTALL UPDATES

Just as you would do with Windows, Ubuntu needs to have the latest security patches installed. Its rising popularity means that it's attracting increased interest from malicious hackers.

Fortunately, Ubuntu has its own update manager and will periodically check for updates. When new updates are ready to be installed, you'll see a warning on the application bar. Click the warning to bring up a list of available updates, and click the Install Updates button to install them.

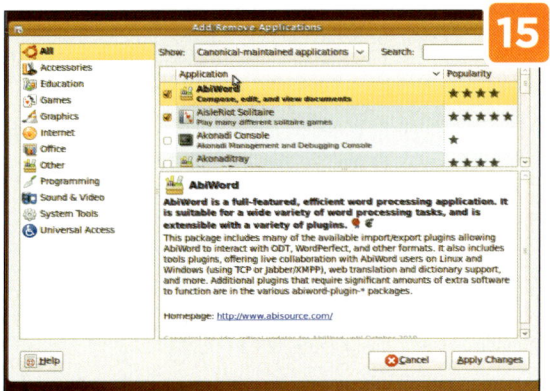

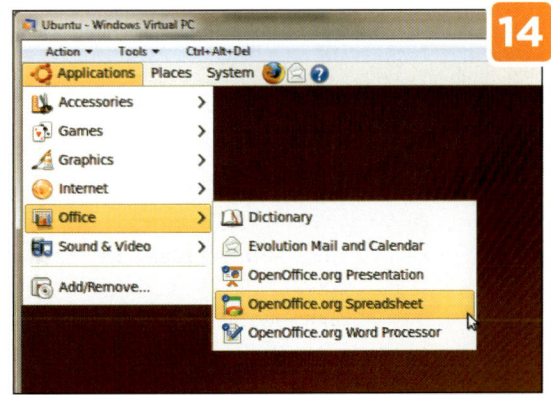

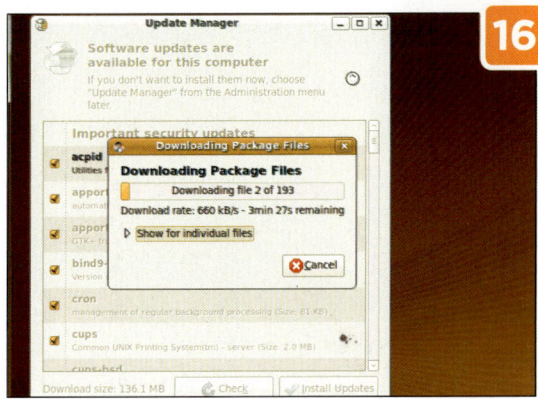

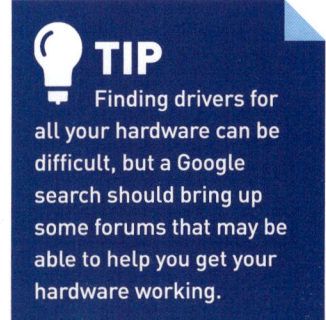

TIP
Finding drivers for all your hardware can be difficult, but a Google search should bring up some forums that may be able to help you get your hardware working.

Make your own NAS

If you have an old PC sitting around doing nothing, you could turn it into network storage for your new PC using FreeNAS. Here we show you how to get to grips with this powerful system

FREENAS IS A free operating system that turns any computer into a network-attached storage (NAS) device. Here we'll take you through installing the software on an old PC. You'll need a PC with at least one hard disk in it and an optical drive. The best installation of FreeNAS uses a USB flash drive. You'll need one with at least 64MB of disk space; you can buy 1GB models for around £3 if you don't have one.

To start, download the ISO CD image of the operating system from *www.freenas.org*. You need to download the LiveCD version. There are two versions for download: one for Intel processors and one for AMD 64-bit processors. Select the right version and download the ISO file to your PC. This file is an image of a CD that needs to be written to a blank disc. If you don't have any CD-writing software, the free CDBurnerXP (*http://cdburnerxp.se*) will do the job.

Once you've written the files to the CD, you can boot from the disc on the computer that you'll be using for FreeNAS. Before you do, however,

there are some configuration options you need to think about. First, for the maximum flexibility you should install FreeNAS on a USB flash disk, leaving your hard disks completely for data storage. For this to work, you need to set your BIOS to boot from USB devices.

To do this, turn on your FreeNAS PC, plug in your USB flash drive and enter the BIOS (normally you have to press Delete, F10 or F12, but look out for a message telling you which key to press). Typically the USB boot options will be under Advanced BIOS Features. There may be an option to boot from USB drives, you may have to select a USB flash drive from the Boot Device menu or the option may be called Boot Other Devices. In our BIOS, the USB drive was detected as a hard disk and we had to select it as the first device in the Hard Disk Boot Priority menu. If your PC can't boot from USB flash drives, you can install FreeNAS to one of your hard disks, but this makes configuration harder later on and prevents you from using this hard disk in a RAID array.

TIP

Booting from a USB flash drive makes FreeNAS easier to configure and gives you more disk space to play with.

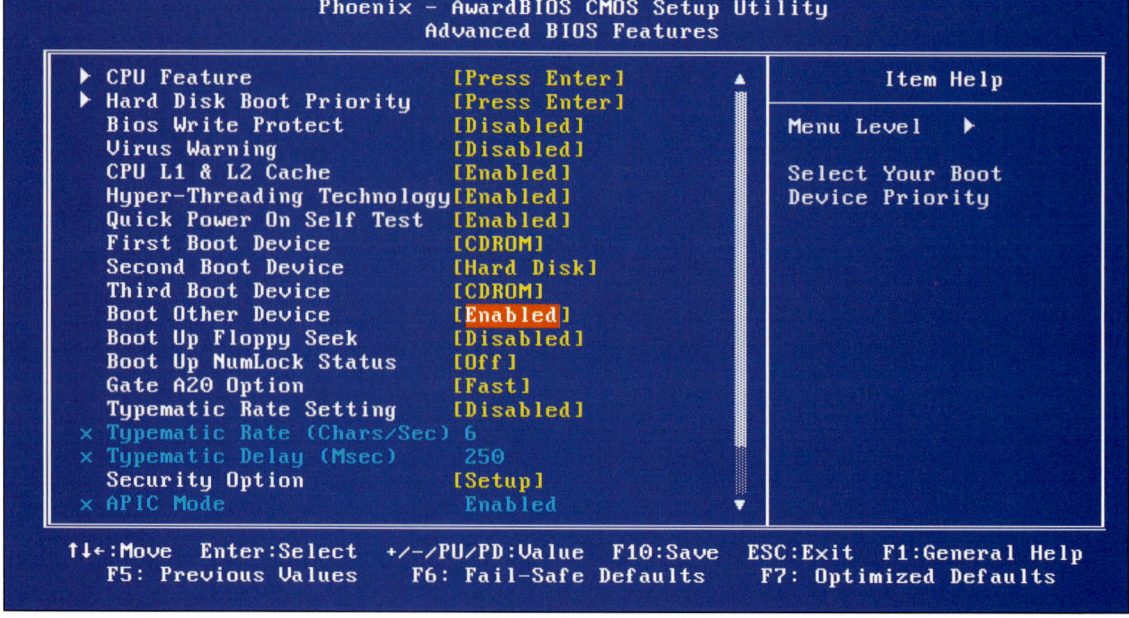

↑ You need to enter the BIOS and set your computer to boot from a USB disk for the optimal FreeNAS installation

Alternatively, you can connect the flash disk to a USB port and boot the PC from the FreeNAS Live CD. Your settings will be saved automatically to the flash drive, so there's no installation at all. However, this makes it trickier to upgrade FreeNAS to a later version.

While you're in the BIOS, make sure that you disable the option to halt on keyboard errors, as your FreeNAS PC won't need a monitor or keyboard connected to it when it's ready.

The other configuration option to consider is whether you want to use RAID. FreeNAS lets you use all common types of RAID (see *http://tinyurl.com/raidlevels* for an explanation). You'll need at least two hard disks to use RAID. The benefits are increased speed and reliability, and you can add extra hard disks to your PC later to increase the storage space. The alternative is to use each disk separately; this is your only choice if you have one hard disk. We'll show you both methods here.

CONNECTING YOUR PC

You're now ready to install the operating system via an Ethernet cable to your router or hub. Before you start, remove any USB flash drives (unless you're planning to start FreeNAS from CD each time, in which case start your computer and go to Step 3), or you'll get an error.

1 Boot from the disc you created. When the Console setup menu appears, insert your USB drive into a spare port, type 9 and then Enter to install FreeNAS to your PC's hard disk. Select option 1 and press Enter. FreeNAS will confirm the partitions that it will create and warn you that your entire USB flash disk will be wiped. Press Enter to continue. Select your optical drive from the list and press Enter. Finally, select the flash drive to which you want to install the OS (it will have a name that starts 'da') and press Enter.

2 FreeNAS will install itself to the flash drive, which should take only a few seconds. When it's finished, you'll get a message telling you that you can remove the optical disc and restart your

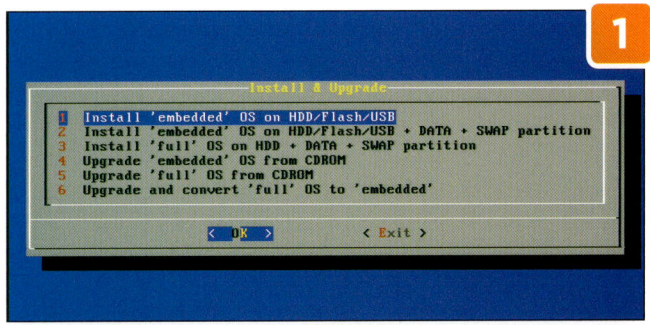

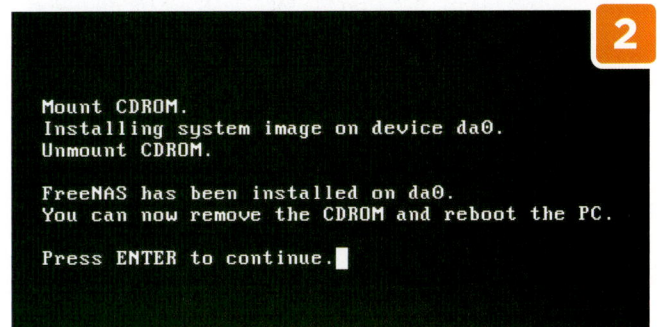

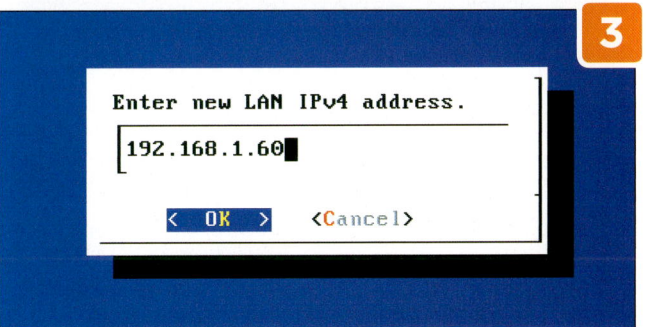

computer. Follow these instructions and make sure your computer is set to boot from USB devices.

3 When your computer restarts, you'll see a similar Console setup menu to the one in Step 1. Type 1 and then Enter to pick the network interface you want to use. Pick the one with (up) in brackets and press Enter. Go to Finish and exit configuration and press Enter, then Enter again.

Next, set the IP address that you want your FreeNAS computer to use by typing 2 and then

Enter. You'll be asked if you want to use DHCP. If your router has an option to fix the IP address it gives to a specific PC (many do), select Yes. Otherwise, select No. In this case you'll have to select an IP address manually.

The easiest way to find a safe address is to follow your router's instructions to access the web management page from your main PC and view the DHCP server settings. The page will contain a start address, such as 192.168.1.1, and either an end address, such as 192.168.1.49, or a number that says how many addresses it hands out, such as 50. In this example, 50 IP addresses would give us a range between 192.168.1.1 and 192.168.1.50.

All you have to do is pick an IP address outside this range. To be on the safe side, we recommend picking an address that's 10 higher than the last DHCP address. So, keep the first three numbers the same and add 10 to the last number – in our example, that would be 192.168.1.60 – and write this address down, as you'll need it later.

Type the address into FreeNAS and press Enter. You'll be prompted for your network's subnet mask. You'll probably have a network that uses 255.255.255.0, so type 24 and press Enter. On the next two screens, enter a Gateway and a DNS address. These are your router's IP address. Type it in both boxes and press Enter. Finally, say No to IPv6 and press Enter. You'll then get a confirmation that the IP address has been configured.

4 FreeNAS is now running, so you can switch to its web-based interface for further configuration. In a web browser on another computer, type the IP address of your FreeNAS server into the address bar. The default username is admin, with the password freenas.

The first job is to change the password. Click on the System menu and select General. Click on the Password tab, type in the old password and then your new password twice. Click Save and you'll be prompted to log into the management page again with your new password.

5 Next, it's time to set up file sharing. To do this, add the hard disks on which you want to share files to FreeNAS. Click on Management in the Disks menu, and then the big plus sign. Select a hard disk from the Disk drop-down menu (hard disks start with 'ad') and type in a description. We

recommend leaving the other settings alone, except for S.M.A.R.T., which is used to monitor your disk's health. Put a tick in this box and click Add. Repeat this step for each hard disk in your system, and then click Apply Changes on the Disks, Management screen.

6 Your hard disks now need to be formatted. To do this, select Format from the Disks menu. Remember that if you're using old disks you'll need to have copied off any files that you want to keep. If you're going to use each disk individually, leave the File system option on its default value of UFS, type in a Volume label and click Format disk. Repeat this procedure for all your disks and go to Step 8.

If you want to use RAID, select Software RAID from the File system menu and click Format disk. Repeat for all your hard disks, and go to Step 7.

7 To create a RAID array, select Software RAID from the Disks menu. Select the type of RAID array you want to create from the tabs and click

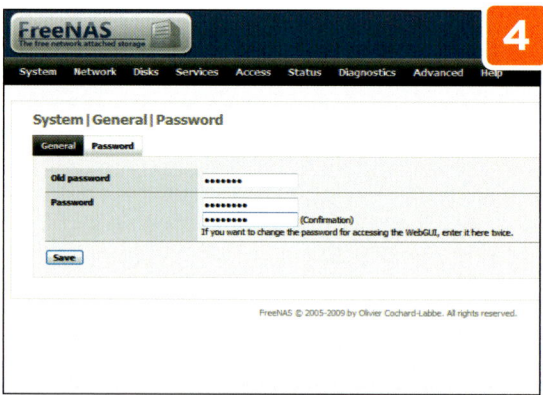

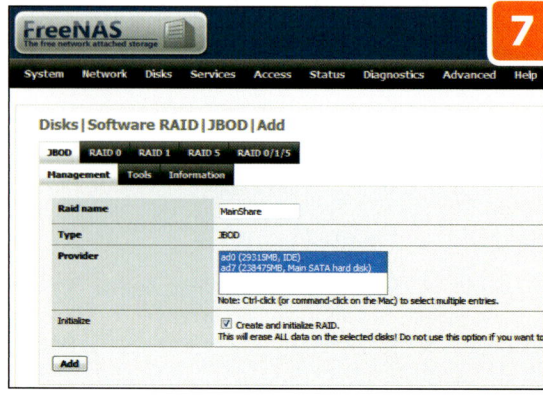

TIP
You can run FreeNAS directly from the CD and store settings on a flash drive if your PC won't boot from USB devices.

the Plus icon. Type in the RAID name (no spaces are allowed), select the hard disks you want to use in the Provider menu, select Initialize and click Add. Click Apply Changes on the next screen.

You have to format your new RAID array, so select Format from the Disks menu. Choose your RAID array from the drop-down Disk menu, type in a Volume label and click Format disk.

8 Now you need to share your disk. Click on Disks, then Mount Point. Select a hard disk or RAID array from the drop-down Disk menu. Type in a Share name and Description, then click Add. Click Apply Changes and your share is ready.

In order for Windows computers to be able to access the share, you need to enable the file-sharing service. Click on CIFS/SMB from the Services menu and put a tick in the Enable box. You shouldn't need to change many of the settings, but there are some you can: NetBIOS name is the name that will appear when Windows computers browse the network, Workgroup is the Windows workgroup in which your server will appear, and

Large read/write should be enabled if your computers run Windows 2000 or later. When you're ready, click Save and Restart.

Finally, you need to select which files you want to share. Click on the Shares tab. Type in the name you want the share to be known by and a comment, and then click the button next to Path. Select the mount point that you created at the start of this step (individual hard disks will have one mount point each and a RAID array has one mount point) and click OK. Click Apply Changes. You can repeat this for every mount point that you have.

9 On your Windows PC, get a Run command up (Windows+R) and type \\<*ip address of your FreeNAS server*>. You'll see an Explorer window with folders named the same as the Shares you've just set up. If you right-click a folder and select Map network drive, you can create a network drive that you can access in Windows just like a normal hard disk. Repeat this step for all the computers on your network that need access to the network share.

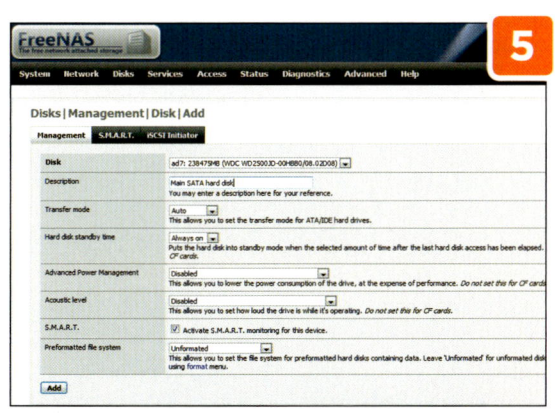

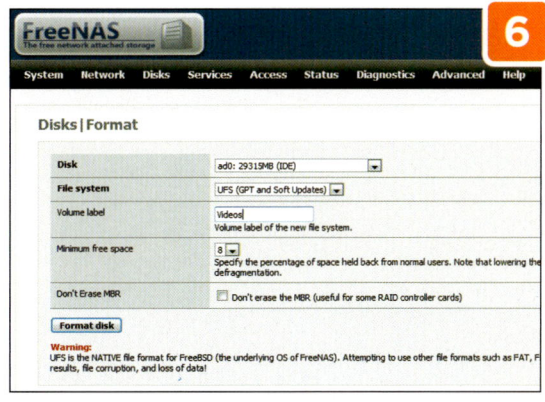

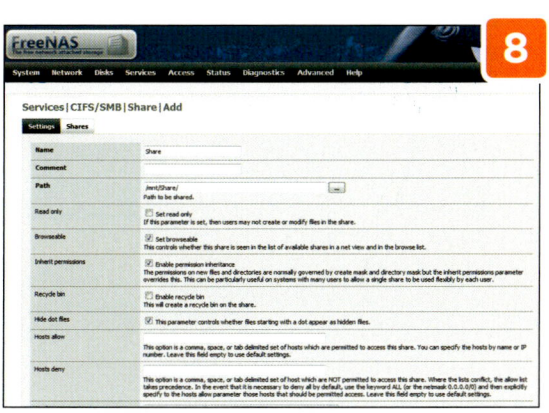

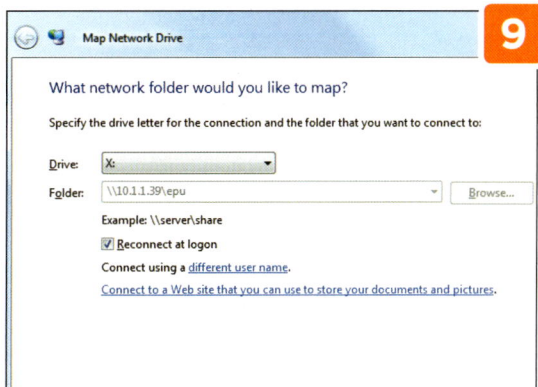

Configure FreeNAS

FreeNAS's advanced features let you add security, share files over the internet and share media with other computers. Here we show you how to set up, configure and use these features

THE FIRST PLACE to start is security. Our default installation of FreeNAS didn't have any usernames or passwords, so anyone could access the computer. While this is fine on a local network, if you're going to use more advanced features that are accessible over the internet, such as the FTP server, you'll need to know how to set up users and groups.

At the time of writing the current version of FreeNAS doesn't let you choose which users have access to each service: anyone with a username and password can access every feature and every share. For home use this shouldn't make any difference, unless you're really keen to restrict access for your family.

↓ Adding users to your FreeNAS computer is very straightforward

BACKING UP YOUR CONFIGURATION
If your system develops a problem and you have to reinstall FreeNAS, you'll need to restore it quickly.

If you don't back up your configuration, you risk losing every file stored in a RAID array. Log on to FreeNAS's web-based management and click Backup/Restore from the System menu. Click Download configuration and save the file to your PC. If you need to restore your configuration, use the same menu, but click the Browse button, select the configuration file you backed up and then click Restore configuration.

It's also worth checking that you have the most up-to-date version of FreeNAS. To do this, go to *www.freenas.org*, click the Download link and select the latest version in the FreeNAS Images list (not the LiveCD list). This will download a .img file. In FreeNAS's web management page, select Firmware from the System menu. Select Enable firmware upload, click Browse, select the .img file you downloaded and then click Upgrade firmware. This will automatically upload the file and upgrade your FreeNAS computer, restarting it when it's completed.

ADDING A USER
To add a new user, go to FreeNAS's web-based management page and log on. Click on the Access tab and select Users and Groups. Click the blue Plus and you'll be prompted to add a user by typing in a username and password. It's best to type in the same usernames and passwords that are used to log into Windows, as this way you'll automatically be able to access network shares without having to authenticate.

You can also assign users to groups. At the moment, all users have access to every service; however, when this is updated in a later version of FreeNAS it will make security easier to deal with as you'll be able to allow or deny a whole group of users access to a service. For now, though, we've put all our users in the Admin group. When you've created one user, click Add, then Apply changes. Click the blue Plus to add another user.

TURNING ON SECURITY
Now you have users, it's time to use them. We'll start by showing you how to secure the network

Access | Users | Add

| Users | Groups |

Login	David
	Login name of user.
Full Name	David Ludlow
	User full name.
Password	••••••••
	•••••••• (Confirmation)
	User password.
User ID	1001
	User numeric id.
Primary group	admin ▾
	Set the account's primary group to the given group.
Additional group	admin
	bin
	daemon
	ftp
	guest
	kmem
	man
	network
	nobody
	nogroup
	operator
	sshd
	Set additional group memberships for this account.
	Note: Ctrl-click (or command-click on the Mac) to select and deselect groups.
Home directory	Enter the path to the home directory of that user. Leave this field empty to use default path /mnt.
Shell access	☐ Give full shell access to user.

Add

share we helped you create on page 101. Select CIFS/SMB from the Services menu. To turn on security, select Local User from the Authentication menu and then click Save and Restart. When you get the message, "The changes have been applied successfully", all your network shares are secure and only authorised users can access them.

To check, type Windows+R to get a Run command and type \\<*ip address of your FreeNAS computer*>. If you created a username and password that matches your current Windows user, you'll be able to access the shares; if you didn't, you'll be prompted to type in a valid username and password.

SMARTER SHARES

You can share an entire Mount Point (hard disk or RAID array), but this isn't always the best use of disk space. It often makes more sense to share only a particular folder. For example, you could give each user their own share to use. A similar argument goes for other services here.

To share a folder, you first need to create one. FreeNAS has a built-in file browser that lets you do this. Click on Advanced and select File Manager, then log on with the same username and password that you use to log on to FreeNAS's

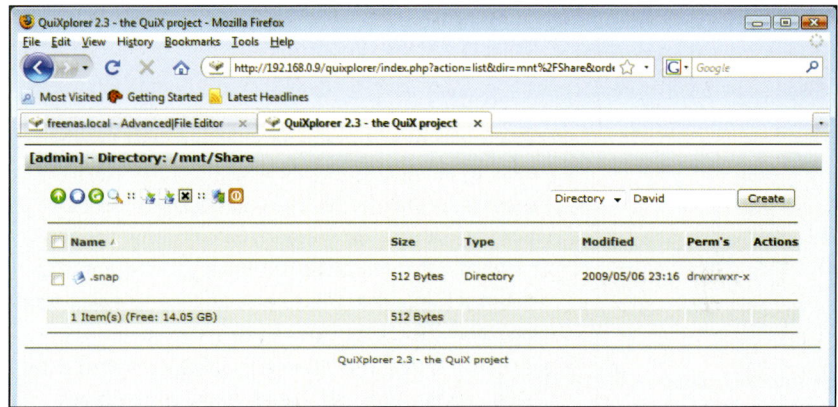

↑ The built-in file browser lets you manage files and folders from the web management console

web-management page. You'll see an Explorer-style file browser that you can use to view every file and folder. To create a new folder to share, you need to know where to put it.

Unlike Windows, which has different drive letters for each hard disk, FreeNAS is based on Linux. We've already explained that for each hard disk or RAID array you have to create a Mount Point, and it's the Mount Point that you need to access. These are stored in the 'mnt' folder, so click on this. Here you'll see a list of folders with the same names as the Mount Points that you created, each one referring to a hard disk or RAID array. Click on one to access it. Select Directory from the drop-down menu, type in a name and click Create to make a Folder.

The new folder will have the wrong permissions and won't let users write files to it. To change this, click on the link under the Perm's column next to the folder you've created (it will look something like drwxrwxr-x). Put a tick in the 'w' box under Public and click Change.

To use your new folder to create a share, click on CIFS/SMB from the Services menu of the main web interface window, and click on the Shares tab. Click the blue plus icon, type a name for your new share (we've chosen the name of one of our users) and a description. Click the button next to Path and navigate to the mnt folder. Click the Mount

↑ You can password-protect your network shares for added security

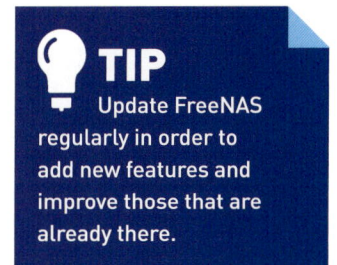

TIP
Update FreeNAS regularly in order to add new features and improve those that are already there.

Point name where you created your new folder, then click your new folder. Click OK, then click Add followed by Apply changes. Your new share will then show up when you get a Run command and type \\<*ip address of your FreeNAS computer*>. It may be prudent to stop sharing the main share, which gives users access to an entire drive, by clicking the red minus icon next to a share's name.

SETTING UP FTP
The problem with network shares is that they're not easy to share over the internet. Fortunately, FTP provides a way for all users to access their files from anywhere. Be warned, though, that the FTP settings are quite basic and give users access to the mnt folder and, therefore, access to every hard disk and RAID array you have installed.

To turn on FTP, select FTP from the Service menu (don't select TFTP, as this is a very basic form of FTP). Put a tick in the Enable box and a tick in the box marked 'Only allow authenticated

↓ You can access your FreeNAS server over the internet using FTP

users. Anonymous logins are prohibited.' This will let only authenticated users access FreeNAS.

You can leave the other settings as they are, although you may want to turn on Resume, which lets users continue downloading a file if it's interrupted, and SSI/TLS, which allows users to make secure connections to your server. However, this latter option will put a bit of overhead on your server, so turn it off if performance becomes an issue. When you're done, click Save and Restart.

To test that it's working properly, open your web browser and type ftp://<*ip address of your FreeNAS computer*>. When prompted, type in a valid username and password, and you'll be able to browse all the files on your PC. This access is very basic, so for more control you're better off with a dedicated FTP client such as FileZilla (*http://filezilla-project.org*).

The next step is to give access to the computer over the internet. The first problem to overcome is that your home has an external IP address that's shared by all the computers on your network. This IP address can change, making it impossible to access your home. Fortunately, with Dynamic DNS you can create a simple URL that's updated regularly so that it always points at your home.

The only point to make is that if your router doesn't support DynDNS.org (the best free Dynamic DNS service), FreeNAS does, so you don't need to download any other software. Select Dynamic DNS from the Services menu, click Enable and type in your DynDNS.org account details.

With Dynamic DNS up and running, you need to configure your router so that it knows to send

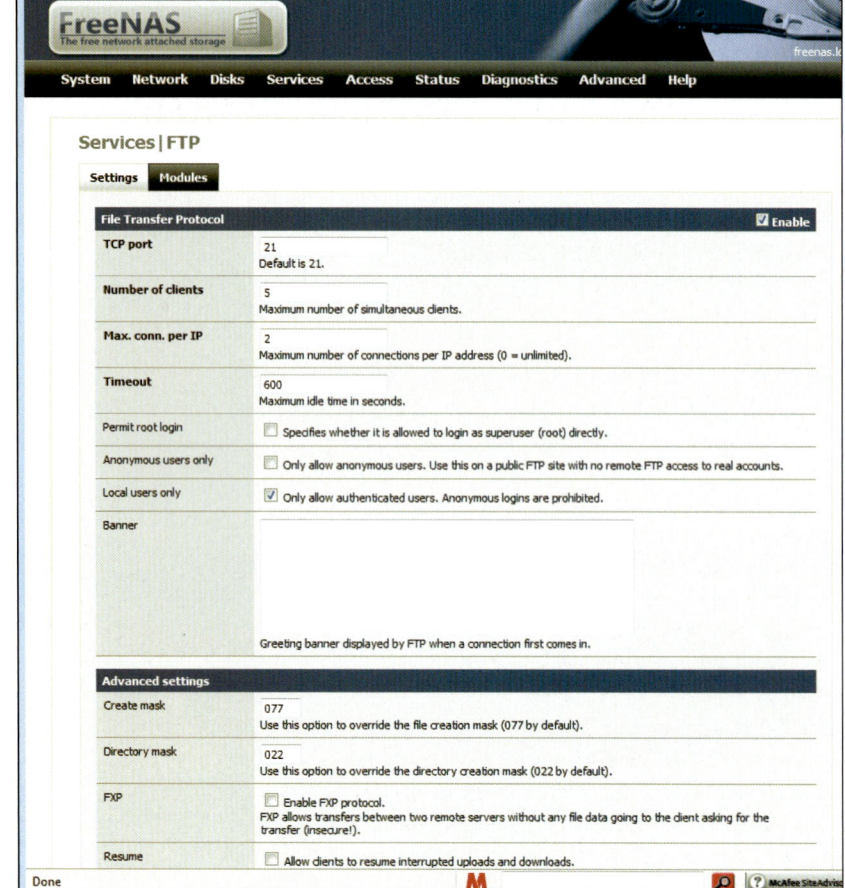

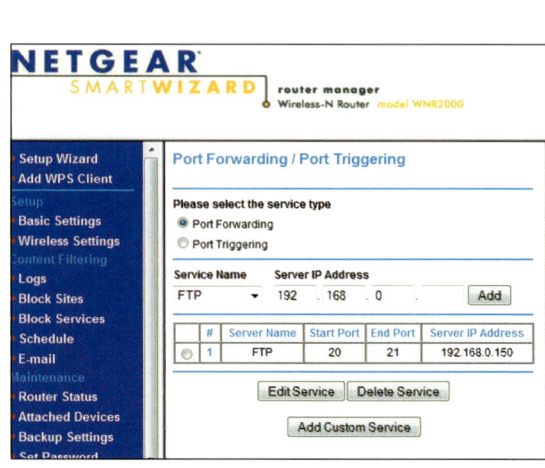

↑ You may need to reconfigure your router to get FTP working properly

incoming FTP requests to your FreeNAS computer. This is fairly straightforward and involves configuring port forwarding (called virtual servers on some routers). You need to configure a new rule that forwards all incoming traffic on Port 21 to the IP address of your FreeNAS computer. Your router's manual will tell you how to do this, and *www.portforward.com* has lots of information about it as well.

Once that's done, you can access your FreeNAS computer from over the internet. In a web browser, you type ftp://*<name of the DynDNS.org URL you created>*, such as ftp://computershopper. homeftp.net. You'd also use your DynDNS.org URL in a dedicated FTP client, such as FileZilla.

SHARING MEDIA FILES

If you want to share your media files, FreeNAS makes this easy. It has support for iTunes sharing, which lets you share your music files with computers running iTunes and some media streamers, and UPnP, which lets you share music with a wide range of media streamers. Both services work in the same way, so we'll just explain how to use UPnP.

First, you need a folder in which to store all your media. This can be an existing folder in a share or you can create one specifically using the instructions above. In either case, make sure that you have network access to this folder so that you can copy new files to it, by creating a new share if necessary.

To turn on the UPnP server, select UPnP from the Services menu and select Enable. Click the button next to Database directory and choose a folder in which to create the media directory. This can be stored anywhere, but for convenience we put ours in a directory called Media, which we also use to house our media files. Click Add, which is next to Content, and add the directory that houses your media. You can add multiple directories by repeating this step.

If you have a media streamer with limited format support, you can use transcoding to turn one file format into another. Put a tick in the Transcoding box, and FreeNAS will convert files into a compatible format. However, this operation is processor-intensive, so turn it off if your PC's performance suffers. If you do turn this feature on, select a Temporary Directory in which to store the transcoded files.

↑ Your FreeNAS computer can share media files using its built-in UPnP server

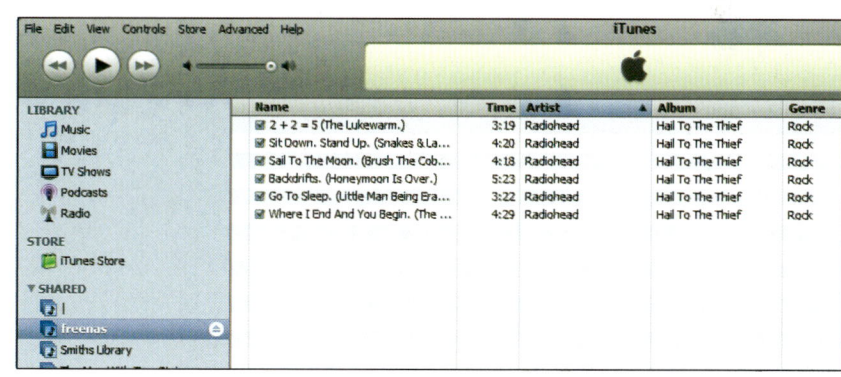

Finally, select Enable web user interface, click Save and then Restart. Your server will now be working. You can click on the URL link to view a web page with the status of your server.

To turn on iTunes sharing, select iTunes/DAAP from the Services menu and follow these instructions. The only difference is that you need to set a password for the administrator's web page, and click the Zeroconf/Bonjour link at the bottom of the page to make sure these two network services are selected and turned on, otherwise iTunes won't detect your NAS.

↑ The built-in iTunes server lets you stream music to other computers running Apple's software

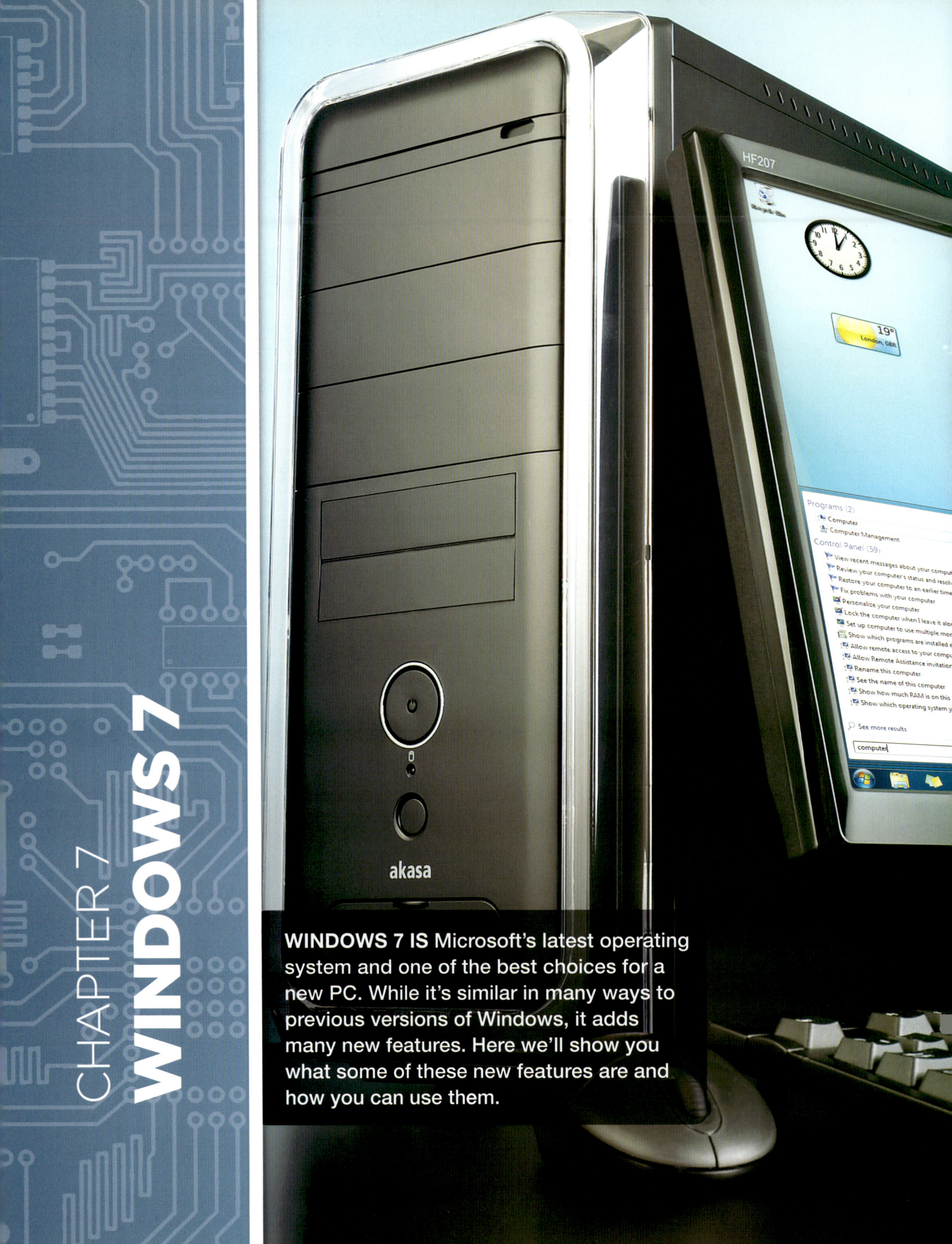

WINDOWS 7 IS Microsoft's latest operating system and one of the best choices for a new PC. While it's similar in many ways to previous versions of Windows, it adds many new features. Here we'll show you what some of these new features are and how you can use them.

IN THIS CHAPTER

The new desktop

Gadgets
Gadgets display simple bits of information, such as the current weather and the time. You can add more by right-clicking the desktop and selecting Gadgets.

Preview windows
Hovering the mouse cursor over a highlighted icon displays a preview of the application's current windows. Hovering the cursor over one of these previews brings that window to the foreground for a better view.

Start menu
Windows 7's Start menu is similar to Vista's. You use it to find programs, documents and Control Panel items. The Shut down button is there to turn off your computer, but you can click the arrow next to it to switch users, hibernate your PC and more besides.

Running taskbar icon
Highlighted icons show you which applications are currently running.

Jump Lists
If you right-click on a taskbar icon you'll see a Jump List, which gives you quick access to recently accessed documents, folders, websites, songs, pictures and more.

Taskbar icons
Non-highlighted icons in the taskbar are used to launch commonly used applications. You can drag and drop your favourite programs here from the Start menu.

Manage your windows

Grab an application and shake the mouse to minimise all other open windows. This is a great way to clear clutter onscreen, so you can focus on a single application. Do the same thing again to restore the other windows.

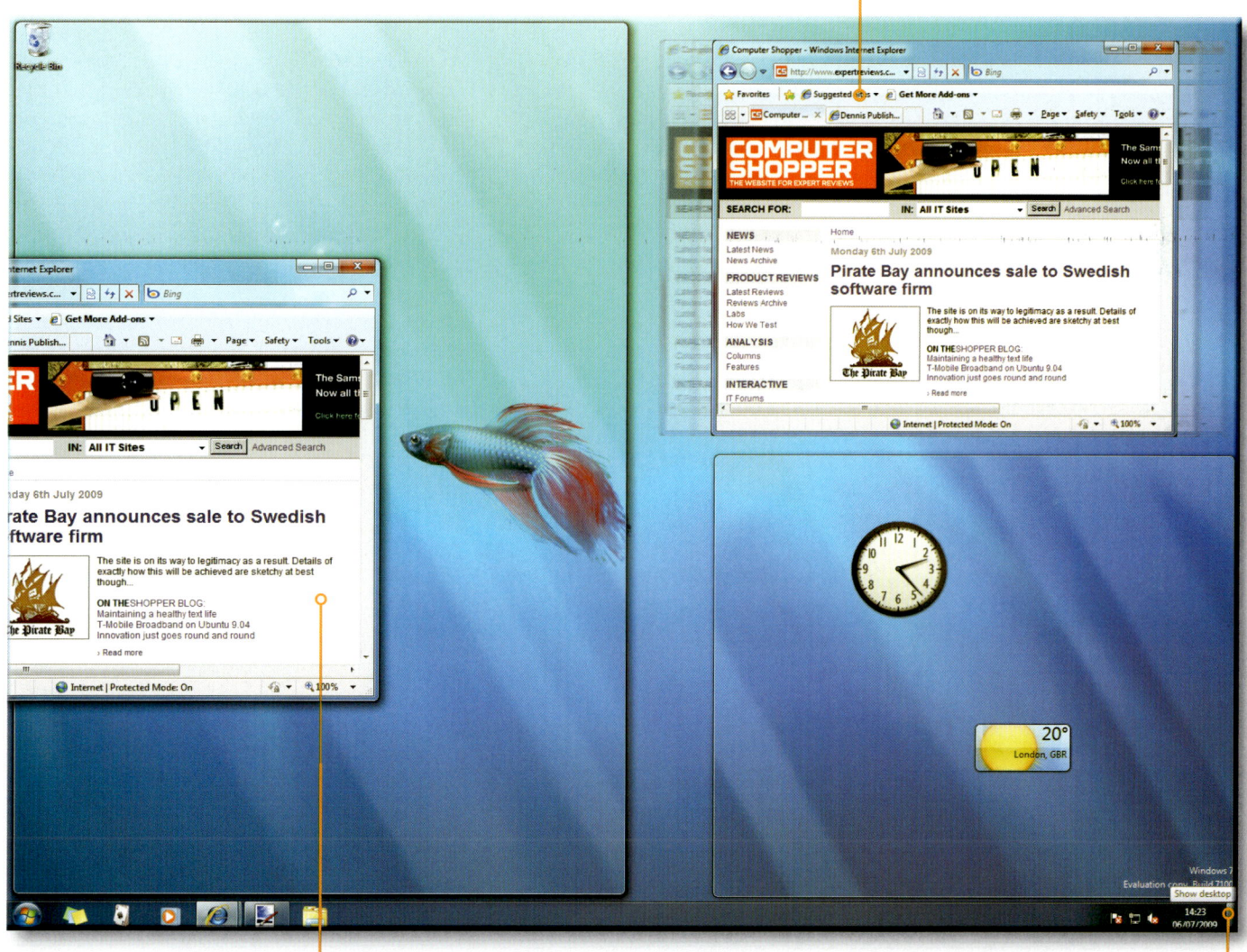

Grab an application and move it to either side so it takes up half your monitor. This is a quick way to compare two applications side by side. Move a window to the top of the screen and it's maximised to take up the whole screen. You can select a window and press Windows and → ← or ↑ for the same effect.

Move your mouse cursor to the bottom right of the screen and all the windows dissolve to an outline. Use this mode to view gadgets quickly and see how many windows you have open. Click the left mouse button to minimise all windows and click it again to bring them back.

HOW TO...
Transfer your files

If you're installing Windows 7 on your new PC, you may want to transfer files and settings from your old system. Here's how

IF YOU'RE BUILDING a brand new Windows 7 PC, the odds are that you've got an old computer that's set up just the way you like it. Rather than starting completely from scratch, you may want to carry over your documents, media files, web bookmarks and so on. Windows 7's Easy Transfer wizard helps you copy these files and settings from the old system to the new, regardless of whether they're on the same machine.

1 RUN EASY TRANSFER
If you're currently running Vista, you already have Easy Transfer. Launch it from the Start menu via All Programs / Accessories / System Tools. In XP, you'll need to insert your Windows 7 disc. Close the installer if it opens, then go to My Computer, right-click on the DVD drive and select Explore (not Open). Browse to the Support folder, then the Migwiz folder. You'll find a file called migsetup.exe: double-click it to run the Easy Transfer Wizard. A welcome screen helpfully explains all the merits of Windows Easy Transfer; feel free to read it, then click Next.

You'll need some form of external storage to house your files during the transfer. If you plan to copy only a small quantity of data, you may be able to use a CD, a DVD or a USB flash drive, but you're likely to have too many files. The easiest option is an external USB hard disk. If your PC is on a network, you can use another computer or a network-attached storage (NAS) device. Choose the method appropriate to you from the choices given. Next, if you're in Vista, confirm that this is your old computer, rather than the new system.

You're now ready to choose what to transfer. The wizard scans to see what files and settings can be transferred, then shows the results in a tick list. In our example it's divided the files into My items (those belonging to your user account) and Shared items. Click Customize to see a list of all the kinds of files that are currently set to back up, including desktop items, Favorites and program settings. If you don't want a particular item kept, deselect it. For finer control, click Advanced at the bottom.

2 SAVE YOUR DATA
Having chosen the files to keep, click through and you'll be asked if you want to protect your backup with a password. Unless there are

➜ Easy Transfer helps you move your documents, settings, emails and more from your old PC.

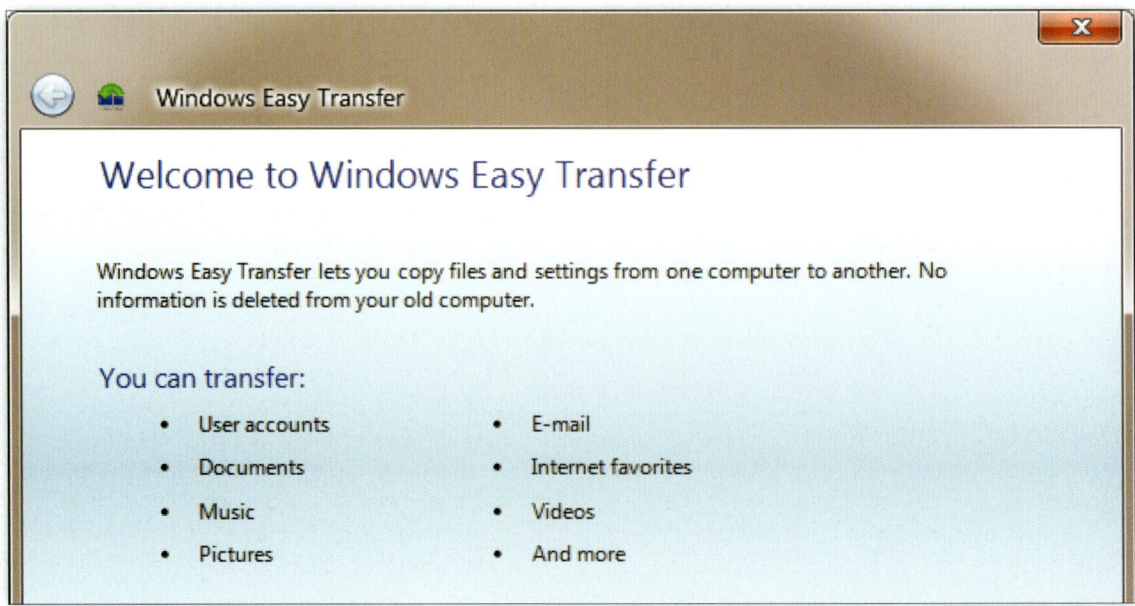

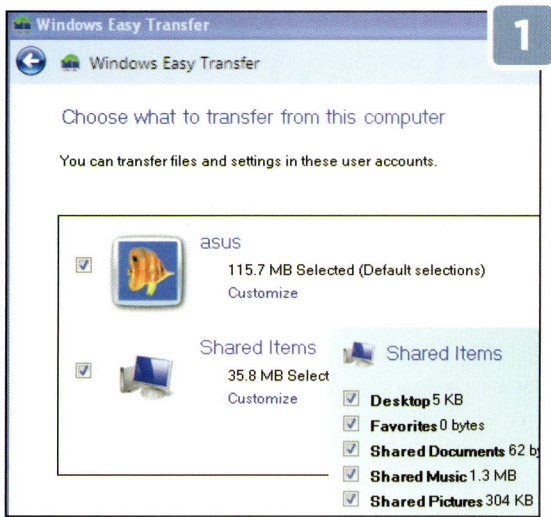

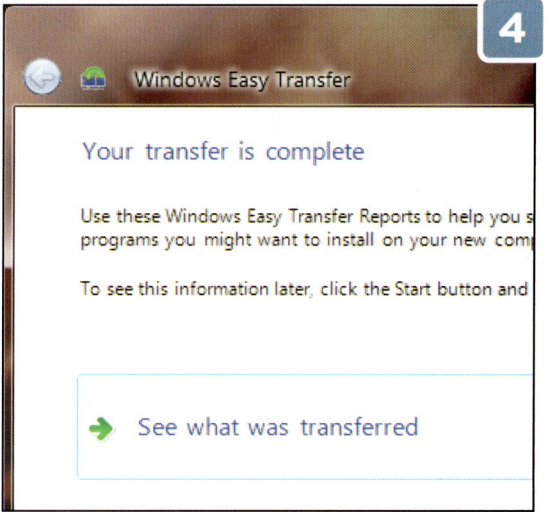

sensitive files, skip this. You'll be asked to name your set of data; choose something you'll recognise later, such as 'Windows XP transfer', and browse to where you'll save your data, as discussed in step 2. In our case it's a USB stick.

You can now start the transfer. A window shows progress. Go for a coffee. You're then told if any files didn't copy; if you need them, copy them manually to a USB drive or other storage for future use. Now, if your new computer doesn't yet have Windows 7 installed, follow the steps on pages 80 to 83, and come back when you're ready to retrieve your data.

3 RUN EASY TRANSFER IN WINDOWS 7
On your new system, click the Start orb and go to All Programs | Accessories | System Tools. Click on Windows Easy Transfer, click through the welcome window and you'll be asked what method you're using. Select the storage you used, and say

this is your new PC. When asked if your files have already been saved to an external drive, plug in your media and click Yes. (If you backed up over a network, make the appropriate choice.)

Select the storage type, browse to your storage device and navigate to the folder you selected earlier. You should see the file you named in step 2 ('Windows XP transfer', or whatever) with the label 'Easy Transfer File'. Select this and enter your password, if you chose one.

4 RESTORE YOUR DATA
Windows 7 scans your backup and shows a window as in step 1. Choose what to restore, or leave everything selected. Click Advanced for tasks such as transferring a whole user account from the old system or mapping an entire drive from Windows XP. Click Transfer to begin the final stage. At the end you'll see confirmation of exactly what was transferred.

💡 TIP
One thing that won't be included in the transfer process is your programs. The only way to preserve these is if you install Windows 7 over a matching edition of Vista and pick the Upgrade option. In all other cases you'll need to re-install each program from its original disc or download, unless you use a utility such as LapLink PCmover (*www.laplink.com/ pcmover*). This is because program installations involve system files.

Keeping track of files

Windows 7 has some great new ways to keep track of all your files, helping you to keep your computer neat and tidy

THOUGH YOU MAY never have known you needed them, Libraries are one of the best things about Windows 7. There are four categories by default: Documents, Music, Pictures and Video. Each section contains all the folders and files you would previously have kept in the relevant folder in My Documents (in Windows XP) or Documents (in Windows Vista).

What's different is that the items in a Library don't have to be stored in the same place. They don't even have to be on your PC's main hard disk. You can include files and folders from anywhere – perhaps an external drive, or another computer on your network – in the same Library.

To see this in action, expand the Documents subfolder within Libraries by clicking the blue disclosure triangle that appears beside Documents when you hover over it. You'll see two entries: My Documents and Public Documents. (These are actual disk folders; right-click on My Documents and you'll see it lives in C:\Users\Name, where Name is your Windows username.)

By default, each Library location includes two folders: My Documents and Public Documents, My Video and Public Video and so on. If you click the 'Library locations' link, you can add a folder and bring its contents into the Library from anywhere. This doesn't move the folder itself, yet the items appear in your Library as if they were all in one place. If you rename or delete something in the Library view, this has the expected effect on the actual item, wherever it's stored.

It's by adding your own items to Libraries that they become truly useful, pulling together items from across your system in categories that make sense to you. The only limitation is the inability to add folders on removable storage, such as a USB flash drive or a DVD. However, you can include folders on other PCs on your network or on a network attached storage (NAS) box.

Just ike the Documents or My Documents folders in previous versions of Windows, Libraries belong to an individual user account. As soon as you have more than one user on your computer, however, you should really have more than one user account. This means everyone will be able to

have their own files in their own places, which others – except an Administrator – won't be able to mess with. This makes extra sense with Windows 7's Libraries. Each family member can arrange their own things as they like, and even put shared files that everybody uses, such as the family music collection, into their own Libraries, organised their own way.

Assuming you're the administrator, everyone else should have a Standard account, which they should log in with every time they use the PC (to switch accounts, click the Start orb, click the triangle next to 'Shut down' and choose 'Switch user'). Standard users can't install software or change system settings – they'll have to ask you to enter your Administrator password. They can set their own desktop background, for example, use software already on the PC, save their own web bookmarks and edit and delete their own files.

You can also set up a Guest account, with similarly limited privileges, for anyone who needs to use the PC on an ad hoc basis.

1 CREATE A USER ACCOUNT
Hit the Windows key and type 'user accounts', then click User Accounts when it appears. Select Manage Another Account, Create New Account. Type the name of the person and make sure Standard user is selected, then click Create Account.

All accounts should be protected by a password, so people can't log in as each other. If younger users forget theirs, the Administrator can reset it. Go back to Manage Another Account, click the name of your new user and choose Create A Password. You'll also be asked for a hint that the user will get if they forget the correct password. Change the picture, too, if you like.

2 SETP UP CONTROLS
You can also apply Parental Controls from here. For example, you can set a maximum age rating for games, so that the user won't be allowed to run unsuitable titles, even if they're already installed on the PC. (This depends on the BBFC and PEGI ratings applied to all games sold

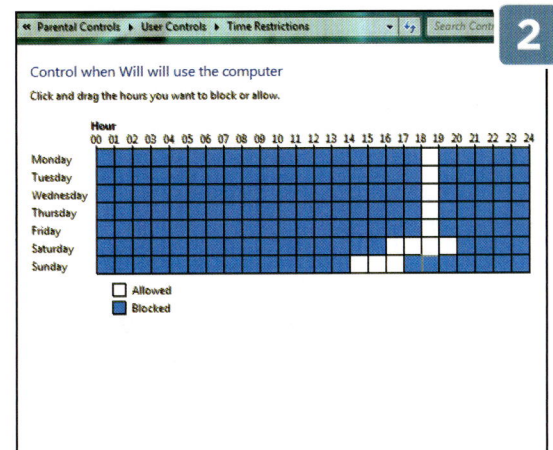

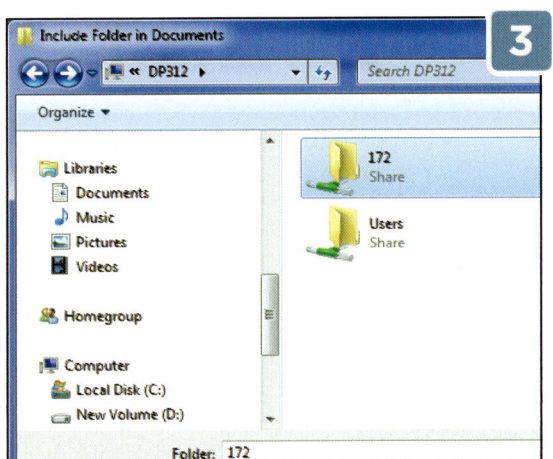

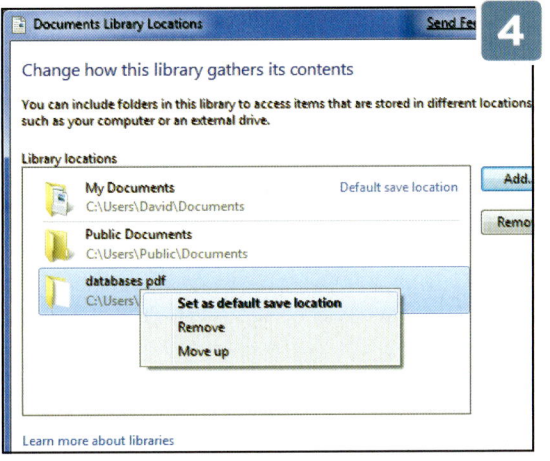

commercially in the UK.) You can also specify which individual games or applications they can access. You can even dictate the exact times of the day and week at which they will and won't be allowed to use the computer.

When the user runs up against one of the controls you've put in place, they'll be invited to contact you if they want to ask you to override it. Of course, it's up to you whether to do so.

If you need more comprehensive controls, Windows Live Family Safety adds web filtering and activity reporting. This is available as part of Microsoft's free Live add-ons.

3 ADD FOLDERS

By default, the only folders in each Library are the standard Documents locations under C:\ Users\. To add folders, click the 'Includes 2 locations' link at the top of a Library view. Then Click Add to start expanding the Library. You can add folders from almost any location, including network folders. The only ones you can't add are removable storage such as USB memory drives and optical drives (CDs and DVDs).

4 SAVE LOCATIONS

As we've said, the strength of Libraries is that they bring together content that's really stored in different places. But what if you actually want to store something in the Library? You can: drag a folder on to your Documents Library, for example, and it moves there. You can have lots of physical files and folders within a Library as well as other locations. They all get stored in the default save location. In the Documents Library Locations dialog box, one of the folders will be marked as the default save location. That's the physical folder to which any files dragged into the Library will be saved. To change it, all you need to do is right-click on another Library folder and select Set as default save location.

Note that if you right-click on an already created Library and select New Folder, that's what you get: a new folder in the default save location.

You're not limited to the supplied Libraries. To make a new Library, click on the top-level Libraries icon, right-click and select New, Library. Enter a name. Your Library won't include any folders until you add some.

> **⚲ TIP**
> Parental Controls take the user accounts concept to its logical conclusion by enabling you to decide exactly what each user can and can't do on the PC. Of course, this is no substitute for human supervision; Windows is clever, but it lacks your parental judgement. Insofar as you do rely on user account controls, remember that if a user knows your Administrator name and password they can just log in as you, so keep these secret.

Sharing files with HomeGroup

Sharing files and resources between several computers is simple with the help of Windows 7's HomeGroup feature

EXPERIENCED WINDOWS USERS will know that file and printer sharing is a well-established technology, though it's only really become commonplace in the home and small office in the past few years, as multiple PCs have become the norm. However, setting up file sharing has always been a tricky business, requiring you to tackle user accounts, permissions and workgroups. Windows 7 makes it much easier with a new system called HomeGroup.

Simply put, a homegroup is a collection of computers that can access the files in one another's Libraries. The beauty of HomeGroup is that, unlike with the previous Windows file-sharing system, at no point do you need to know the name or network address of any of the computers with which you want to share files.

Once your homegroup is up and running, you'll see it in the Windows Explorer navigation pane, with a list of all the other computers in your homegroup that are online. Simply click on one and you'll be able to access its Libraries as if they were your own. You can even incorporate files from your homegroup into your own Library.

This could raise some concerns about the security of your files, so there are a few points we should make clear. You don't have to share all your Libraries: on each PC, you can choose which of your Pictures, Videos, Music or Documents Libraries to share. By default, Documents is disabled, so you can let other family members listen to your Dire Straits albums without giving them the ability to snoop on your statements. You can also manually mark specific files or folders as private to prevent access.

As an extra level of security, all the folders you share will be read-only to other users in the group, so you don't need to worry about anyone accidentally deleting or corrupting your files. Nor will the kids be able to fill your hard disk with temporary files and unwanted downloads. But if you do want to enable other users to edit a particular file, or let them add files to one of your folders, that's easy to set up.

The bane of any file-sharing arrangement has always been that the PC containing the files you want might be switched off. Even Windows 7, clever though it is, hasn't cracked the challenge of talking to a system that's powered down. The good news, however, is that there's a workaround: while browsing files or folders that reside on a different PC, you can tell Windows to make them available 'offline'. After you do this, you'll find that, magically, you can access them even when the other computer isn't available.

Of course, there's a trick to it. When you make a file from another machine available offline, Windows creates a hidden copy of it on your own hard disk. Later, if it can't access the file over the network, it silently shows you this local copy instead. It all happens transparently. The other user might change the file, of course, but Windows synchronises its copy with the original whenever it can – and files won't get changed on the other PC while it's turned off. So for most purposes it's just like working with the actual file.

⬇ HomeGroups make it easy to share files and printers between Windows 7 PCs

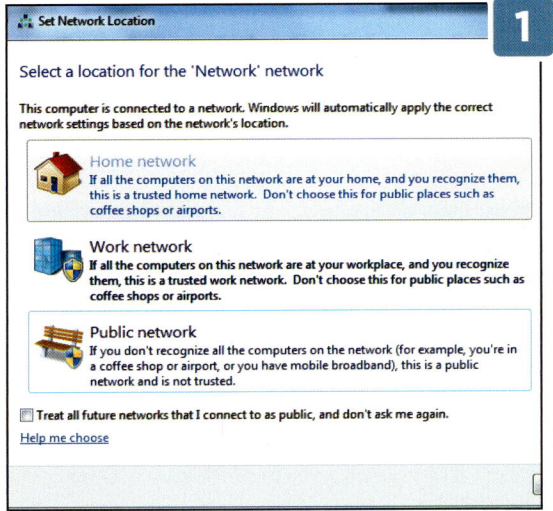

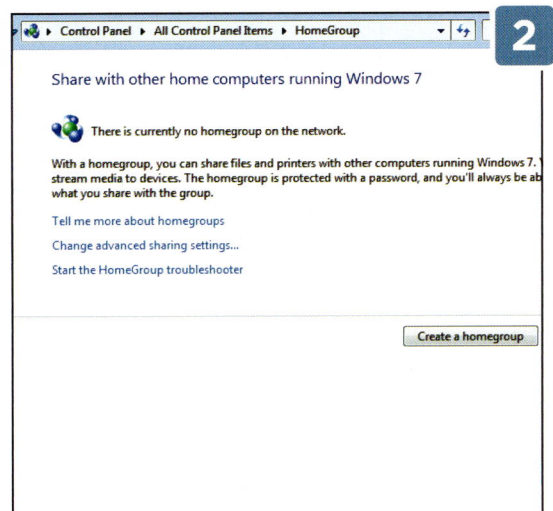

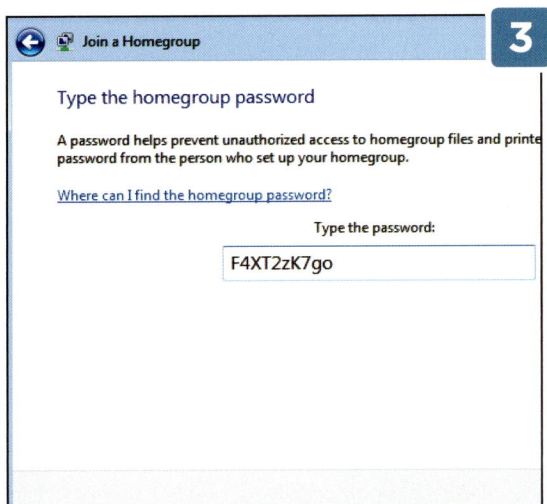

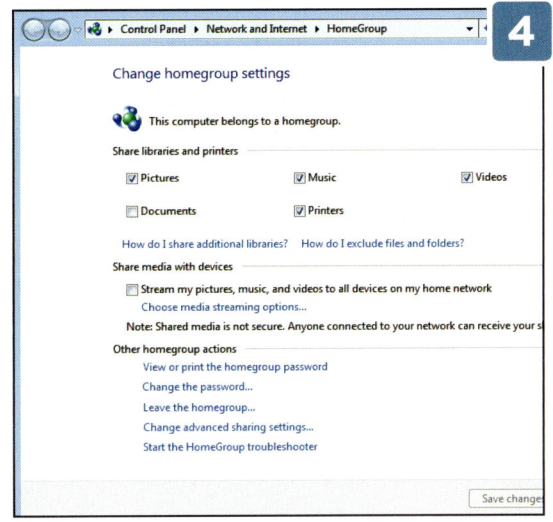

HomeGroup beats Windows Vista's file-sharing wizards because it requires very little configuration. The catch is that it works only with other Windows 7 PCs, but if that's what you have it'll save you a huge amount of effort. Standard file sharing can still be used with other machines.

1 MAKE YOURSELF AT HOME
Windows 7 should prompt you to create a homegroup the first time each PC connects to a network. You can only use HomeGroup if you're on a network designated as Home, rather than Work or Public. You can set this option in the Network and Sharing Center under 'View your active networks'.

2 CREATE A HOMEGROUP
Now go to Control Panel and select Network and Internet, then HomeGroup. Click Create HomeGroup. Select 'Libraries to share' and click

Next. Save the default password or make up your own secure password.

3 ADD PCs
On another Windows 7 PC, bring up HomeGroup from the Control Panel. Click Join HomeGroup. Select 'Libraries you want to share from this PC' and click Next. Type the password that you established in step 2 and click Next. Once the PC is connected to the homegroup, you can share files and printers with your other machines via the HomeGroup icon in Windows Explorer.

4 CHOOSE WHAT TO SHARE
To adjust which files a PC is sharing, open HomeGroup from the Control Panel. You can also choose to make your media available to network-streaming devices. To stop sharing a file or folder, click on the 'How do I exclude files and folders?' link for instructions.

TIP
HomeGroup is designed to be as simple as possible. However, that means it's not very versatile. When you share files and folders using HomeGroup, your sharing settings affect everybody in the group. If you want to create a more complex sharing system – for example, to give your partner access to your Documents Library but not your kids – you have to go back to the old way of sharing folders.

CHAPTER 8

NEW PC ESSENTIALS

EVEN THOUGH YOUR new PC is up and running and you've installed your operating system, you're not quite finished if you want your computer to be the best it can be. We'll show you which free utilities no computer owner should be without, and our guide to taking a complete image of your fresh PC will show you how to make a complete backup of your PC, including the operating system, applications and data.

IN THIS CHAPTER

Essential tools

ONCE YOU'VE BUILT your PC and everything is working perfectly, you may feel that your computing experience isn't quite complete. This is because, unlike a Mac OS installation, very little extra software is installed with Windows. You get a primitive word processor called WordPad, an image program called Microsoft Paint, which has barely changed since 1992, and very little else. There's no way to create complicated word-processing documents, do your accounts in a spreadsheet or edit photos.

More importantly, as Windows doesn't come with a virus scanner, you're left wide open to all kinds of internet threats. Windows XP can't even burn files to DVD, and Vista's disc-authoring capabilities leave much to be desired. Both versions also lack a credible alternative to Apple's iPhoto image organiser, although Windows 7 is an improvement .

⬆ Microsoft Office 2007 looks great and is very powerful, but it's expensive and most people won't touch half its features. OpenOffice is compatible with Office file formats, and is a credible and free alternative

In the not too distant past, you had to splash out on products such as Microsoft Office, Adobe Photoshop Elements, Norton Internet Security and Roxio Easy Media Creator to make your PC usable. Recently, though, a few software packages have emerged that offer the same features for free. As you'll see, OpenOffice is an impressive office suite, Paint.NET is a powerful image editor, AVG Anti-Virus will keep you safe online and CDBurnerXP lets you burn discs to your heart's content. Furthermore, Google's Picasa will let you organise your photos and share them online.

We've also covered some smaller free utilities that will make your new system easier and more fun to use, as well as keeping your data secure. Read on to find out about the essential free software to install on any new PC.

OpenOffice.org
OpenOffice.org 3

DOWNLOAD DETAILS **www.openoffice.org**
FILE SIZE **130MB**

As far as office software is concerned, a clean installation of Windows will come with an unimpressive word processor and nothing else. Fortunately, you don't have to splash out on the full version of Microsoft Office to give yourself powerful word processor and spreadsheet applications.

OpenOffice.org includes both of these essentials, as well as a presentation program, the Draw vector drawing package and the Base database application. The Writer word processing, Calc spreadsheet and Impress presentation applications are all compatible with Office file formats up to Office 2003, and can open and save documents either in Microsoft's formats or in the suite's OpenDocument format.

There's very little missing from the applications, and most are easy to use. Writer has a spellcheck, and a selection of styles and fonts, as well as word count and table of contents generation features. We can't really see anything missing from what Calc can do, as it supports all the functions and formulas we've ever needed. It even handles charts better than Excel 2007. Impress looks like an older version of PowerPoint, and comes with a couple of different templates

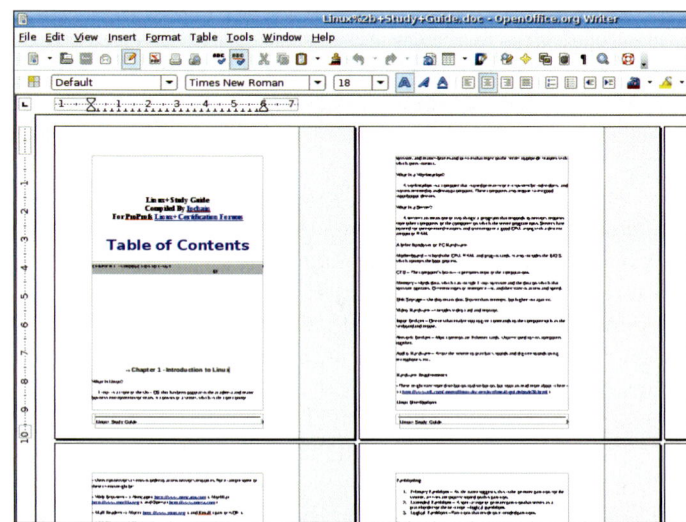

⬆ Packed with features, OpenOffice.org is an essential download

to get you started. The last two applications are more niche, but could still be useful. Draw is a reasonable program, but we found it the most fiddly part of the suite to use and it took us a while to master it. Base is a powerful SQL-compatible database, which lets you create searchable linked data tables.

OpenOffice.org may not look as flashy as Microsoft Office 2007, but there's little missing in the way of features and it's free, rather than £167. It's an essential download for every new PC.

AVG Technologies
AVG Anti-Virus Free Edition

DOWNLOAD DETAILS **http://free.avg.com**

FILE SIZE **47MB**

Even though Microsoft claims that Windows 7 is more secure than any previous version of the operating system, you'd be mad to go online without security software on your PC. A good security suite will protect you against viruses, but will also spot other malware, such as spyware and adware, which can lead to anything from a few annoying pop-ups to your banking logon details being passed on to unscrupulous criminals.

As new viruses and spyware programs are discovered all the time, your security suite needs to be continually updated to maintain the appropriate level of protection. Most security software companies make you pay a subscription to receive the updates, but AVG offers both its software and the subscription for free for non-commercial use. There's no catch, either.

The AVG software includes a virus scanner, which can be set to scan your hard disk at regular intervals, a resident shield that lives in your computer's memory and detects viruses as they appear, an email scanner and a program, which scans links

↑ AVG's anti-virus application will help protect your computer

in search engine results to check whether or not they lead to malicious websites. Recently, AVG also added a spyware resident shield, so you're protected against all the threats the internet has to offer.

If you're seriously worried about security threats, consider a paid-for program, such as Kaspersky Internet Security 2009, but AVG Free is certainly a credible home alternative.

Rick Brewster/Ed Harvey
Paint.NET

DOWNLOAD DETAILS **www.getpaint.net**

FILE SIZE **1.5MB**

While Windows has a reasonable image viewer as standard, Microsoft Paint is laughable as an image editor. Adobe Photoshop Elements is our favourite image-editing program, and, at around £50, is fair value. However, a good free alternative is Paint.NET. It's not the only free image-editing application for Windows, as you can also download GIMP from *www.gimp.org*. GIMP's user interface may make your head hurt, though, which is why we prefer Paint.NET.

The program is a tiny download of just 1.5MB, though if you have Windows XP, you'll also need to install Microsoft's .NET framework, which is a free download from *www.microsoft.com*. It has a clean interface that's reminiscent of Photoshop, with floating palettes and information windows. The package supports all the usual image-editing functions, such as layers, cropping and levels and curves adjustments. It also has several image effects as standard. You can save images in most standard formats, including JPEG, BMP, GIF and TIFF, and compressed image settings are handled with a clear preview to show you what your saved image will look like.

It does have a couple of omissions, most notably an Unsharp Mask feature, which is a popular method to sharpen an image.

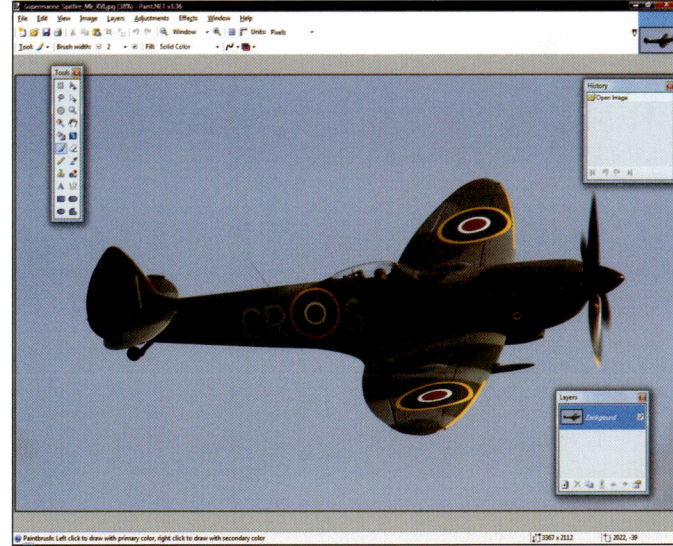

↑ Paint.NET's clean user interface is reminiscent of Photoshop's

However, the application has an active user community producing plug-ins to use with the software, including an Unsharp Mask plug-in. You will have to search through the forums to find what you need, though.

Paint.NET is astonishing for a free program, and has the advantage of being a small download. It may take you a bit of work and research to add all the features you will need, but it's well worth the effort.

Google
Picasa 3

DOWNLOAD DETAILS http://picasa.google.com
FILE SIZE **6MB**

Picasa 3 is a fantastic photo organisation and editing program from Google. It's a relatively small download, and is easy to install and set up. You should be careful when installing the program that you select the options you want, as by default it'll add shortcuts to your desktop, Quick Launch and System Tray, and set Google as your default search engine.

Picasa will scan your PC for any images when you first run it, read the time data encoded in each photo and arrange your pictures by date. The Library view displays all your photos as thumbnails, and double-clicking on a picture takes you into the editing view. This gives you most of the editing options you'll need to make your photos presentable, such as cropping, red-eye reduction, straightening and contrast and colour adjustment. There are also several effects, including Sharpen, Sepia, Black and White and Soft Focus.

Once you're happy with your pictures, you can view them as a slideshow, with a lovely fade effect between each photo. The best thing about Picasa, though, is its online storage. To use this you'll need a Google Mail account, which you can get at *http://mail.google.com*. Once you have an account, you simply

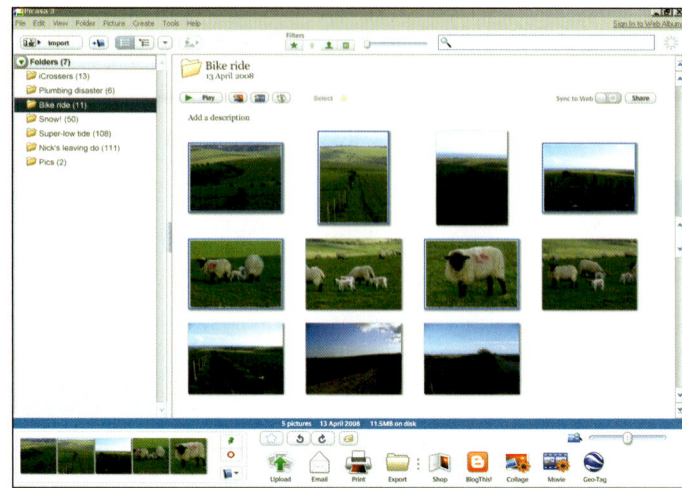

⬆ You can share your pictures online with Picasa 3

select the pictures you want to upload and click the Web Album button. You can upload photos in a quality suitable for viewing in a web browser, or upload bigger files that are good enough to print. Once your photos are online, you can make the album publicly available, or restrict it to only the people you invite to view your pictures. Google gives you 1GB of storage for free, which is enough for around 5,000 photos at web-quality settings. Vista users should try the built-in Windows Photo Gallery first before downloading Picasa, though.

Canneverbe Limited
CDBurnerXP

DOWNLOAD DETAILS http://cdburnerxp.se
FILE SIZE **2.9MB**

Windows 7, Vista and XP all have built-in CD-burning capabilities, and the later versions of the operating system can also burn DVDs, but these applications are fairly primitive and not particularly easy to use. CDBurnerXP is a powerful free program that makes it easy to burn data files to disc, turn audio files into a music CD and create CD and DVD images.

As with Paint.NET (page 119), if you're running Windows XP, you'll need to download and install the .NET Framework to use CDBurnerXP. The program itself is only a small download, and is simple to install.

The main interface will be familiar to anyone who's used a CD-burning program such as Nero. To create a CD, you just need to drag and drop files from the folder view at the top of the screen into your disc compilation at the bottom. You don't have to choose which type of disc you want to burn before you start your compilation, as CDBurnerXP automatically chooses the right file system depending on which type of disc is in the drive.

Once you've created your compilation, you just click the Burn icon to create your disc. You can also select Save

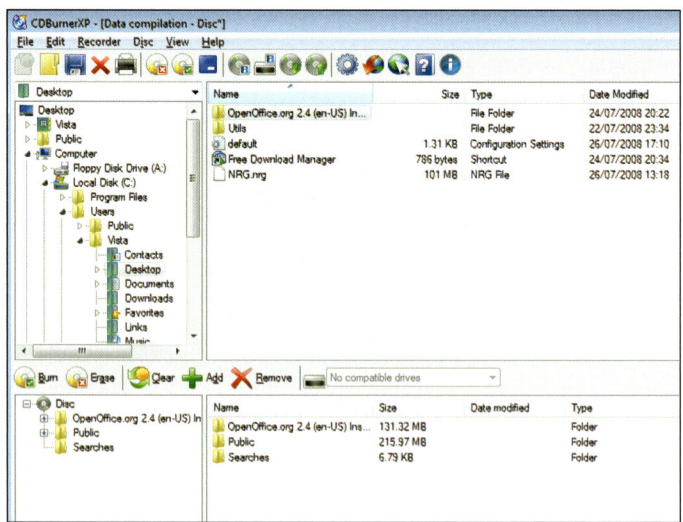

⬆ CDBurnerXP makes it easy to burn data files to CD

compilation as ISO file from the File menu to create a disc image to burn later. Usefully, the program also has the option to convert NRG and BIN image files, as used by Nero and some other CD-burning programs, to the more compatible ISO format.

Commercial applications such as Nero and Easy Media Creator have some impressive video disc-authoring features, but for most people CDBurnerXP will be the only disc-burning program they'll need.

Free Download Manager
Free Download Manager

DOWNLOAD DETAILS www.freedownloadmanager.org

FILE SIZE **5.6MB**

Essentially, Free Download Manager makes downloading files faster. When you start to download a file, the program splits the file into blocks and downloads all of them simultaneously. We found downloads were often four times faster using this program. You can also pause and resume downloading most files.

The application also has some other powerful features. You can use it to download movies from various video-sharing sites, such as YouTube and Google Video, and you can automatically convert these from the FLV format to more compatible formats such as MPEG4. Free Download Manager can also be used as a BitTorrent client, so is the only program you need to install to take care of all your downloads.

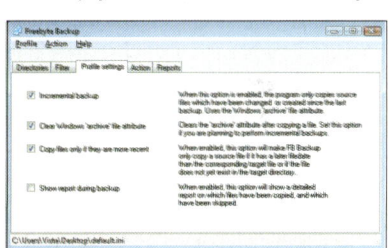

↑ You can download video from sites such as YouTube

Freebyte.com
Freebyte Backup

DOWNLOAD DETAILS www.freebyte.com/fbbackup

FILE SIZE **785KB**

Freebyte Backup is a simple program that lets you back up the contents of your PC's hard disk to an external hard disk. To make a backup, you simply add the drives and directories to be included, then specify any files you want to exclude from the backup, either by the date they were created or by file type. You then just click the Start button and the files you specified will be backed up.

Once you've made your first backup, you can set the software to copy only files that are new or have been changed since the last time you backed up your PC, which drastically cuts down the amount of time the process takes. Automatic backups can be scheduled using the Windows Task Scheduler, although this can be tricky to configure.

↑ Back up your data with Freebyte

Nathan Moinvaziri
ExtractNow

DOWNLOAD DETAILS www.extractnow.com

FILE SIZE **940KB**

Even though Windows-supported ZIP files are the most common form of archive, there are many other kinds. ExtractNow can extract the majority of archives, including the popular RAR format, and CD and DVD image ISO files.

The program is particularly useful for extracting batches of archives. You just have to drag files into its window, click Extract and the program will extract each archive's contents into the folder where the archive is situated. You can also associate archive file types with the program, so it will open automatically when you double-click on an archive in Windows.

ExtractNow is an easy way to deal with different types of archive without having to install multiple programs, and it's a tiny download. The only thing that it doesn't let you do is create files, but Windows has this functionality built in.

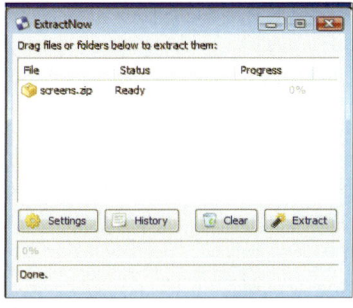

↑ ExtractNow can deal with different types of archive

VideoLAN
VLC media player

DOWNLOAD DETAILS www.videolan.org

FILE SIZE **9.3MB**

Playing back audio and video files on a PC can be tricky. Even though all PCs come with Windows Media Player, there are many types of file that it doesn't support, so you'll need to install specific audio and video codecs to play them. Windows XP doesn't even have support for DVD movies as standard.

Finding out which codec is missing from your system can be a tricky business, but VLC takes much of the pain out of this process. It will play most types of audio and video files, including DVDs. It's simple to install, and will launch automatically when you double-click on a compatible file type. It can even play files that are incomplete. With built-in support for DVDs, it's one of the most comprehensive media players and it's completely free. VLC is the simplest way to play back media files.

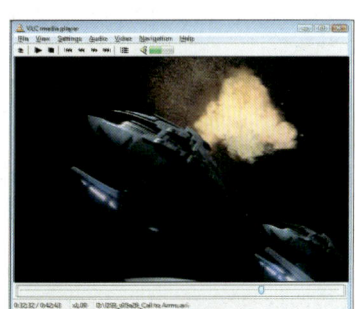

↑ VLC lets you play DVDs as well as most other media files

Saving power with your new PC

THE RISING COSTS of electricity and increasing concerns over the environment are two very good reasons to consider ways of cutting down on power consumption. PCs are one of the worst offenders in the home, but other devices connected to them, such as printers, monitors and external hard disks, all have their part to play.

Fortunately, there are several things you can do to save power and make your computer more efficient. We'll show you how much power your devices really use, how much it costs you to run them and how to save money by putting your devices into standby mode.

COST OF LIVING

First, it's worth explaining how costs are calculated. Every electrical device draws power, measured in watts (volts x amps). This is the figure used to describe light bulbs – a 100W bulb draws 100W of power. Over an hour this would be a watt hour. Electricity companies then charge your consumption based on the number of kilowatt hours (kWh) you're using. As a kilowatt is 1,000W, you first have to convert the wattage of any measured product into kilowatts by dividing by 1,000. So, a 100W light bulb uses 0.1kW. Over an hour, this would be 0.1kWh. If your electricity company charges you 11p per kWh, your 100W light bulb would cost you 1.1p per hour to run. In reality, most electricity companies use a two-tier system of charging. A fairly common tariff is 14p per kWh for the first 728 kWh per year and then 12p for each kWh thereafter.

For our calculations we've assumed the higher figure of 14kWh. While this means that we've ended up with higher costs overall, it gives us a fair comparison between each device. You can try our Google Docs spreadsheet for calculating running costs by visiting *http://tinyurl.com/powersaver*. You'll need a Google account to access it, but can

⬆ Devices left on can use a huge amount of power, which will cost you a small fortune

↗ Devices such as the Intelliplug can help you save power

DEVICE	POWER WHEN ON	STANDBY POWER	TYPICAL COST PER YEAR*
PC	129W	3W	£40
Laptop	32W	3W	£17
LCD monitor	29W	2W	£8
Inkjet printer	Varies**	3W	£2
Network storage	41W	1W	£34
LCD TV	158W	3W	£33

*We've assumed a typical day's use for each product (eight hours a day for PCs, four hours a day for TVs), using standby modes where appropriate and being turned off at the plug when not in use

**Inkjet printers typically use between 10W and 30W to print a page of paper, but this is for a short amount of time, so the standby power is the biggest factor

sign up for a free one on that web page. Once you've accessed the spreadsheet, select Copy spreadsheet from the File menu to edit it in your own account. All you need to do is set your kWh cost and, for each device, type in its power usage figures, the number of hours a day it's on, off (at the socket) and in standby mode and the sheet will work out the rest.

MEASURING YOUR DEVICES
Measuring electrical devices is easy. All you need is a plug-in power monitor, such as the Plug-In Mains Power and Energy Monitor (£28, *www. maplin.co.uk*). This plugs into your wall socket, and then you just plug the electrical device you want to test into it. The reading on the screen tells you how many watts your device is drawing. Using the calculations above, you can work out how much a device will cost you each year.

You'll be quite surprised at the results. For example, a typical PC uses around 120W when on, while an LCD monitor will use around 29W (149W in total). If you were to leave both on all day every day for a year, you'd be using 1,305kWh per annum, which would cost a staggering £183 a year. However, putting a PC into standby mode means that it uses only around 3W, which is similar to an LCD monitor's 2W in standby mode. Turning them off at the plug when you're not using them would save more money, as you're not drawing any power.

Typically, a computer that's on eight hours a day with no standby modes turned on would cost around £61 a year to run. If you were to set the PC to go into standby mode when not in use for, say, three hours a day, it would cost £47 per annum to run – a saving of around £14 every year. The same can be said of every device that you use. The table

(above) shows typical usage figures for electrical devices you have in your home.

COMBATTING THE PROBLEM
To save money, devices need to use less electricity. For PCs, this means adjusting Windows' power-saving settings so that your computer powers down automatically after a period of inactivity. For other devices, you need to power them down when they're not in use. Ideally, you should switch devices off at the plug, because many still draw power when they're in standby mode. For example, the average LCD TV draws 3W when in standby mode. If this was to be left on all year, it would cost you £3.67 every year. That's not a huge amount of money, but multiply this sum for every device you own and it adds up to a small fortune. For computer devices, such as printers, switch them off when you're not using them.

If the thought of having to switch off a plug under a desk sounds like too much hassle, then consider buying a product such as OneClick's Intelliplug (£17, *www. oneclickpower.co.uk*). This has a master socket for your PC and two slave sockets that get power only when your PC is turned on. It's ideal for your monitor and printer, as they'll be on only when your computer is.

You can try other power-saving techniques, too. For example, if you've got network storage, check to see if there's a sleep mode. Setting your storage to shut down overnight when you won't be using it can save you money every year. Follow this advice for all your electrical kit and you could knock more than £100 every year off your electricity bills.

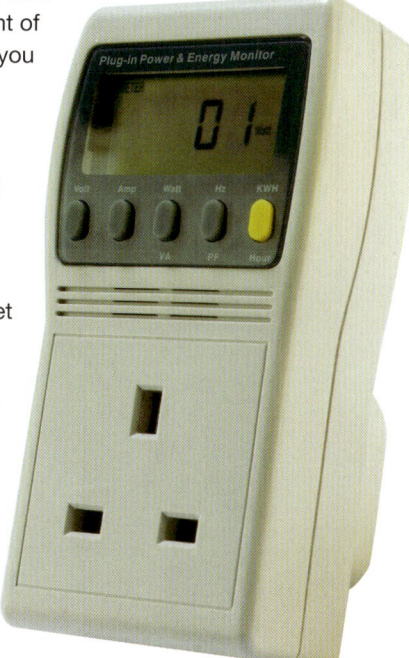

↑ Measuring how much power your devices use could be a real shock

Making an image of your hard disk

NOW YOU'VE FINISHED building your PC, installed Windows and downloaded all the drivers and extra software you need, you'll understand just how much work is needed to get a computer up and running from scratch. Beyond simply getting it working, there's all the additional hassle associated with ensuring that Windows looks and feels right, setting up all your applications the way you like them, and organising all your favourites and home page in your web browser.

It's hours of work, so imagine how you'd feel if your PC suddenly shut down, taking your hard disk with it. Thankfully, this is very unlikely, but a more probable scenario is that as time goes on Windows will become increasingly bloated. Over the years, you will install and uninstall any number of extra applications and additional hardware, which will leave a large number of extra files and services on your hard disk. These will slow your PC down to a crawl, and reinstalling everything from scratch isn't a huge amount of fun.

This is where using a disk-imaging program can save you a world of trouble. It will take a complete copy of your hard disk, including the operating system, your applications, all your settings and every file on your hard disk.

NO MORE REINSTALLING

When restored, the image will take your computer back to the day that the image was made. Instead of having to reinstall Windows when it's no longer working the way you want it, you can just flash the image back and return to when you first installed Windows, complete with all your original settings and applications. So instead of hours of work, with a disk-imaging application it takes only a fraction of the time.

The best thing is that you're not just limited to taking one image. With the right software, you can also schedule images to occur regularly, so that you're constantly making a backup. If you should suffer a problem, you simply restore your computer back to the last good image – a little bit like a super System Restore.

Disk-imaging applications also include standard file backup options, so you can take less regular images, which use a lot of disk space, but still protect all your data.

HARD DISK

Ideally, you should store images on an external hard drive so you won't lose them if your main hard disk fails. This also means that you can restore the image to your old hard disk (or to a new one in the case of a major problem), getting up and running again in a short period of time. You could also back up to a secondary partition on your primary hard disk.

NORTON GHOST

We can't stress the importance of using disk-imaging software enough, particularly when you build a new PC, as you can create an amazing recovery disc just like the one you'd get with a new computer from a manufacturer. Over the next few pages, we'll show you how to image your PC using the best application on the market: Norton Ghost 14. We used the download version of Ghost, which costs £40 and is available from *www.symantec.co.uk* (click on the online store). This is identical to the boxed version, although the installation steps may differ very slightly. You'll also have to download the recovery CD image file, which we'll show you how to use later.

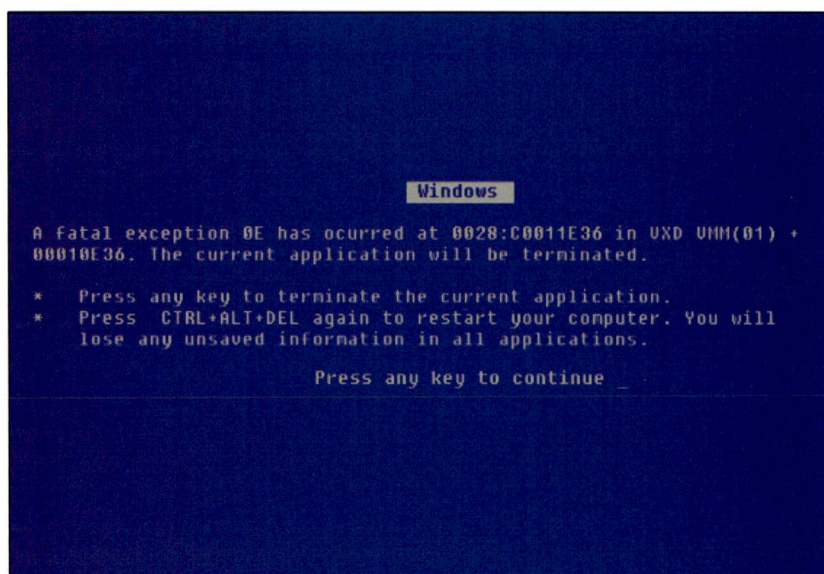

↑ To recover from a system error quickly, you need a disk image of your hard disk

HOW TO...
Make a hard disk image

1 INSTALL GHOST

Run the Ghost installation program and follow the wizard. The software should install quickly and automatically, without asking you any questions. When it's finished, you'll be prompted to restart your computer. Do this and wait for your PC to load Windows again. When prompted, enter the product key that you were provided with when you bought the application, click Next, and then click Next again to run LiveUpdate and to download the latest version of the software. Restart your computer again if prompted.

2 CHANGE SCHEDULE

After LiveUpdate has finished, the Easy Setup application starts. This automatically sets up a scheduled imaging job and a scheduled file backup job. These tend to be a bit extreme, though, so you should change some settings.

First, under My Computer Backup, click the box next to Schedule to specify when you want a backup taken. The default is set for every Sunday and Thursday, but once a week should be sufficient. These backups record only the changes to files since the last image to save on disk space.

Ghost is also set to create a full new image set, which takes up a lot of disk space, once every three months. This should be fine for most people.

3 ADD TRIGGERS

You can also set Ghost to run a backup when certain triggers are detected. Click on the General link under Event Triggers, and select the options you want – Any application is installed, for example. Be warned that using any of these options will increase the amount of disk space you'll need for backups, so use them carefully. When you're happy with your settings, click OK.

4 MANAGE FILES

Ghost will also take regular file backups. It's set by default to back up the Documents, My Video, My Pictures and My Music folders, Internet Explorer favourites and desktop settings. Click on the blue text to the right of Select at the top of the screen to add more options. Click OK when you're done. You can now change the schedule for this backup in the same way as in Step 3.

Finally, Norton Ghost tries to pick a suitable backup destination, such as an external hard disk.

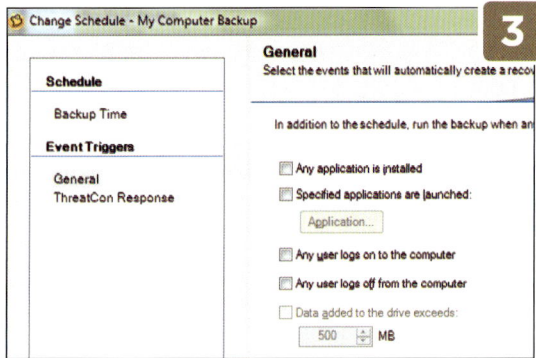

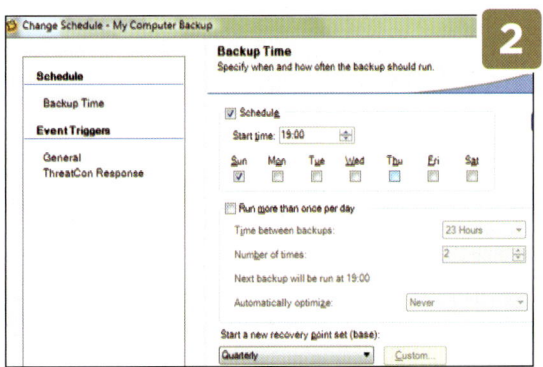

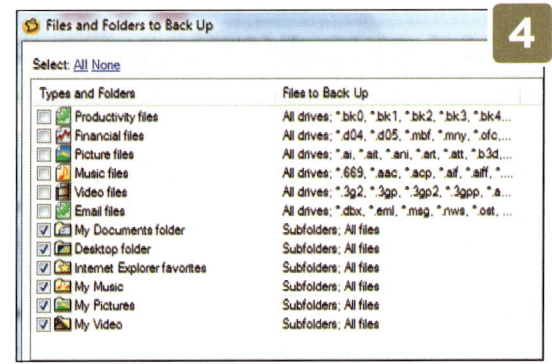

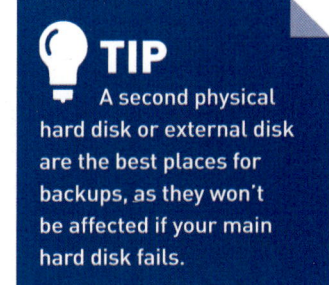

TIP
A second physical hard disk or external disk are the best places for backups, as they won't be affected if your main hard disk fails.

You can also back up to a separate partition, like the one we created when we installed Windows in Chapter 6. This will be safe from Windows crashes, but not hard disk faults, so an external hard disk is the safest option. Use the secondary partition if you don't have an external disk. Click OK, select Run first backup now and click OK again.

5 MANAGE BACKUPS

While your backups will run to the schedule you set, you can modify this or choose to start a backup manually if, for example, you've just saved a lot of new files or made a major system change. Start Norton Ghost and select Run or Manage Backups. The next window will display your current jobs. Select one and click Run Now to run it. You can Change schedules and edit what's being backed up by clicking Edit Settings. With the default My Documents Backup, you can now add your own custom files and folders.

6 RECOVER FILES

If you want to recover individual files, click Recover My Files from Ghost's main screen. You can search for a specific file or click Search to find all your backed-up files. Right-clicking a file or folder lets you view the different backup versions and recover the one you want. You can also restore files from an image. Click Recovery Point, select

the backup you want and choose Explore from Tasks. You can browse the image in the same way as a regular folder and drag files to your computer.

7 RECOVER A HARD DISK

You can restore an image to a hard disk by selecting the Recover My Computer link from Ghost's Welcome page. Select the Recovery point you want and click Recover now. Provided the Recovery point isn't for your boot partition (the one with Windows on it), Ghost will restore the image. If it is for your boot hard disk, Ghost can't recover it while Windows is running. Instead, you need to follow Steps 8 to 12 to create a recovery CD.

8 CREATE A RECOVERY CD

If you bought the download version of Ghost, you should have also downloaded the recovery CD image file. This needs to be recorded to a CD. You can do this with CD-writing software such as CDBurnerXP (see page 120). If you don't have CDBurnerXP, you can download ISO Recorder from *http://isorecorder.alexfeinman.com*. Version 2 is for Windows XP and version 3.1 is for Windows 7 and Vista, so make sure that you get the right one. Install the software.

Browse to the directory to which you downloaded Norton Ghost and look for the ZIP file (NGH140_AllWin_EnlishEMEA_SrdOnly.zip). Open

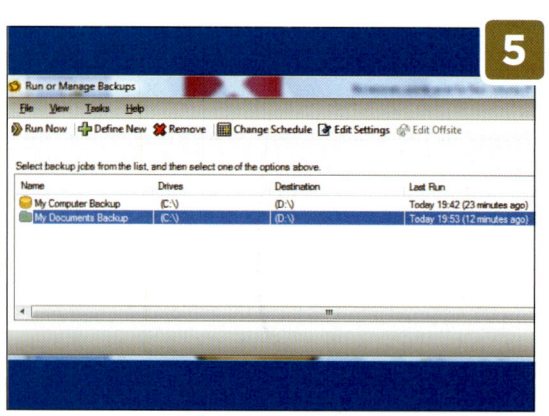

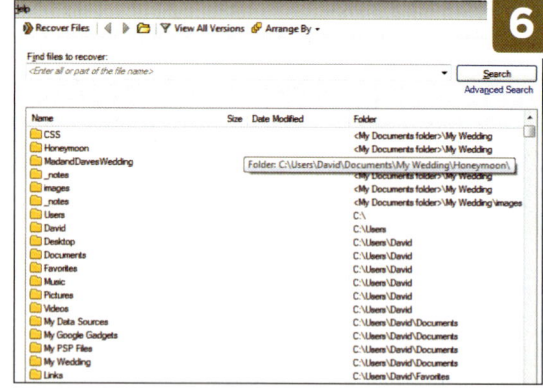

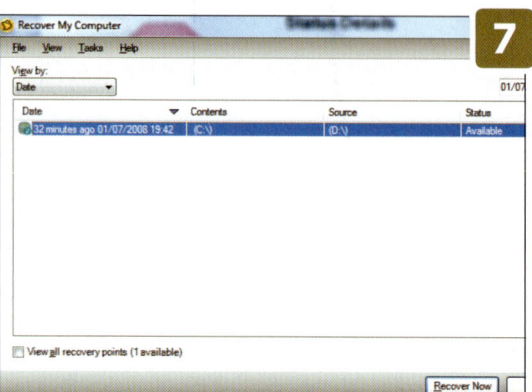

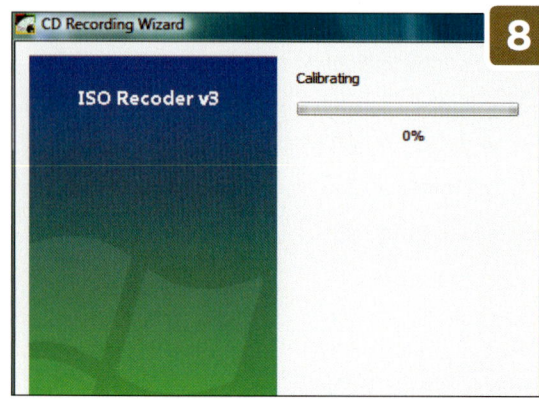

this by right-clicking on it and selecting Extract. Right-click on the resulting ISO file and select Copy image to CD. Click Next and then Finish when the operation is done. You now have a bootable restore CD.

9 BOOT FROM YOUR RESTORE DISC

Make sure that your BIOS is set to boot from your optical drive (see page 70) and then restart your PC. You'll be prompted to hit a key to boot off the CD, so make sure you're ready. When the Windows loading screen starts, click Accept to accept the Norton Ghost licence agreement.

There are several options on the next screen. Click on Analyze to perform system tests, and Check Hard Disk for Errors to run a system scan on your hard disk. The Virus scanner is useful only if you've also got Symantec Anti-Virus, otherwise the definitions will be too old. You can also click on Explore your hard disk.

10 ADD DRIVERS

While this recovery disk will recognise most hard disks, it can't identify them all, particularly if you're running RAID. If the image you want to restore is saved on a networked hard disk, then you may have to install a driver for the network adaptor, too. To do this, click on Utilities and then Load drivers. You need to use the Explorer-like window to navigate to a folder with the relevant driver in it. You can plug in USB drives or use a CD, so adding extra drivers shouldn't be hard. You should also have them available if you had to add extra drivers when installing Windows.

11 RECOVER YOUR COMPUTER

Click on Home and Recover my Computer. Select the recovery point you want to restore (if the list is blank, select View by filename and click Browse to find it) and click Next. Click Finish and then Yes to start recovering your PC. The files will then be restored to your computer.

Once it's completed, you can reboot your computer and it will be back to the exact state at which you made the recovery point.

12 RECOVER FILES

Alternatively, you can use this interface to recover individual files from a restore point. Select Recover from the main screen and then Recover My Files. Navigate to a recovery point, select it and click OK. You'll then be presented with the Symantec Recovery Point Browser.

You can navigate through this like an ordinary disk. When you find the file or files you want to recover, you just have to select them and click Recover Files. You can then choose where to restore the files to, such as another drive.

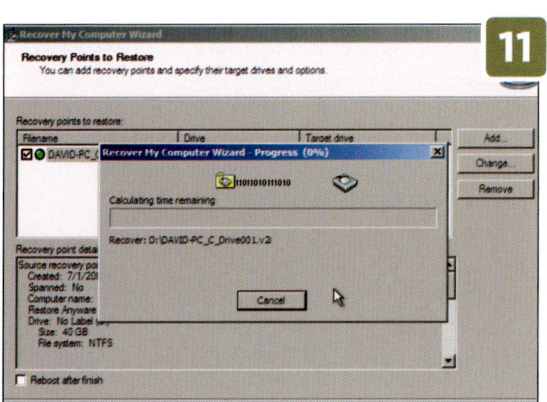

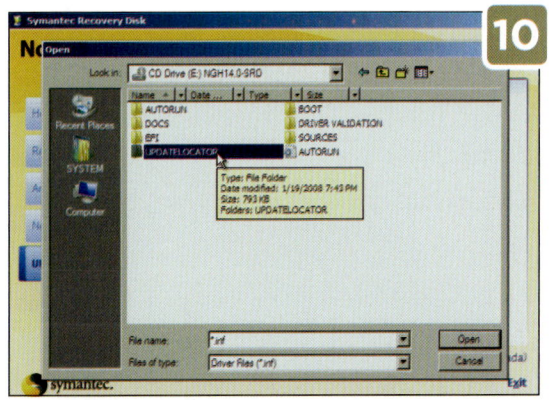

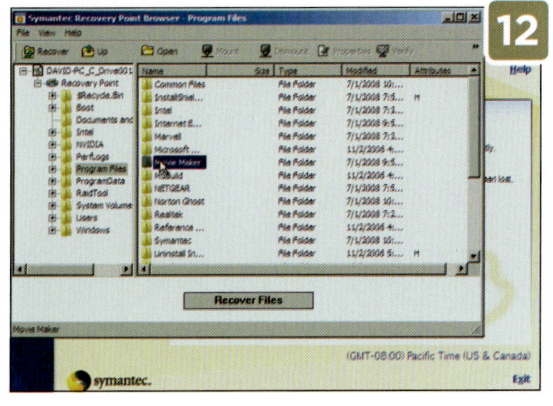

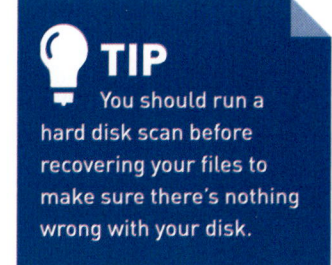

TIP
You should run a hard disk scan before recovering your files to make sure there's nothing wrong with your disk.

CHAPTER 9
TROUBLESHOOTING

HOPEFULLY THIS BOOK has given you everything you need to build the perfect PC. However, you may have run into problems along the way or simply haven't understood some of the terms we've used. Don't worry – we haven't abandoned you. In the next few pages, we'll give you some essential troubleshooting and problem-solving tips. There's also a glossary, so you can look up any terms you don't know.

IN THIS CHAPTER

Top 10 tips for solving boot problems

If you're having trouble getting Windows to start, these tips will help you get it up and running with the minimum of hassle

THERE ARE MANY reasons why a PC won't boot into its operating system. Many are easy to cure, while others take a little more time.

1 CHECK YOUR USB DEVICES

USB devices are often the cause of PCs refusing to load Windows. The boot sequence appears to be running correctly, but just before you see the Windows splash screen, the PC appears to hang or freeze. You'll either see a black screen, or a white cursor flashing in the top left of the screen. Usually this is caused by USB devices, particularly memory card readers. Check whether you've left a flash drive in a USB port or a memory card in a reader (or digital camera or camcorder) that's connected to your PC. Many printers also have memory card readers. Remove any cards and press your PC's reset button to reboot it.

2 CHECK FOR OPTICAL DISCS

It's easy to leave a bootable CD or DVD in a drive accidentally. This could cause your PC to refuse to boot, or to boot into an application other than your operating system. It may not be obvious that your PC is booting from an optical disc, so check that your drives are empty and reboot.

3 CHECK THE BOOT ORDER

BIOS settings are critical for booting, so if you see a message such as "NTLDR is missing. Press Ctrl+Alt+Del to restart" you should enter the BIOS and check the boot sequence. When you see the POST screen, press Del (some computers will require you to press F2, F10 or F12, but most display a message telling you which key to press). Look for an Advanced BIOS Options menu and a Boot Sequence menu within that. Ensure that the primary boot device is the hard disk that has your operating system on it. If you have more than one hard disk and don't know which one Windows is on, you may have to try setting each as the primary device and rebooting to see if it fixes the problem. CD-ROM and floppy drives can boot before the hard disk, but this will slow the boot time down.

4 LISTEN FOR STRANGE NOISES

Listen for any unusual noises coming from your PC. As your PC boots, you should hear

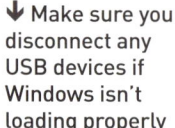
⬇ Make sure you disconnect any USB devices if Windows isn't loading properly

↘ Overheating can cause the dreaded blue screen of death

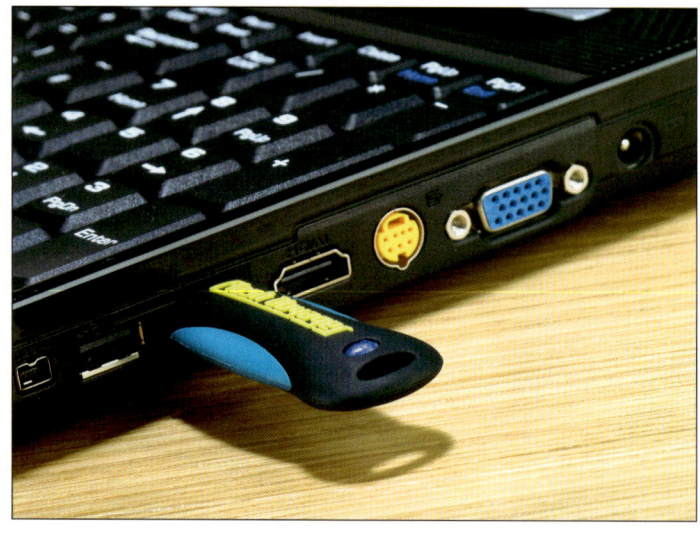

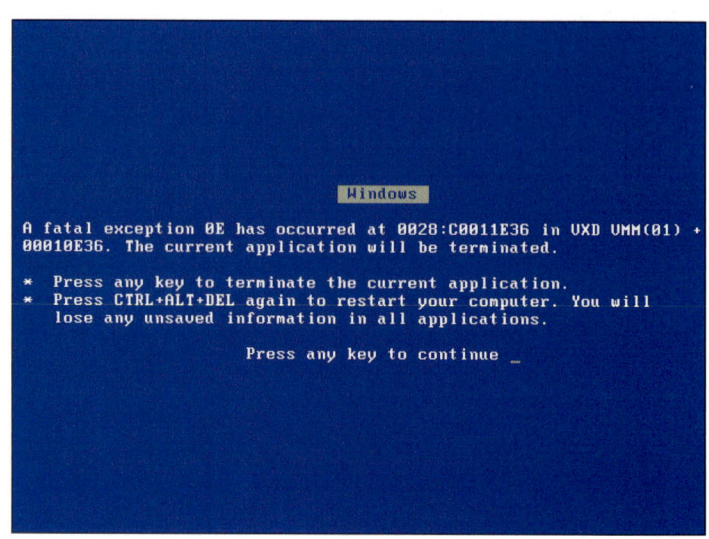

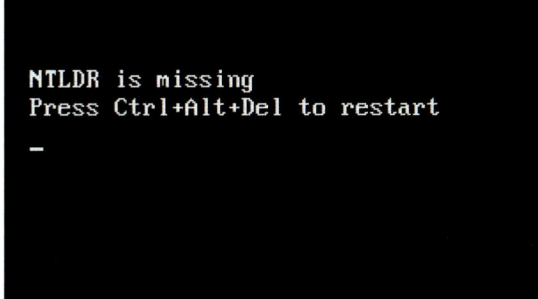

```
NTLDR is missing
Press Ctrl+Alt+Del to restart
-
```

⬆ If you see a message such as this, you should check the boot order in the BIOS

flurries of clicking from the hard disk, but if there's a rhythmic scraping or chirping noise, your hard disk may have failed. In this case, turn to page 124 to find out how to restore a backup to a new disk.

5 CHECK YOUR CABLES

Wake sure that no cables have become dislodged. Start with power cables and both ends of your monitor's cable. If you don't find any problems, remove your PC's side panel and check internal cables, particularly the hard disk's power and data cables. Many modern graphics cards require one or two power cables, so check these are properly connected. Without a power cable, some graphics cards emit a high-pitched noise.

6 RESET THE BIOS

Overclocking can cause boot problems, so you should check your motherboard's manual to see if there's a way to boot the PC at standard speeds without losing all your BIOS settings. If not, you'll need to reset the BIOS (this is also known as resetting the CMOS). The same manual should document the procedure, which usually involves moving a motherboard jumper to a reset position, although in rare cases you may find a switch or button on the outside of the PC.

7 CHECK FOR OVERHEATING

Your PC may be overheating and it may fail to boot after an unexplained 'blue screen'. Wait for at least 30 minutes to allow the components to cool down and try turning on the PC again. Meanwhile, investigate potential reasons for overheating, such as a broken fan. You should ensure that your PC isn't placed next to a heat source such as a radiator.

8 BEEP, BEEP!

If your PC is making an unusual beeping noise, you'll need to refer to your motherboard manual to diagnose the problem. If you don't have a manual, we've provided a list of common BIOS

⬆ Check the power cables if your graphics card is emitting a high-pitched noise

beep codes on page 134. Some motherboards have LED displays that you can use along with thedescriptions of each code in the manual to determine the status of the POST sequence. These often make it much simpler to solve the problem as you can see precisely how far the PC makes it through the boot process before failing. Knowing this information should make it obvious which component is causing the problem.

9 CHECK HARDWARE AND SOFTWARE

If you've recently installed a piece of hardware and you see a blue screen when your PC boots, the cause is probably the new hardware. Uninstall it and see if it fixes the problem. It could also be caused by new software, so try and boot into Safe Mode by pressing F8 repeatedly after the initial POST screen. It's also worth noting that you'll probably see a blue screen if you've recently swapped the hard disk for one from a different PC and tried to boot from it.

10 UNPLUG YOUR HARDWARE

If none of the tips above has helped you solve the problem, you should disconnect any unnecessary hardware. All a PC needs to show a POST message is a motherboard, a processor, one memory module, a graphics card and a power supply. All other hardware can be unplugged. If the PC now boots, begin reconnecting other components one at a time until the problem returns. If it still doesn't boot, it's likely to be a hardware failure. At this point, it's worth trying to borrow components known to be working, and swapping them with yours to find out which of the core parts is defective.

Fixing boot problems

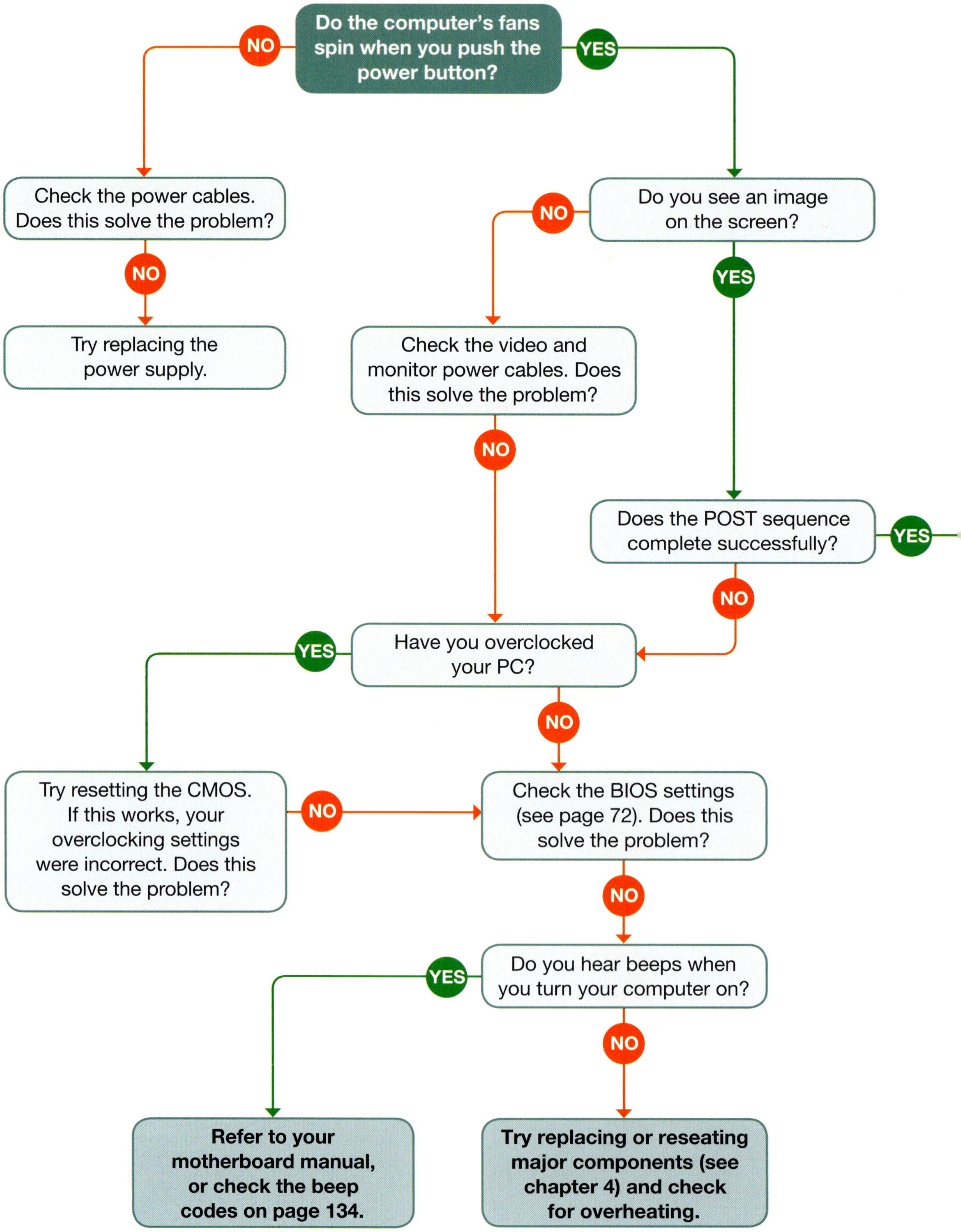

Do the computer's fans spin when you push the power button?

NO → Check the power cables. Does this solve the problem?

NO → Try replacing the power supply.

YES → Do you see an image on the screen?

NO → Check the video and monitor power cables. Does this solve the problem?

NO → Have you overclocked your PC?

YES → Does the POST sequence complete successfully?

YES →

NO →

Have you overclocked your PC?

YES → Try resetting the CMOS. If this works, your overclocking settings were incorrect. Does this solve the problem?

NO →

Check the BIOS settings (see page 72). Does this solve the problem?

NO → Do you hear beeps when you turn your computer on?

YES → Refer to your motherboard manual, or check the beep codes on page 134.

NO → Try replacing or reseating major components (see chapter 4) and check for overheating.

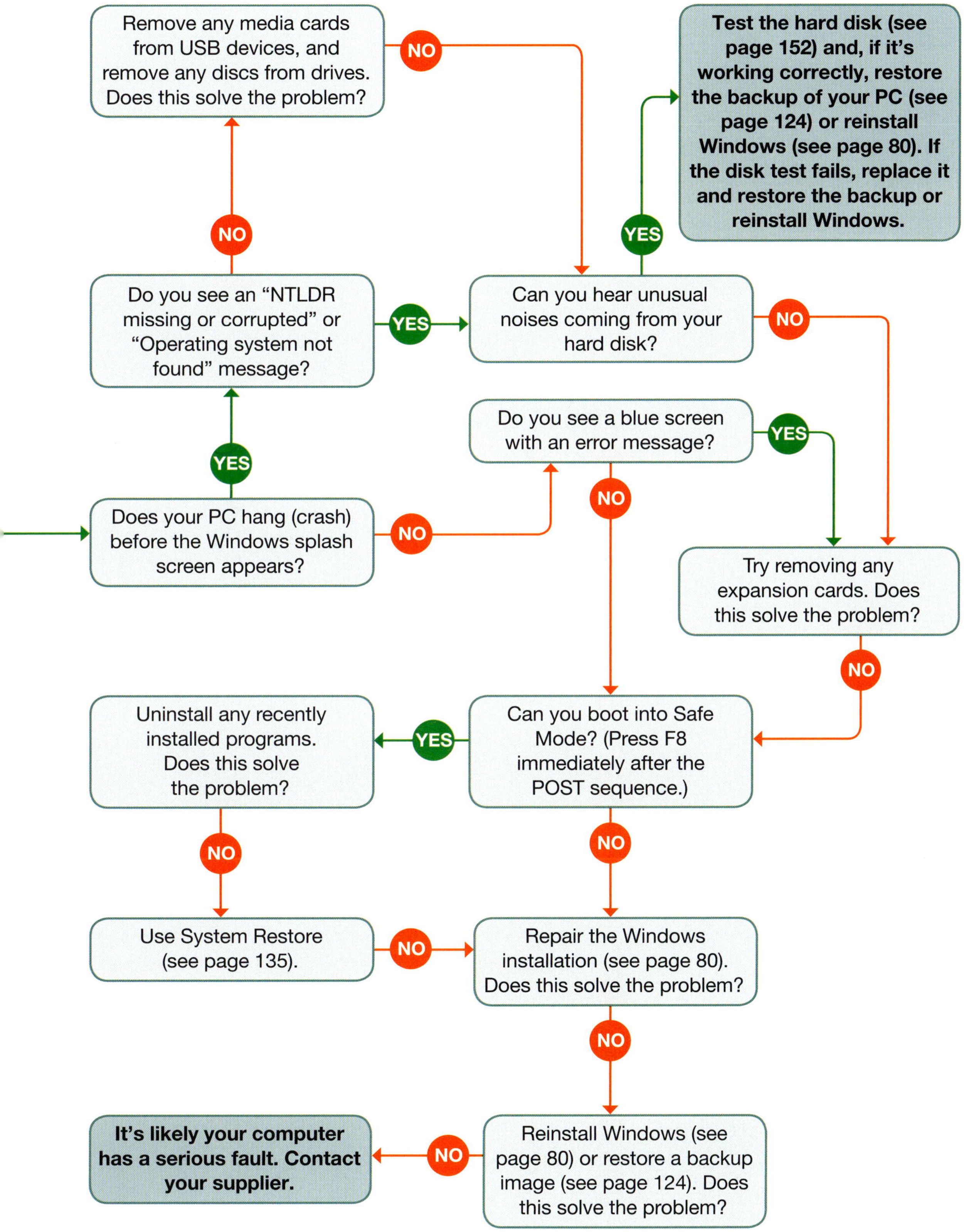

Remove any media cards from USB devices, and remove any discs from drives. Does this solve the problem?

NO →

Test the hard disk (see page 152) and, if it's working correctly, restore the backup of your PC (see page 124) or reinstall Windows (see page 80). If the disk test fails, replace it and restore the backup or reinstall Windows.

NO ↑

YES ↑

Do you see an "NTLDR missing or corrupted" or "Operating system not found" message?

YES → Can you hear unusual noises coming from your hard disk?

NO →

YES ↑

Do you see a blue screen with an error message?

YES →

NO ↓

Does your PC hang (crash) before the Windows splash screen appears?

NO →

Try removing any expansion cards. Does this solve the problem?

NO ↓

Uninstall any recently installed programs. Does this solve the problem?

YES ← Can you boot into Safe Mode? (Press F8 immediately after the POST sequence.)

NO ↓

NO ↓

Use System Restore (see page 135).

NO → Repair the Windows installation (see page 80). Does this solve the problem?

NO ↓

It's likely your computer has a serious fault. Contact your supplier.

NO ← Reinstall Windows (see page 80) or restore a backup image (see page 124). Does this solve the problem?

BIOS beep codes

If your PC makes a beeping noise when it boots, it may be trying to send you a message. Here's how to interpret the noises

WHEN YOU SWITCH on or reset your PC it performs a diagnostic test called a Power-On Self Test (POST) to check that all the components are present and working correctly. First, it checks core components such as the system clock, processor, RAM, keyboard controller and graphics card. If any device fails this part of the POST, you'll hear a series of beeps from the PC. After the graphics card has passed its test, the BIOS can then indicate any errors onscreen, such as the classic "Keyboard error or no keyboard present. Press F1 to continue" message.

Beep codes differ depending on the BIOS manufacturer, but here are some common codes for popular BIOSes.

AMI BIOS

- **ONE BEEP** All OK
- **TWO BEEPS** Memory parity error (reseat or replace memory)
- **THREE BEEPS** Memory read or write error (reseat or replace memory)
- **FOUR BEEPS** Motherboard timer problem (replace motherboard)
- **FIVE BEEPS** Processor or memory error (reseat or replace processor and memory)
- **SIX BEEPS** Keyboard controller failure (replace motherboard)
- **SEVEN BEEPS** Processor exception interrupt error (reseat or replace processor)
- **EIGHT BEEPS** Display memory read or write failure (reseat or replace graphics card)

- **NINE BEEPS** ROM checksum error (replace BIOS chip or motherboard)
- **10 BEEPS** CMOS shutdown read or write error (replace BIOS chip or motherboard)
- **11 BEEPS** Bad cache memory (replace cache memory if possible)
- **ONE LONG, THREE SHORT BEEPS** Memory error (reseat or remove any memory recently added and reseat all other memory)
- **ONE LONG, EIGHT SHORT BEEPS** Graphics card error (reseat graphics card)

AWARD BIOS

- **ONE LONG, TWO SHORT BEEPS** Graphics card error (reseat or replace graphics card)
- **ONE LONG, THREE SHORT BEEPS** No graphics card, or graphics memory error (install or replace graphics card)
- **TWO SHORT BEEPS** Memory error (reseat or replace memory)
- **ONE HIGH-PITCHED BEEP** Processor overheating
- **ONE HIGH-PITCHED BEEP, ONE LOW-PITCHED BEEP** Processor error

PHOENIX BIOS

Phoenix BIOSes produce a series of beeps separated by a pause. For example:
beep… beep beep beep… beep… beep would be 1-3-1-1

- **1-1-4-1** Level 2 cache error (reseat or replace the processor)
- **1-2-2-3** BIOS ROM checksum (replace BIOS chip or motherboard)
- **1-3-1-1** Memory refresh test failure (reseat or replace memory)
- **1-3-1-3** Keyboard controller failure (replace the motherboard)
- **1-3-4-1** Memory failure (reseat or replace memory)
- **1-3-4-3** Memory refresh test failure (reseat or replace memory)
- **1-4-1-1** Memory refresh test failure (reseat or replace memory)
- **2-1-2-3** BIOS error (replace BIOS chip or motherboard)
- **2-2-3-1** IRQ problem (remove expansion cards or replace motherboard)

HOW TO...
Restore your system

If you're having problems, System Restore – which is built into Windows – allows you to return your PC to a working state

1 TURN ON SYSTEM RESTORE

First, press the Windows-Break keys. Click the System Protection link. Make sure that the C drive has the Protection option set to On. If it doesn't, select drive C, click Configure, select 'Restore system settings and previous versions of files' and click OK.

There must be at least 200MB of free space on your hard disk for System Restore to work. If there isn't, you'll need to clear out unwanted files.

Use the slider to specify how much disk space System Restore is allowed to use; the more it has, the more restore points it can keep.

2 CREATE A RESTORE POINT

Every time you make a significant change to your system, such as installing a new application, Windows automatically creates a restore point. It's good practice to create a restore point manually before you make any changes, though, so you know that you have something to fall back on.

To create a restore point, press Windows-Break and click the System Protection link. Click the Create button, type in a name for the restore point and click OK.

3 RESTORE YOUR SYSTEM

When your PC has a problem, you can revert to any saved restore point. If you know which software is causing the problem, remove it using Uninstall a Program. If it's a driver, turn off your PC and remove the relevant hardware, too. Next, with your PC running, open System Restore from the Start menu. Click Next and Windows 7 will choose a restore point automatically, but you can select a different one from the list if you wish. Pay close attention to the date: use the latest point when you're sure the system worked properly. Allow the restore to finish and your PC to restart.

4 EMERGENCY RESTORE

If something has gone really wrong, your PC may not even boot into Windows. While the PC is booting, keep pressing F8. Instead of the normal Windows startup routine, you'll be offered a menu. Choose Safe Mode with command prompt. Log on as an administrator, and at the command prompt type c:\windows\system32\restore\rstrui.exe (in Vista, type c:\windows\system32\rstrui.exe). This starts System Restore, and you can then choose a restore point to go back to.

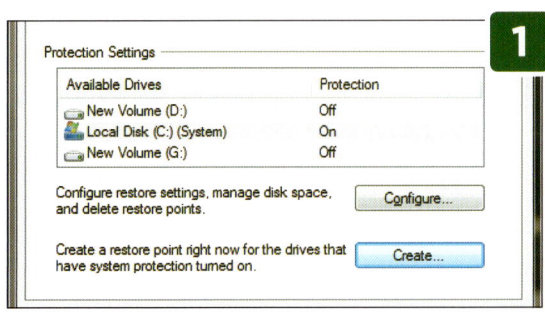

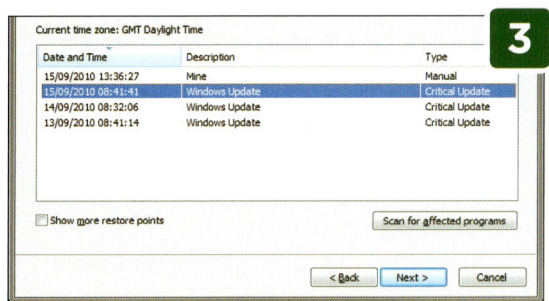

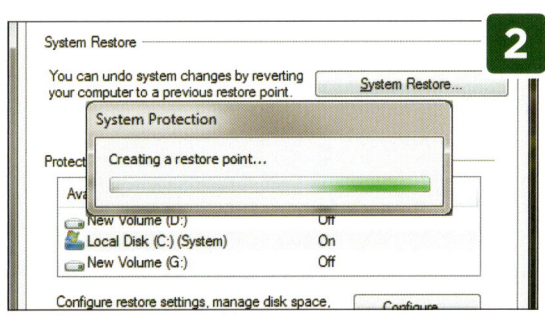

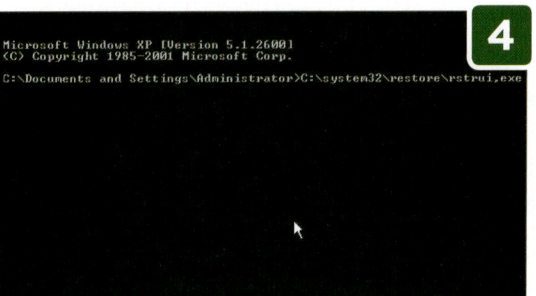

Windows problems

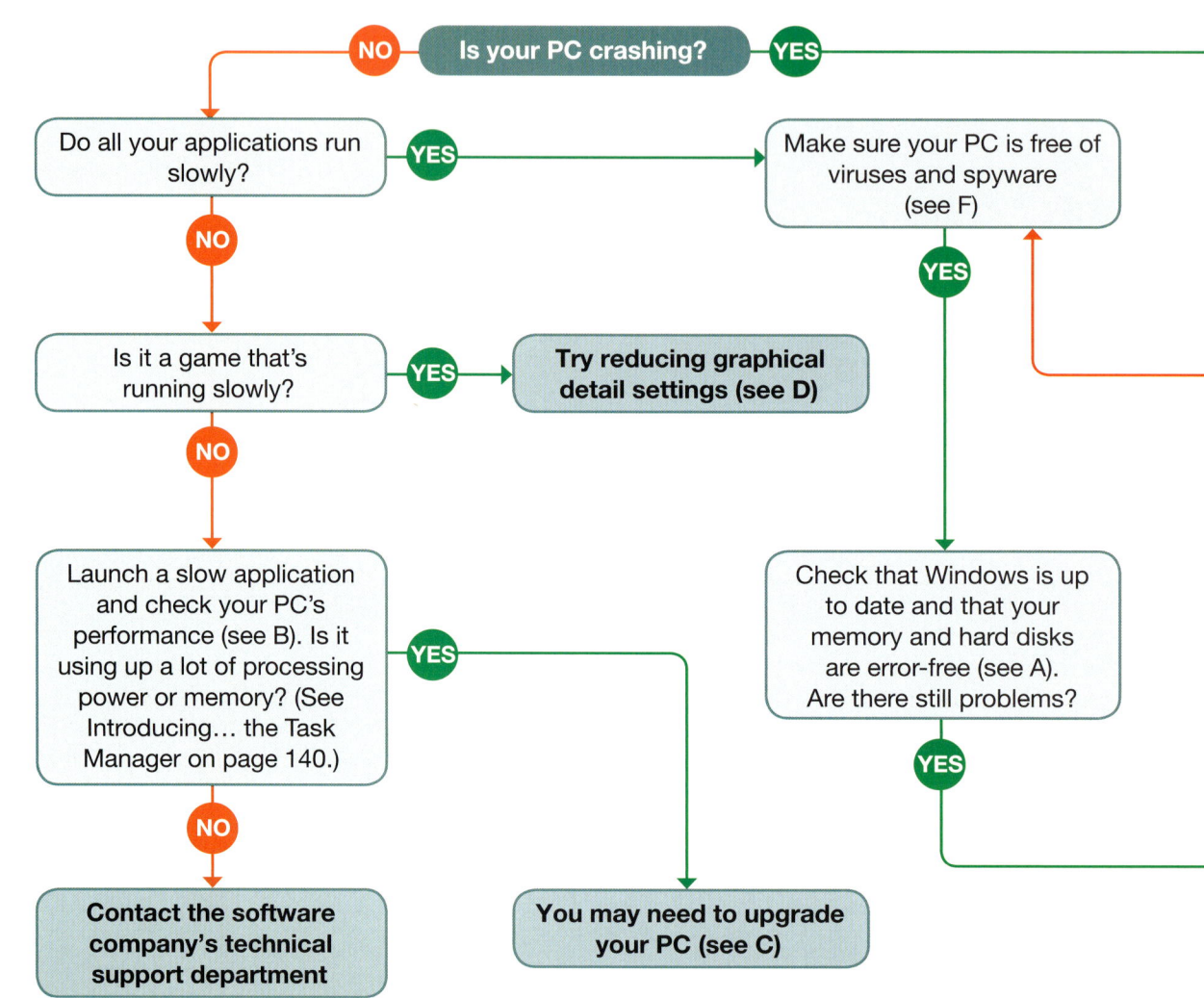

Is your PC crashing? — NO → Do all your applications run slowly?

Is your PC crashing? — YES → Make sure your PC is free of viruses and spyware (see F)

Do all your applications run slowly? — YES → Make sure your PC is free of viruses and spyware (see F)

Do all your applications run slowly? — NO → Is it a game that's running slowly?

Is it a game that's running slowly? — YES → Try reducing graphical detail settings (see D)

Is it a game that's running slowly? — NO → Launch a slow application and check your PC's performance (see B). Is it using up a lot of processing power or memory? (See Introducing... the Task Manager on page 140.)

Make sure your PC is free of viruses and spyware (see F) — YES → Check that Windows is up to date and that your memory and hard disks are error-free (see A). Are there still problems?

Launch a slow application and check your PC's performance (see B). Is it using up a lot of processing power or memory? — YES → You may need to upgrade your PC (see C)

Launch a slow application... — NO → Contact the software company's technical support department

Check that Windows is up to date and that your memory and hard disks are error-free (see A). Are there still problems? — YES → You may need to upgrade your PC (see C)

THE A TO G OF FIXING YOUR PC

A Test your memory using Memtest, which you can download for free (see page 128). If it finds any errors, you may need to replace some of your PC's RAM. Contact your PC's technical support line. It's also worth checking that your hard disk has no errors by using the error-checking tool in Windows. Just right-click on the drive, choose Properties and click the Tool tab. Press the Check Now button.

Finally, make sure that Windows has the latest updates. Open Automatic Updates in the Windows Security Center, which is available in the Control Panel.

B If an application is running slowly, it's worth finding out how much of your computer's processing power and memory it is using.

Close all your other applications and press Ctrl-Alt-Del simultaneously to open the Windows Task Manager (see page 140). In the Processes tab you'll be able to see what percentage of your processor power and how much memory (divide by 1,000 for a rough figure in megabytes) each program is using. If it's hogging all the processing power or most of your RAM and is still slow, your PC is struggling with this program.

C If your application needs more system resources, you may need to upgrade your PC. If you're short on memory, an upgrade is relatively simple. Check your manual to see what kind of memory your PC accepts or go to *www.crucial.com* and use the online system scanner.

D Modern games can be incredibly demanding. If your graphics card is struggling, it will produce a low frame rate, which causes the game to pause and stutter. Run the game and find the graphics settings in the options menu.

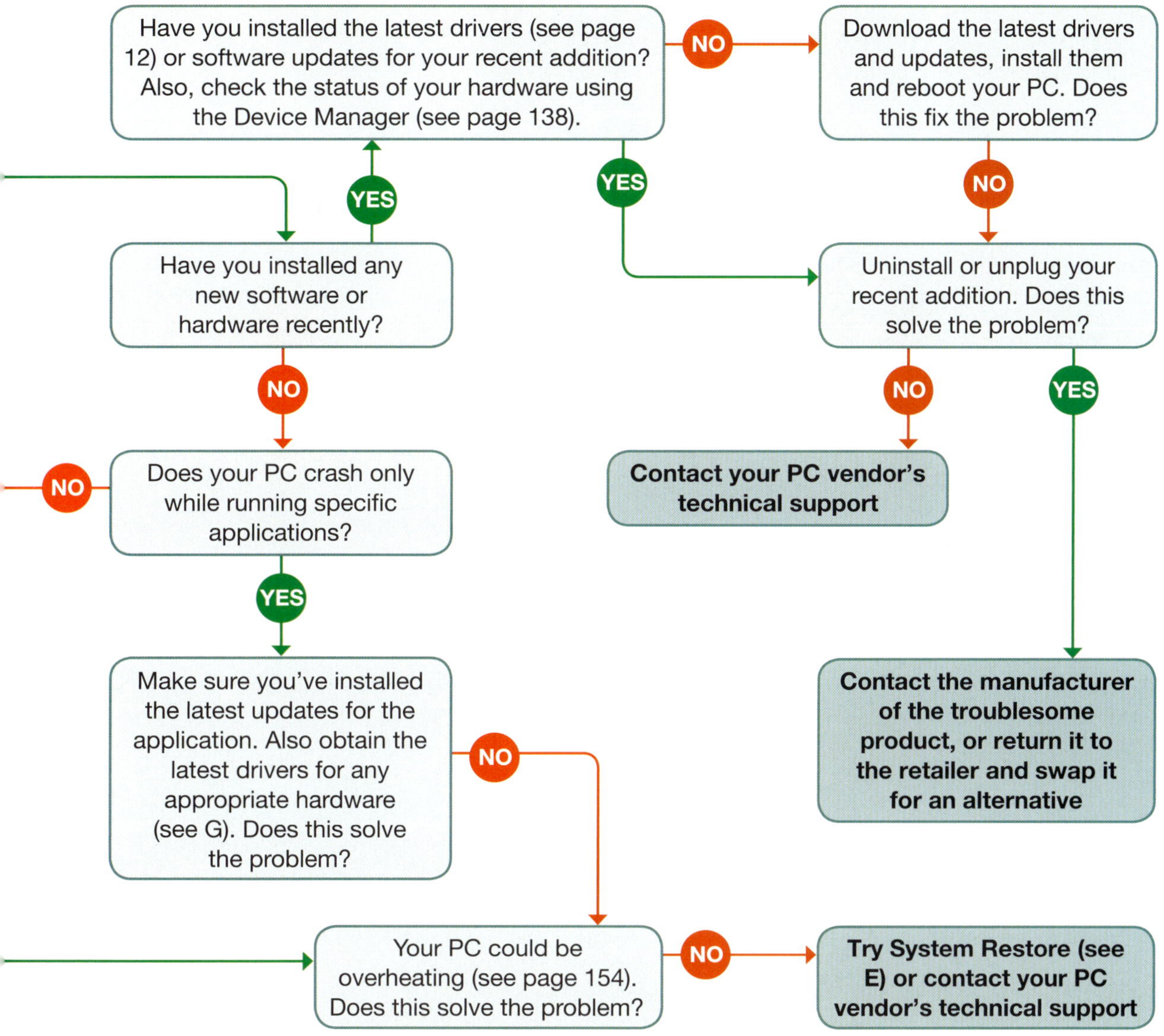

Have you installed the latest drivers (see page 12) or software updates for your recent addition? Also, check the status of your hardware using the Device Manager (see page 138).

NO →

Download the latest drivers and updates, install them and reboot your PC. Does this fix the problem?

YES ↑

YES ↓

NO ↓

Have you installed any new software or hardware recently?

Uninstall or unplug your recent addition. Does this solve the problem?

NO ↓

NO ↓

YES ↓

Does your PC crash only while running specific applications?

NO →

Contact your PC vendor's technical support

YES ↓

Make sure you've installed the latest updates for the application. Also obtain the latest drivers for any appropriate hardware (see G). Does this solve the problem?

NO →

Contact the manufacturer of the troublesome product, or return it to the retailer and swap it for an alternative

Your PC could be overheating (see page 154). Does this solve the problem?

NO →

Try System Restore (see E) or contact your PC vendor's technical support

---

Try turning off anti-aliasing (AA) and anisotropic filtering (AF) first to see if this improves your frame rate. If not, reduce the resolution to 1,024x768 or lower.

Make sure that you have the latest patches for your game and the latest drivers for your graphics card by going to Nvidia's or ATI's website, or check your laptop manufacturer's site if you have built-in graphics.

E Your PC keeps a record of any changes made to its settings. If you encounter a problem, you can restore the settings from an earlier date. In Windows

7, the System Restore tool is under Programs, Accessories, System Tools. Alternatively, you can simply type System Restore into the search box. Follow the instructions to restore your PC to the state it was in before your problem started.

F Slow performance may be a sign that your PC is running some undesirable software. This can include such nasties as viruses, privacy-invading spyware and aggravating advertising pop-ups. These programs can be grouped together under the term malicious software (or malware, for short).

Run a virus scan to find any malware on your PC. If you don't have anti-virus software, download AVG Free Edition from *http://free.avg.com* and run a full scan.

G If certain types of program such as games cause your PC to crash, check that you have the latest drivers for any hardware that's responsible for running them. Update your graphics card drivers if your PC crashes when playing games or video; update sound card drivers to solve audio playback troubles; and find new TV tuner drivers for any TV card-related problems.

Introducing... the Device Manager

THE DEVICE MANAGER allows you to view all the hardware inside your computer. It's also the place to go when you're having problems with hardware, as it can help diagnose faults and update device drivers. To open the Device Manager, go to the Control Panel, Hardware and Sound, Device Manager.

You can launch the Device Manager in different ways: it's quicker to right-click on My Computer, then Properties, then Device Manager.

DEVICE SQUAD

You may never have visited the Device Manager before, as there's usually no reason to. When you install a piece of new hardware, you'll also install any drivers from CD. This process automatically

copies files to the appropriate places and the hardware is added to the Device Manager list.

Although you can enable and disable hardware from the Device Manager, it's often more convenient to do so from other places in Windows. The same is true for updating drivers. While you can manually initiate a driver update from an item's properties page in the Device Manager, there's usually no need to, since most drivers downloaded from manufacturers' websites automatically remove old versions and install the new ones.

However, when your hardware stops working as it should or you can't automatically update drivers, the Device Manager comes into its own. The default view of devices by type shows a collapsed tree structure, where just the headings are shown,

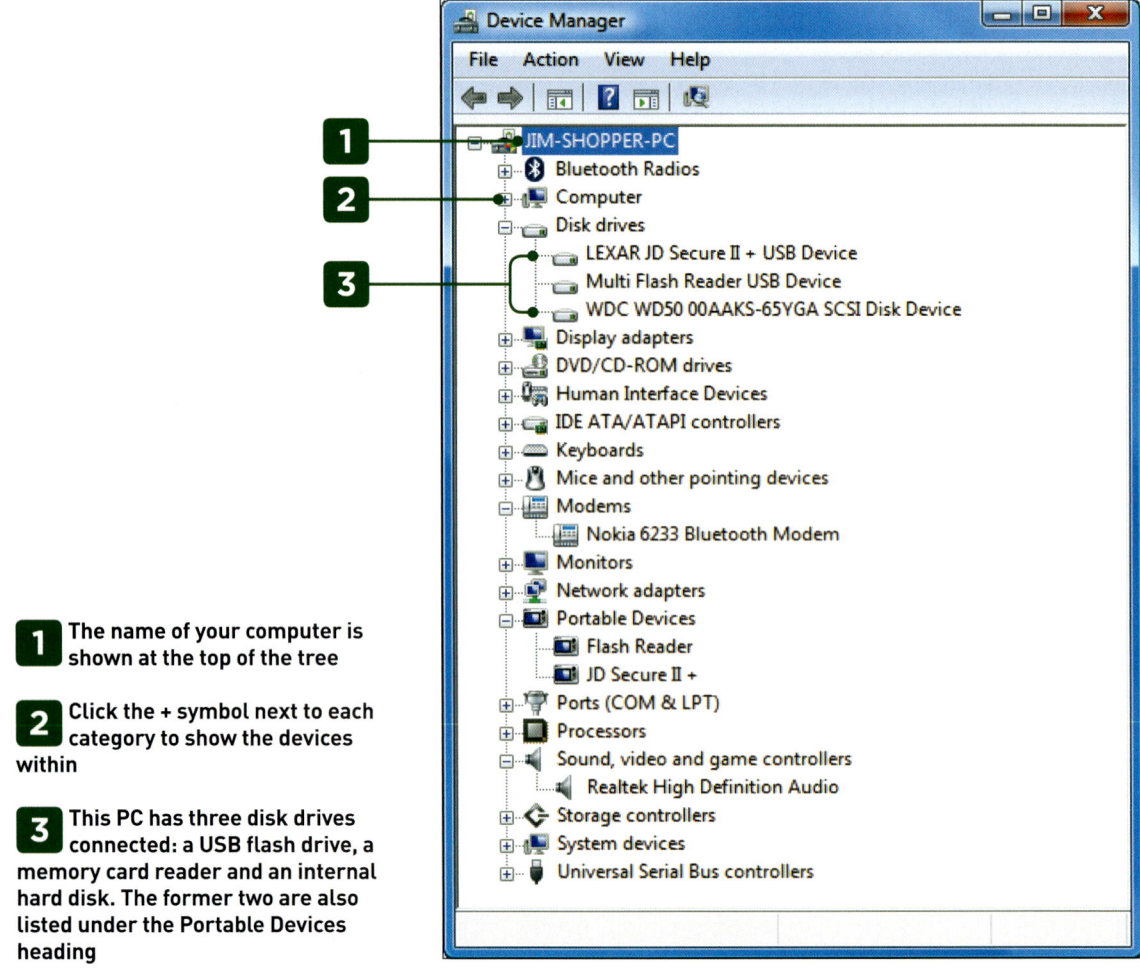

1 The name of your computer is shown at the top of the tree

2 Click the + symbol next to each category to show the devices within

3 This PC has three disk drives connected: a USB flash drive, a memory card reader and an internal hard disk. The former two are also listed under the Portable Devices heading

but it will automatically expand any category that contains a problem. You may see a yellow exclamation mark next to a component's name, or an arrow pointing downwards. The exclamation mark might mean that the hardware drivers aren't installed, or that the hardware itself cannot start. An arrow denotes that the hardware is disabled.

For this example we'll assume that your Windows desktop is showing enormous icons and you can't adjust the resolution in the Display Settings dialog.

1 OPEN THE DEVICE MANAGER
Scan down the Device Manager list until you come to the Display adapters entry. Click the + symbol, and you should see an exclamation mark, which means the drivers aren't installed. If there's no Display adapters entry, look for Other devices, which should have Unknown device listed.

2 CHECK THE DRIVER
Right-click on this, or on the name of the graphics card, and choose Properties. Click on the

Driver tab and you'll see details of the currently installed driver, if there is one. You may see Microsoft listed next to Driver Provider, but you should install the latest driver from your graphics card manufacturer, such as Nvidia, AMD or Intel.

3 DOWNLOAD THE NEW DRIVER
Visit the appropriate manufacturer's website to obtain the latest driver and download it. If necessary, unzip it into a folder on your hard disk. If the file is a self-executable – ending in .exe – you can run it at this point. If not, return to the Properties page you navigated to in Step 2, and click the Update Driver... button. Click the Browse my computer for driver software button.

4 INSTALL THE DRIVER
Click the Browse... button on the next window that appears. Navigate to the folder where you unzipped the drivers and click Next. Windows should install the drivers, and you may see the screen flicker during the process. You may also have to reboot your PC to finalise the installation.

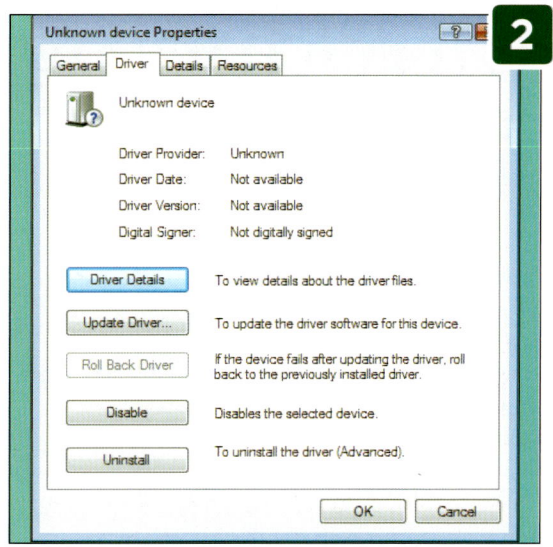

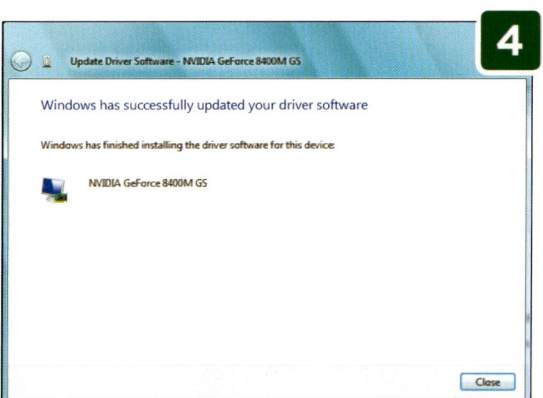

Introducing... the Task Manager

WHEN YOU ENCOUNTER a problem in Windows, your first stop should almost always be the Task Manager. This allows you to shut applications down, view system information – such as the load under which the processor and memory are working – and much more besides.

The Task Manager is particularly useful for identifying troublesome applications or services that are hogging your PC's resources, such as memory or processor time, and slowing it down. It can also help you monitor the size of Windows' page file, as well as keep tabs on network activity.

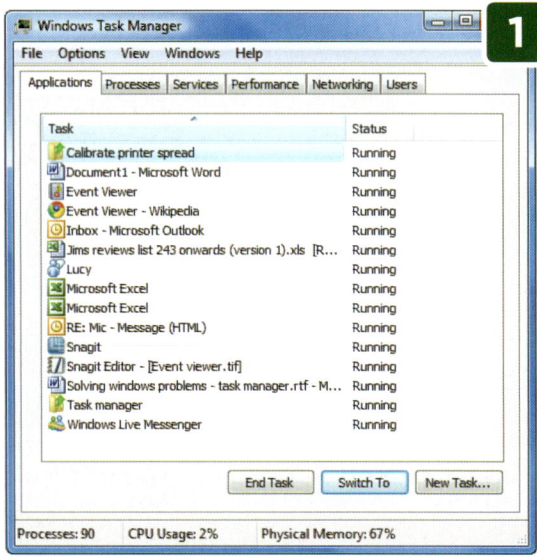

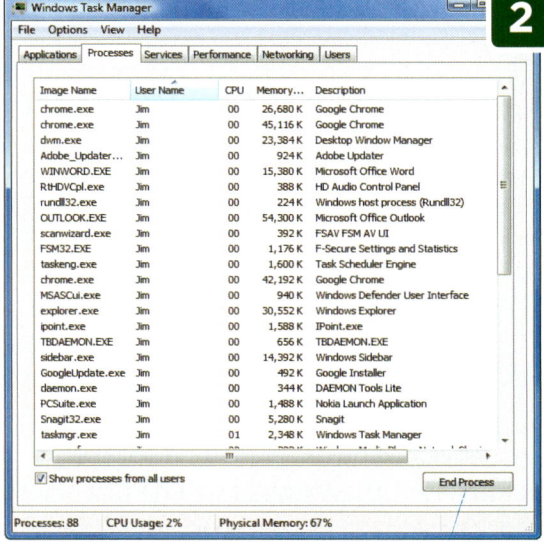

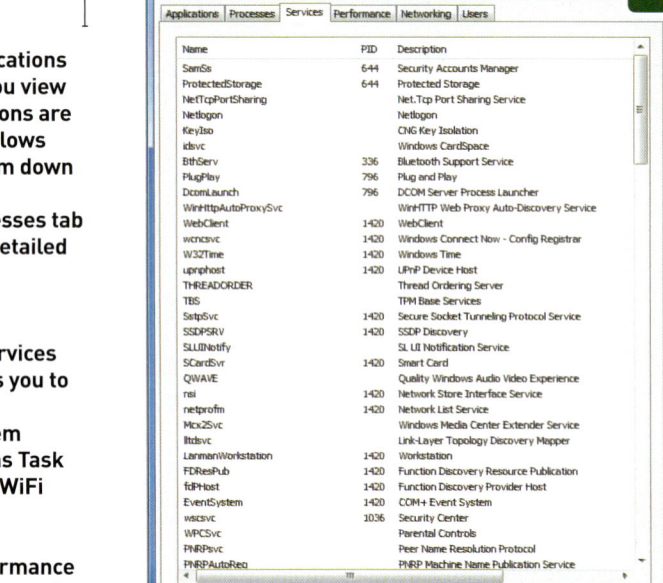

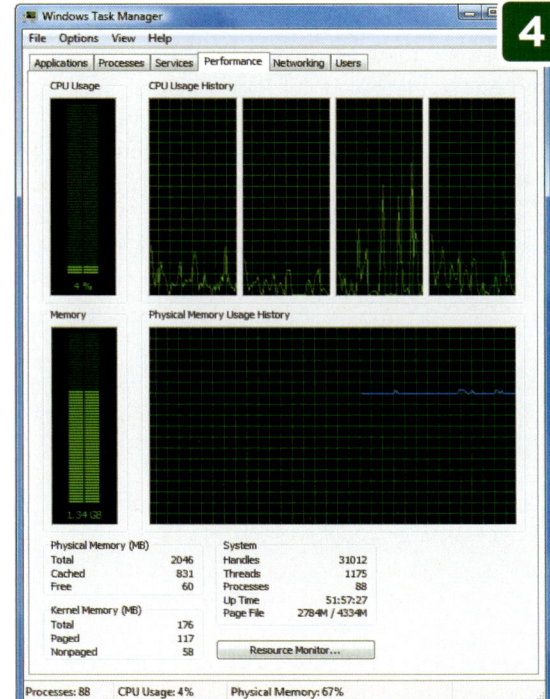

1 The Applications tab lets you view which applications are running, and allows you to shut them down

2 The Processes tab shows a detailed list of all your programs

3 Vista's Services tab allows you to start, stop and configure system services such as Task Scheduler and WiFi configuration

4 The performance tab shows graphs of processor load and memory usage

The fastest way to open the Task Manager in all versions of Windows is to press the Ctrl-Shift-Esc keys at the same time. A window will open that sits on top of any existing windows, and will remain that way until you either minimise or close it.

The first tab shows the list of running applications. This is useful when an application won't shut down, as you can highlight it in the list and click the End Task button. If the application has crashed and you've been unable to save your work, forcing it to end will probably cause any changes since you last saved the file to be lost, unless the application has an auto-save or auto-recovery feature. For this reason, it's sometimes best to wait for programs that are not responding to come back to life rather than forcing them to quit. Any more than a few minutes of non-responsiveness, however, probably indicates that a program really has crashed.

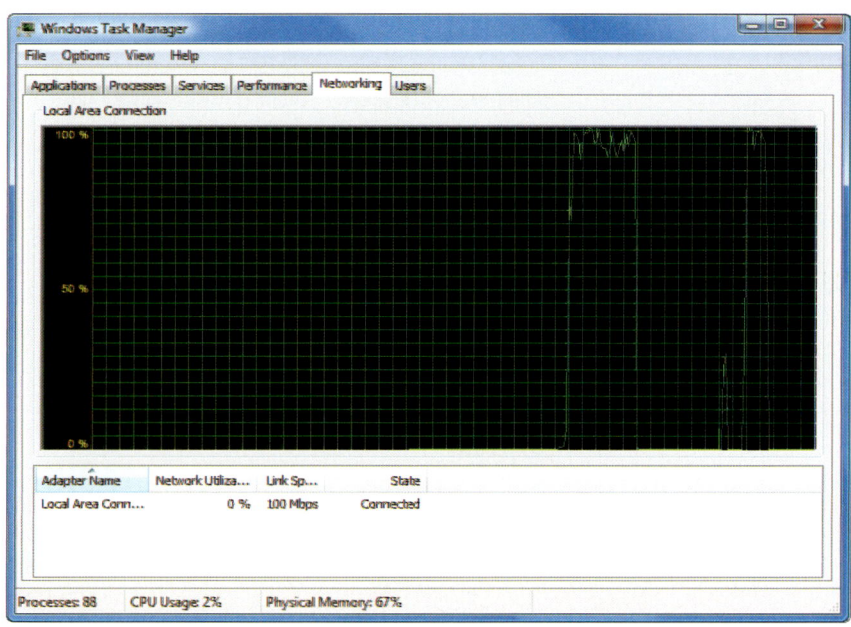

PART OF THE PROCESS

The Processes tabs lists which programs are running in much greater detail, showing memory and processor usage. Processes using an unusually high amount of the processor or memory may be malfunctioning and may need to be ended and restarted. In many cases, an application listed in the Applications tab will translate to several processes, and you'll sometimes need to use the Processes tab when you can't end a program from the Applications tab. It can be difficult to determine what a process does, but Windows 7's Task Manager additionally shows a description of the process, although you may have to scroll right or expand the Description column to see it fully.

You can sort the list of processes by any column. A useful way to do this is by Owner. You'll see your username, plus any other users currently logged on, and 'system', which is the operating system's processes. You should be able to end any processes next to a username without a problem, except that the program or service will no longer function until you restart it or reboot. Ending system processes is more dangerous, as you might cause Windows to crash or stop working properly. However, the worst that will happen is you'll need to reboot your computer.

The beauty of the Processes tab is that you can choose additional columns of information. From the View menu, choose Select Columns… and you'll see a list of options. We'd recommend ticking I/O reads and I/O writes, as this shows which processes are thrashing the hard disk and memory. Any process that is constantly reading and/or writing could have a problem, and you should investigate it further by finding out what the process is for.

Next is the Services tab. This is similar to the Processes tab, and lists each service's process ID (PID) which is often included in error messages. This can often help you identify troublesome services and end them.

The Performance tab shows several graphs: one for each processor core and one for page file usage. On the left you can see the current processor and page file usage.

If either of these is very high, it could explain why Windows is running slowly. The reason could be because you're running a demanding application or an application has crashed. If youleave your computer in Sleep mode rather thanturning it off, the page file size will build up andslow Windows down. A reboot should fix this issue.

↑ You can see how much bandwidth is being used in the Networking tab

Introducing... the Event Viewer

THE EVENT VIEWER presents detailed system logs, which are special files that record significant events that happen on your computer, such as when an application encounters an error or when the computer enters a standby power state.

The Event Viewer is similar to an aeroplane's black box recorder. It lets you see a summary of your PC's health, and can help you pinpoint which application has caused a problem, as well as providing error codes that can be useful for Google searches.

To launch Event Viewer, either type it into Vista's search bar, or right-click on Computer in the Start menu and choose Manage. Event Viewer is the second item in the System Tools list.

FINDING YOUR WAY AROUND

Although the Event Viewer is designed to be user-friendly, it can still be daunting for many people. It's really designed to assist technicians diagnose faults, but even the non-technical can glean useful information from it.

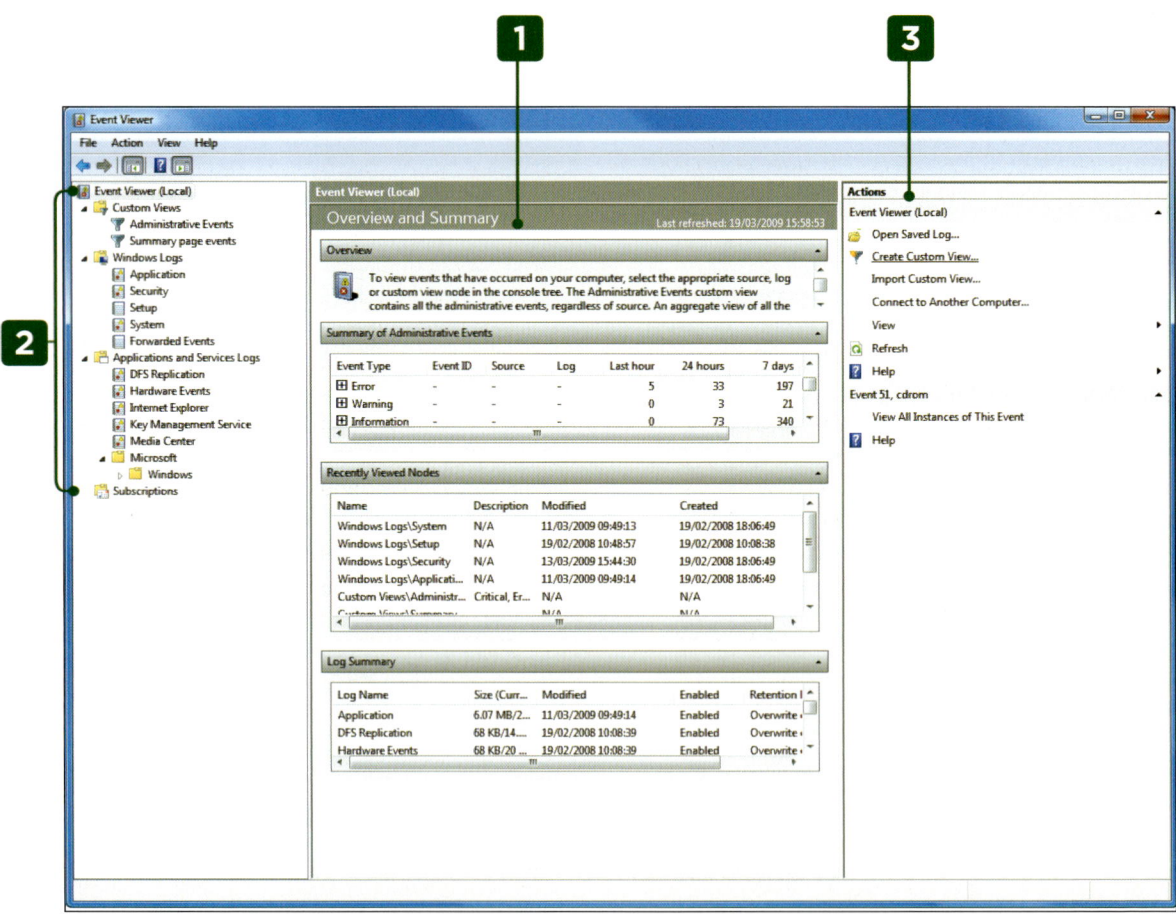

1 The Overview and Summary panel lets you see at a glance the number of errors and warnings

2 You can jump quickly to any of the logs using the tree in the left pane

3 The Actions pane on the right-hand side of the Event Viewer lets you quickly create custom views, as well as changing the view and refreshing the overview. Actions are context-sensitive, and change depending on the current view

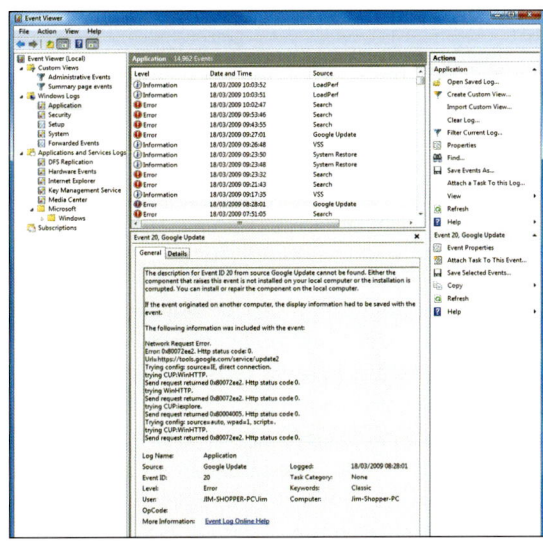

↑ **The detailed information on each error can help you diagnose problems**

If you know a particular application isn't working as it should, you can search for it in the Application log, which is listed under Windows Logs on the left. Let's say that Google's Updater application isn't working. Click on Application beneath Windows Logs and the listing will appear in the middle pane. You can scroll down the list until you see Google Update in the Source column. Highlight the event and you'll see the error details in the pane below. You may have to resize the window to see the full width of the description as it doesn't automatically wrap the text to fit.

The general description should explain the nature of the error; for example, a required component wasn't found or the installation is corrupted. In this case, reinstalling the application should fix the problem. You may also see a particular filename mentioned, which may help to identify the problem, and an error code, such as

Error: 0x80072ee2. Copying and pasting this into Google along with the application name may shed more light on the problem if the description doesn't make it obvious what you should do next.

SYSTEM LOG

The System log covers operating system events, and can be useful for diagnosing problems with hardware drivers. For example, your PC may be refusing to go into sleep mode or refusing to wake up from it. The System log may show warnings such as 'Display driver nvlddmkm stopped responding'. This could indicate that it's your graphics card driver causing the problem, and that updating the driver may cure it.

Most of the log will likely contain Information entries, which tell you when services started and stopped. They may also give warnings, such as the one shown in the screen below: "Windows cannot store Bluetooth authentication codes on the local adapter. Bluetooth keyboards might not work in the system BIOS during startup." Again, this can explain why certain problems are occurring.

CUSTOM VIEWS

You can create custom views in the Event Viewer, which allow you to see relevant information more easily, instead of having to wade through thousands of entries in each log. To create a custom view, click Create Custom View… in the right-hand pane of the Event Viewer. You can then select what time period the view should cover, which event types to include, and how to filter them, whether by log or by source.

A simple custom view could filter the errors and warnings from the application and system logs over the previous 24 hours. When you name and save the custom view, it will appear in the Custom Views section in the left-hand pane.

↙ **This alert warns that Bluetooth keyboards may not work in the BIOS**

↓ **Creating custom views is a good way of keeping track of relevant information**

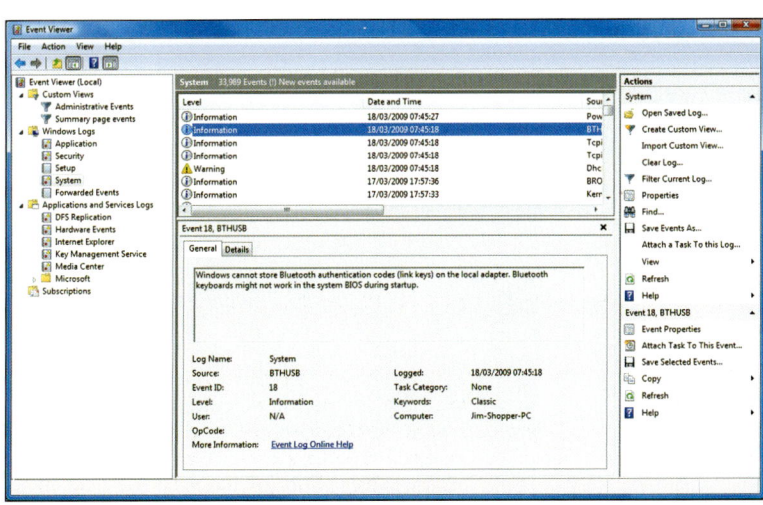

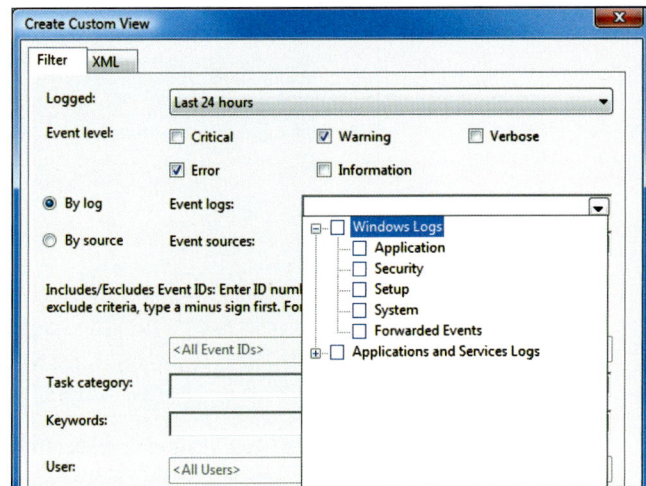

Top 10 tips for solving peripheral problems

1 CHECK ALL CABLES
We've said it before, but it bears repeating: check your cables. Whatever problem you're having with your peripheral, make sure the cables are properly connected at both ends and that they're not damaged. If something won't turn on at all, check the fuse in the plug, as these do fail occasionally. Keep a couple of 3A and 13A fuses to hand so you can quickly swap out a suspect fuse.

2 TRY ANOTHER USB PORT
When USB peripherals aren't working properly or aren't being correctly detected by Windows, try unplugging the cable and plugging it into a different USB port. This forces Windows to redetect the hardware and reinstall the drivers, and often solves annoying problems.

If a peripheral isn't behaving properly, check if it's plugged into a USB hub. If it is, disconnect it and reconnect it to a port on your PC or laptop, as some devices, including Apple iPods, don't like being connected via a USB hub.

3 DRY IT OUT
If you accidentally spill liquid on any of your peripherals, unplug all their cables immediately. Place them somewhere hot and dry, such as an airing cupboard, for at least 24 hours to allow them to dry out. There's no guarantee this will save them, but it often works. If you spill a sticky liquid on a peripheral, don't be tempted to pour extra water on to flush it out – this could cause more damage. If it fails to work after the drying out

process, try disassembling it. Most warranties won't cover damage caused by spillages (but check first), so you have nothing to lose by disassembling a peripheral. Remote controls often benefit from being taken apart, as liquid can be trapped between the rubber membrane and the circuit board, preventing buttons from working.

4 PS/2 WARNING
Don't forget that PS/2 peripherals aren't hot-pluggable. If you forget to connect a PS/2 keyboard or mouse to your PC and you only realise when you see an error message during the POST sequence or when the device doesn't work in Windows, don't plug it in. Turn the PC off first, and then connect it, even if it means holding down the power button after booting into Windows. You won't cause any damage to Windows.

5 USE THE RIGHT PORT
A classic mistake is to reach behind your PC to plug in a USB device without looking and inadvertently insert it into the Ethernet port. USB plugs are exactly the same width as a network socket, which means it feels like you've inserted the USB cable correctly as the plug is held tightly in place. It's only when Windows refuses to detect the device that you're aware something's not working properly.

6 KNOW YOUR COLOURS
The same goes for audio connections, as sound cards tend to use minijack sockets for

↑ **Make sure video cables are screwed in securely**

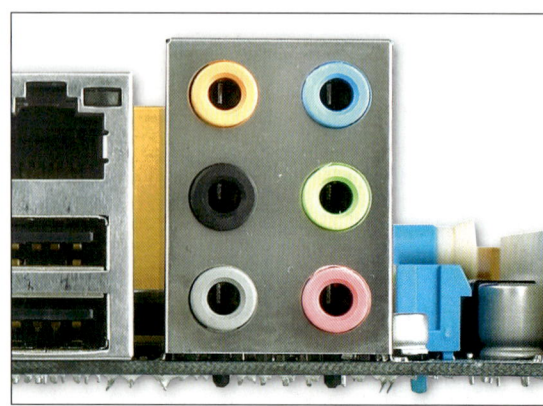
↑ **Know your sound card colours**

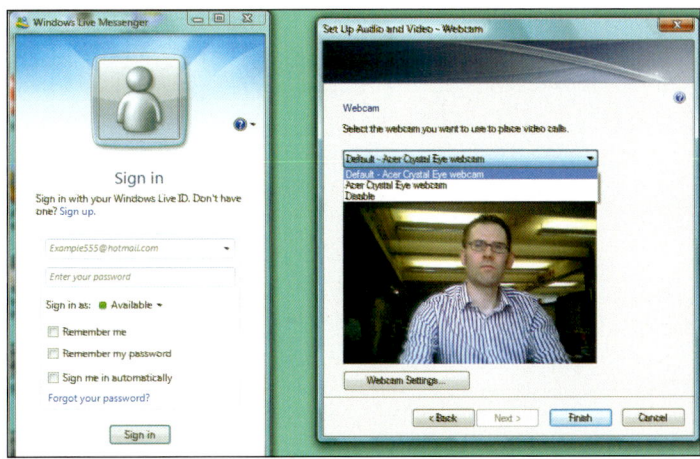

everything and rarely have labels next to them. Here's a quick guide to the colour coding:

Green Main stereo output, usually used for front speakers or headphones

Pink Stereo microphone input

Light blue Stereo line input

Black Rear surround speakers

Orange Centre speaker and subwoofer output

Grey Middle surround speakers for 7.1 systems

7 CHECK WEBCAM SETTINGS

If you're having problems with your webcam, such as a lack of video, check the settings of the program that's using it (usually this will be an instant-messaging application such as Windows Live Messenger). Look for a webcam settings option in the menus and make sure you select the webcam from the list of video devices when asked.

If you don't see the make and model of the webcam listed, it may be because the drivers aren't properly installed. If reinstalling the latest drivers from the manufacturer's website doesn't solve the problem, try rebooting your PC and plugging the webcam into a different USB port.

8 ELIMINATING ECHOES

It's common to have problems with webcam audio. If you're using the webcam's built-in microphone, make sure it's selected correctly in a similar way to the video in tip 7. If you hear an echo through your speakers during a web chat, try turning the microphone level down and asking the other person to turn their speaker volume down. If the problem persists, try wearing headphones or a headset with a microphone, as this will eliminate the feedback loop.

9 CRT WARNING

Don't attempt to fix your monitor by opening it up. This is an important safety tip. There are high voltages inside a monitor, and you could seriously injure yourself, even if the monitor has been unplugged from the mains. Whatever component might need replacing, it's almost always more cost-effective to replace the monitor with a new one. You'll probably end up with a better-quality monitor and a higher resolution in the process.

10 AVOID DATA LOSS

Eject your USB storage devices rather than just removing them. It's a pain ejecting a flash drive or memory card when you want to remove it from your PC, especially as it may seem to do no harm. However, if you pull it out before Windows has finished writing files to it (and this can happen a while after you save a document, due to Windows' delayed writes policy) you could easily lose work or corrupt files on the USB device. If Windows' eject method is too inconvenient, install a program that allows you to remove USB devices quickly, such as the free USB Disk Ejector, which you can download from *http://quick.mixnmojo.com/usb-disk-ejector*.

↖ **If you're having webcam problems, ensure your camera is properly selected in the application you're using it with**

↑ **Eject your USB disks before unplugging them to avoid losing files**

← **Don't attempt to open up and repair a monitor yourself – there are dangerous voltages inside**

Solving sound problems

IT'S A FAMILIAR situation: you turn on your computer and fire up your media player to listen to some music. The file appears to play, but there's no sound coming from your speakers. It's a common and frustrating problem, but is usually easy to fix.

First, check the obvious. Are your speakers switched on and the volume turned up? Are the audio cables correctly connected to your PC? If you have a laptop, does it have a mute button, or a Function key combination that allows you to mute and unmute the sound?

Next, check whether the sound is muted within Windows. You may see an icon that looks like a speaker cone in the Notification Area at the bottom of your desktop. If not, click the < button to expand the view to see all icons. Single-click on the speaker and you should see a volume slider and a Mute tickbox. Ensure that the box isn't ticked and that the volume slider isn't set to minimum. If you don't see an icon, click Start, All Programs, Control Panel. Click on the Hardware and Sound link, then Sound to launch the dialog box for all sound controls.

MULTIPLE SOUND DEVICES

Another common reason for hearing no sound is because you have multiple audio devices connected to or installed on your computer. For example, you may have recently installed a Skype handset or headset. In effect, this is a sound card in itself, and Windows can inadvertently make this the primary sound device, meaning that all sounds, whether from Windows Media Player, Internet

Explorer or another application, are being routed to the handset instead of your speakers. You can either unplug the device, which should fix the problem instantly, or you can select a different audio device in the Control Panel.

Navigate to the sound properties in the Control Panel as described above. In Windows 7, there are separate tabs for Playback and Recording, allowing you to select different devices for each option very easily. Click on the Playback option, right-click on the audio device you want to use and click 'Set as default'. If the device is greyed out you will first need to right-click on it and select Enable.

If this doesn't solve the problem, you may need to check your sound card's audio mixer, which provides volume controls for different devices, such as the microphone, line-in and WAV. To open the mixer, click on the speaker icon in the Notification Area and click the Mixer link.

DEVICE MANAGER

If you still have no joy, check that the sound card is working properly by opening Device Manager (see page 138). Scroll down the list of hardware until you come to Sound, video and game controllers. Expand the tree by clicking the + symbol, and look for any yellow exclamation marks or red crosses. Exclamation marks mean there's a problem with the hardware – drivers may not be correctly

↓ **Make sure the volume sliders aren't set to zero and that they're not muted**

↘ **Surround-sound speakers such as Creative's Gigaworks G500 require multiple audio connections**

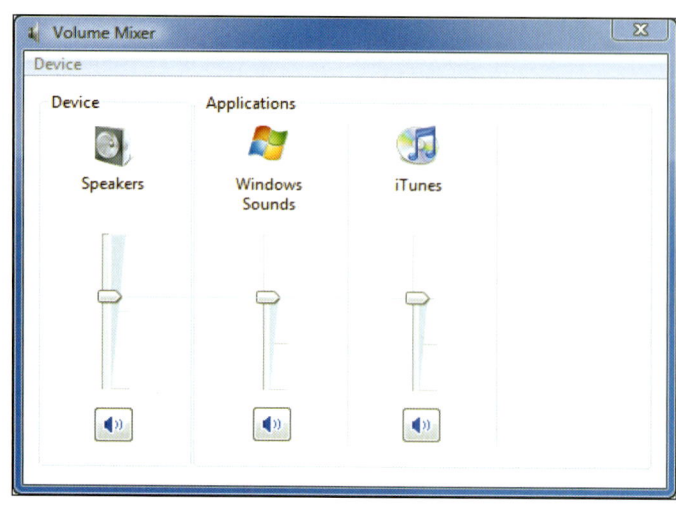

↘ Skype handsets can play havoc with your audio settings

↖ Most sound cards have lots of identical-looking minijack inputs and outputs

installed or the hardware itself is malfunctioning – while a red cross means the hardware is disabled.

If you see an exclamation mark next to your sound card, you'll need to reinstall the driver. This should be included on a disc that came with your computer, but if you don't have one, you'll need to download the drivers. Most PCs and all laptops have built-in sound cards, which means it's fairly easy to identify the make and model. For PCs, you can either search on the manufacturer's website or the motherboard manufacturer's site. For laptops, it's usually best to visit the manufacturer's website. You can recognise a built-in sound card by the fact that its ports are located with others on the rear of your PC, rather than on a separate card adjacent to the main ports.

If you see a red cross, you can try re-enabling the hardware by right-clicking on it and choosing Enable. You may still need to install the drivers after doing this.

CHECK THE BIOS

You may find that there are no sound devices listed in Device Manager. In this case, you should reboot your computer and enter the BIOS (for more on this, see page 72). In the BIOS, look for a menu titled Integrated peripherals, and scan the list for AC'97 or HD Audio. If it's disabled, you simply need to enable it, save the changes and exit the BIOS. When you reboot, Windows should detect new hardware and either install drivers automatically or prompt you to locate them.

If the sound card is enabled in the BIOS but doesn't show up in Device Manager, the hardware is probably faulty and you'll need a new sound card. The easiest option is to buy a USB sound card, as this won't require you to open up your PC. This is your only option if you have a laptop. If you don't mind opening your PC, you can buy a PCI sound card or, if you have a modern motherboard with PCI Express slots, a PCI-E 1x sound card.

↑ Make sure that the correct playback device is set as the default option

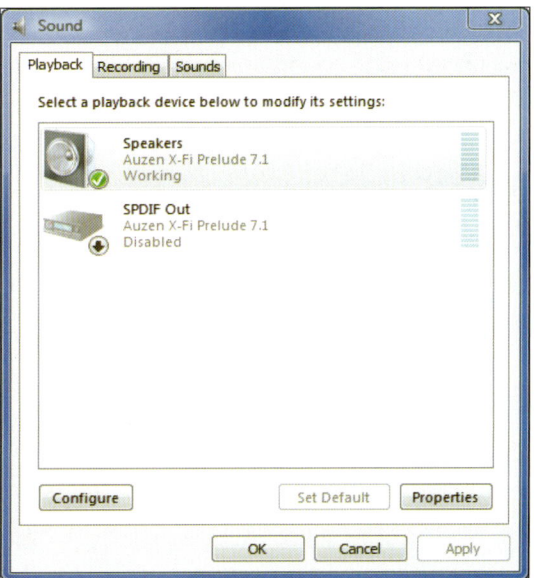

↑ Playback and Recording devices are displayed on separate tabs in the Sound section

Solving monitor problems

AS WITH THE other peripherals covered in this chapter, monitor problems may or may not be fixable. Here we'll address a few common problems that you can solve without calling your display manufacturer.

The most obvious problem is that there's no image on the screen. You need to find out if the fault lies with your PC or your monitor. As we've already shown in Chapter 2, there are several reasons why your PC may refuse to boot, and some of them could cause the screen to be blank.

It's worth checking the basics first. Ensure that the power and signal cables are firmly attached to the monitor, as well as to the wall socket and the PC. If your monitor is plugged into a power strip, make sure that both the wall switch and any switches on the power strip are turned on.

Most monitors, whether CRT or LCD, show a warning message if no input signal is detected. If you see such a message, it's clear that the display is working. Some monitors have multiple inputs, so you need to select the appropriate one to view the incoming signal. There should be a dedicated button on the monitor for this, but it may be hidden in the onscreen menus.

If you do see a Windows screen but it's showing incorrect colours, disconnect and reconnect the video cable at both ends and tighten it securely. A loose cable is a common cause of colour corruption. If you're using a VGA cable with

↑ **LCD screens can warn you if there's no signal or if a signal is out of range**

an LCD screen and you see fuzzy text or the entire Windows desktop is shifted off one edge, use your monitor's Auto setting to re-sync the signal. If this doesn't work, try using the manual clock and phase options in the monitor's menu system.

Another common LCD problem is stuck pixels, where a dot constantly shows one colour (red, green, blue, white or black) irrespective of what Windows is showing. If this is the case, it's worth trying a free utility such as UDPixel from *http://udpix.free.fr* to see if it can be changed. Such applications rapidly change the colours onscreen for several hours in an effort to coax the pixel into life. UDPixel is helpful as it can show the five possible colours across the whole screen to help you identify where any defective pixels are located.

On older CRT monitors, you may see dark patches in the corners or at the edges of the screen. It's often possible to correct these by using the monitor's degauss function in the menus. If this doesn't work, move any magnetic sources such as unshielded speakers away from the monitor.

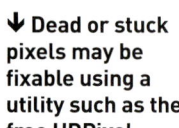

⬇ **Dead or stuck pixels may be fixable using a utility such as the free UDPixel**

A GUIDE TO INTERFACES
VGA

VGA (also known as D-sub) has been a standard PC video connection since 1987, and is the most basic PC graphics connection. The VGA connector supports resolutions of up to 2,048x1,536. VGA connectors carry an analogue signal made up of the component colours – red, green and blue – as well as horizontal and vertical timing data.

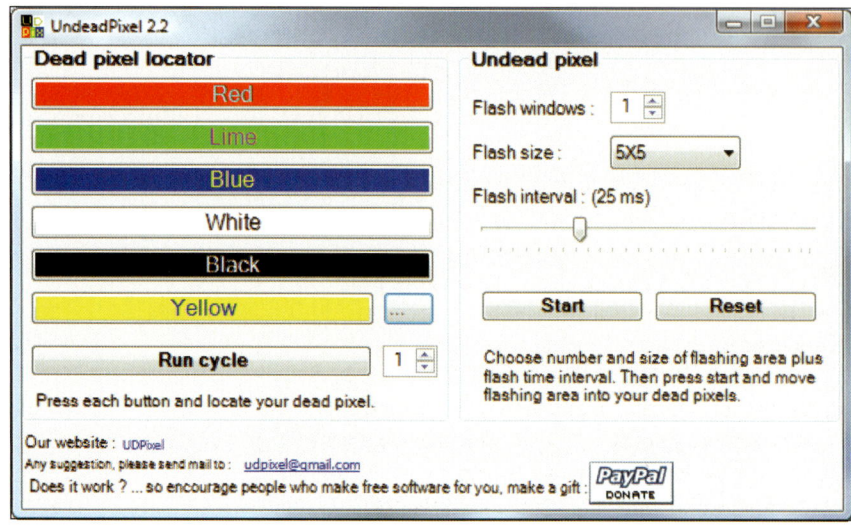

VGA was designed for CRT monitors, which required this timing data to draw the picture using an electron gun firing in a series of lines at phosphors on the screen. LCD monitors paint the same picture using different voltages applied to rows of pixels, so they need to convert this timing data. This is done automatically and rarely causes problems, but for fine control you should look for Pixel Clock and Phase settings on your monitor's onscreen display menu. Test patterns are available on the web to help you set these up correctly.

DVI

The next step up from VGA is DVI, which supports a maximum resolution of 2,560x1,600 (the highest any consumer connection can currently offer) and can carry both analogue and digital signals. Most modern video cards have two DVI outputs. One of the most practical advantages of using a monitor with a DVI input rather than a VGA connection is that you don't need to fiddle with timing data, because in its native resolution a DVI output transmits data for each pixel on an LCD screen.

There are five main types of DVI connection (see the picture on the right), which makes it a bit more confusing than other connectors. DVI-A (Analogue) supports only analogue signals, and has the fewest pins on its connector. DVI-D (Digital) is a digital-only version found on most modern LCD monitors, and can be distinguished by the narrower flat pin, which doesn't include four pins arranged in a square around it.

DVI-I (Integrated) allows for both analogue and digital signals, and is standard on most modern video cards. DVI-I has a wider flat pin, plus the four analogue signal pins. This means that a male DVI-D connector can fit into a female DVI-I port, allowing you to connect your digital monitor to your

⬂ **There are several types of DVI cable**

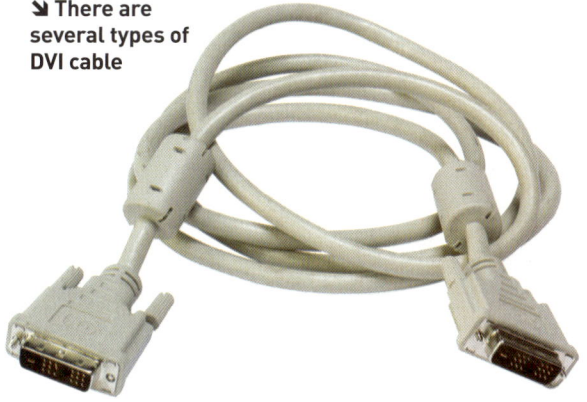

PC; you can also connect a DVI-to-VGA adaptor to this port or DVI-A cable, so you can plug in analogue monitors. A male DVI-I connector won't fit into the narrower flat pin on a DVI-D female port, so you can't connect incompatible devices.

To make things more confusing, there are also dual-link versions of DVI-I and DVI-D. These support higher bandwidth connections for displays over 1,920x1,200, such as huge 30in models, which can support resolutions of up to 2,560x1,600. Dual-link connectors can be distinguished by the six extra pins in the middle of the two banks of nine pins. To use dual-link, you'll also need a graphics card with a dual-link output.

HDMI

DVI has a few limitations compared to the newest standard, HDMI. As well having a standard connector to make things simpler, HDMI also carries high-definition audio and remote control signals. This means you can reduce the number of wires connected between your monitor, speakers and PC. The remote control features allow devices made by the same manufacturer to communicate with each other, so you can set timers to record TV programmes, for example.

HDMI also supports High-bandwidth Digital Content Protection (HDCP) encryption as standard. This is a copy-protection system that is standard on multimedia devices such as Blu-ray players, and you won't be able to watch copy-protected films without it. HDMI is backwards-compatible with DVI, so with the right adaptors, you can connect from a DVI port on your PC to an HDMI-equipped monitor, and vice versa. HDCP is not always enabled on DVI ports, however, so it's worth checking that both your PC and your monitor will support it.

DISPLAYPORT

The final type of connector is DisplayPort, a new digital connector that supports resolutions up to 3,840x2,160 over a single cable. This input is available on only a few current monitors, but it is becoming increasingly common on a number of graphics cards.

DisplayPort isn't compatible with HDMI or DVI, although the DisplayPort connector can pass both of these signals through. This allows graphics card manufacturers to create products that are compatible with DisplayPort and DVI monitors.

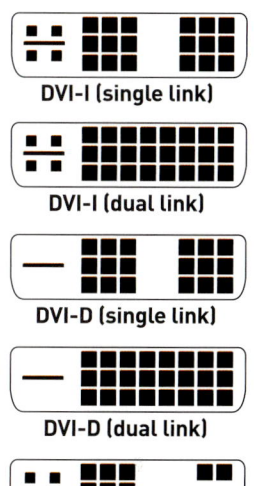

DVI-I (single link)

DVI-I (dual link)

DVI-D (single link)

DVI-D (dual link)

DVI-A

Testing memory

MEMORY IS ONE of the most important components in your PC. It stores every aspect of the programs and data that you're currently running, from the window showing your holiday snaps to the spreadsheet with your accounts. Memory also holds important Windows data, such as device driver information and the core components of how Windows works.

A problem with memory can, therefore, be incredibly serious. For example, if your memory should corrupt a critical part of Windows, when the processor tries to use this data it can end up causing a serious system crash. This can result in damage to Windows and the loss of important data that you may have been working on.

To prevent this happening, it's worth running some diagnostic tests on your computer using the free Memtest86+ (*www.memtest.org*). This utility runs directly from a bootable CD before Windows has started and performs a series of tests on your system memory. Any problems reported here could lead to major problems in Windows. The step-by-step guide opposite shows you how to run the test, but here we'll explain what to do with the results.

ERRORS

An error doesn't automatically mean that you have a major problem with your memory. First, try checking the BIOS to find out what speed your memory is running at (see page 72 for instructions on how to do this). If it's running faster than it's supposed to, then you could be pushing it too much. Our guide on testing for system heat

on page 154 is also worth checking. If your system's temperature is too high, then your PC could be suffering from its effects.

It's always worth checking the obvious things, too. If you didn't plug your memory all the way in, it may be detected but cause intermittent faults. Try unplugging your memory and reseating it. Once you've done this try, run the Memtest86+ program again to see if the problem has disappeared. If it hasn't, it's time to try a new tack.

SWITCH SLOTS

It could be that one of the memory slots is causing the problem. Try switching memory slots on your motherboard and rerunning the test. If you're getting the same error, there's probably something wrong with your memory. You can attempt to find out which stick of RAM is causing the problems by taking out all the memory bar one stick and running the tests again. By rotating the stick of installed memory, you'll be able to track down the offending module.

As processors access memory through their own onboard caches, your processor could be causing the error. If you change your memory and the problem persists, you should change the processor or motherboard.

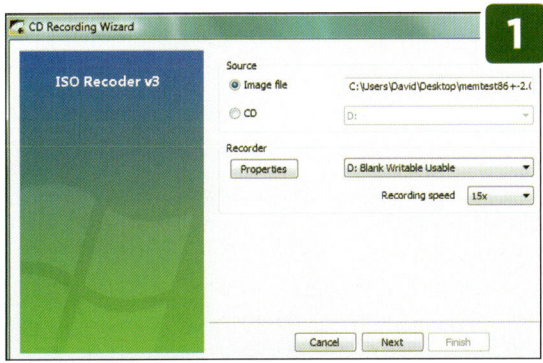

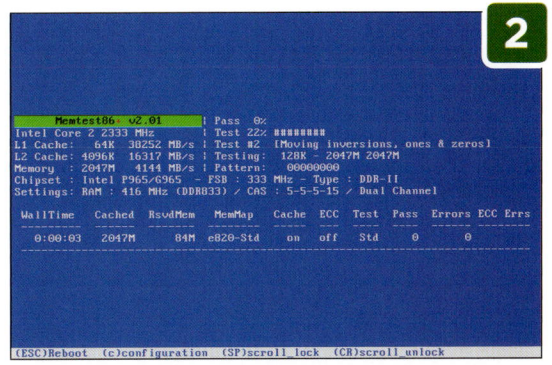

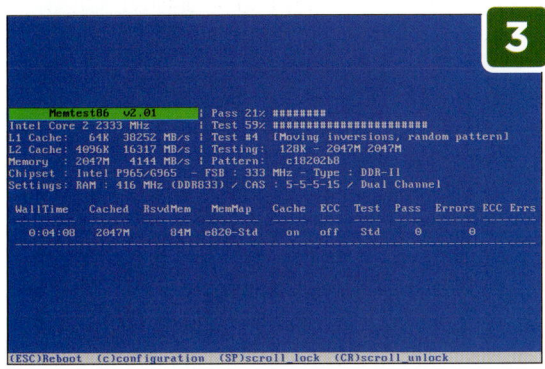

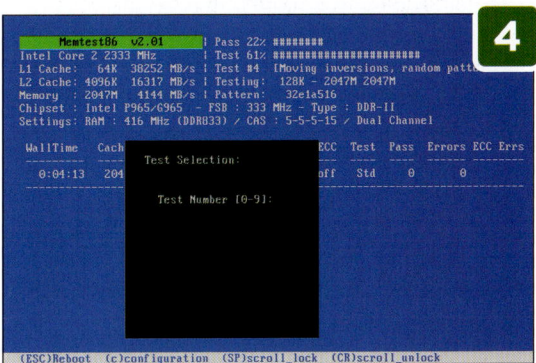

HOW TO...
Test your memory

1 CREATE BOOT DISC

Memtest86+ runs from a CD. Download the ISO file from *www.memtest.org* and save it to your hard disk. If you already have a CD-burning utility such as CDBurnerXP, you can follow the instructions for writing the ISO file to CD. If you haven't, download the free ISO Recorder from *http://isorecorder.alexfeinman.com*. Version 2 is for Windows XP and Version 3 is for Vista and Windows 7, so make sure you get the right one.

Once the software's installed, find the ISO file you downloaded, right-click on it and select Copy image to CD. Put a blank disc in your optical drive and click Next.

2 BOOT FROM THE CD

Put the CD that you just created into your drive and restart the computer. Make sure that your BIOS is set to boot from the optical drive. The CD will automatically load the test environment and start running the tests.

On the screen, you'll see system information and the current test status. The test can take 20 minutes or more to run, so you should leave it running. When it finishes, you'll either get details of the errors discovered or a message saying that your memory has passed the test.

3 COMPARE DATA

The details on the screen show you the speed at which your memory is running. This is displayed after the settings heading, in brackets after DDR. You should compare this to the speed at which it's supposed to be running. If the detected speed is faster than the memory's rated speed, you could have a problem. However, don't worry about small fluctuations in speed, such as a difference of around five per cent. It's common for the timings to be slightly wrong and components made to run a bit quicker than their rated speeds.

4 CONFIGURE TEST

If you want to configure which test to run, you need to press C while the initial test is running. You may need to reset your computer and boot from the CD you created to get this option. In the menu, press 1 to access the test selection. Press 3 to select the test you want to run, and then type a number from 0 to 9 to run that test. You can find a list of the tests on the Memtest website.

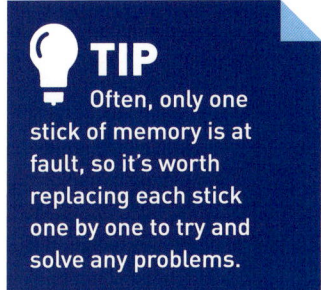

TIP
Often, only one stick of memory is at fault, so it's worth replacing each stick one by one to try and solve any problems.

Testing your hard disk

WE'VE ALL BECOME used to having masses of storage space, which most of us stuff full of gigabytes of photos, videos, music and important documents without a second thought. As wonderful as this all is, hard disks are mechanical and therefore quite sensitive. They can fail rapidly and, even if they don't lock up completely, they can cause problems with some files.

Although you should make regular backups of your data, it's also worth checking your hard disk if you're suffering from problems to make sure that it's working properly. Don't worry if you find a problem, as you can use the guide on taking an image of your PC (see page 124) to save your installed operating system and restore this to a new hard disk.

We'll show you how to test your hard disk for free using Hitachi GST's Drive Fitness Test application (*www.hitachigst.com/hdd/support/ download.htm*). Although it's made by Hitachi, it works on all brands of hard disks. It's run from a bootable CD, which we'll show you how to make.

HOW HARD DISKS WORK

The problem with hard disks is that they're mechanical, and are therefore prone to faults. Inside the sealed enclosure are a series of platters, which are disks stacked above each other. These platters, like floppy disks, store data magnetically, and are written to and read by heads that sit just above the surface. Hard disks are therefore very sensitive to movements, as sudden jerks can make the heads touch the platter and destroy any data that's stored on the disk.

If you get problems when you run Drive Fitness Test, make sure your hard disk is firmly attached inside the case and that your computer is standing on a level surface. We've known of a computer that was kept on an old wobbly desk constantly having problems with corrupted Windows files.

PROBLEM DETECTION

Other problems can affect a disk, including lots of bad areas on the disk (known as sectors). These might be detected in normal use only when you fill your disk up and your computer starts trying to access these areas. By running a system scan beforehand, you can detect these bad sectors

now. These will be marked as bad by the hard disk, which prevents data being written to them, but you should replace the hard disk if you find that you get a large number of bad sectors.

Mechanical problems are also a big worry. A damaged disk can make a horrible, metallic clunking sound. While there's little that can be done to prevent this in the long term, running diagnostic tests that access the whole disk can warn you of potential mechanical failure in the future by giving the hard disk a good workout.

Heat, as for other components, can cause massive problems inside a hard disk, so make sure that the inside of your PC is kept cool, and add more cooling if necessary (see page 154 for more information).

Modern hard disks have built-in S.M.A.R.T. technology. This lets your BIOS and other applications talk to the disk and see if there are any problems. S.M.A.R.T. can also notify you of an impending disk failure before it happens.

Finally, the interface between the hard disk and your PC can cause problems if it's damaged. In this case, there's nothing you can do but replace the hard disk. It's worth checking that the cables are plugged in firmly first, though.

HOW TO...
Test your hard disk

1 CREATE BOOT DISC

Drive Fitness Test runs from a CD that you can create yourself. Download the ISO file from *www.hitachigst.com/hdd/support/download.htm* and save it to your hard disk. If you already have a CD-burning utility, you can use that to write the ISO file to CD.

If you don't have a CD-burning application, download the free ISO Recorder from *http://isorecorder.alexfeinman.com*. Version 2 is for Windows XP and Version 3 is for Vista and Windows 7, so make sure you get the right one. Once the it's installed, right-click on the ISO file and select Copy image to CD. Put a blank CD into your optical drive and click Next.

2 BOOT FROM THE CD

Put the CD in your optical drive and restart your PC. Set the BIOS so that your optical drive is the first boot device (see page 72). You'll be given a menu with a choice of two options. Select the second option, press Enter and accept the licence agreement. The Drive Fitness Test program will then detect your hard disks, and ask for confirmation that this list is correct. Select Yes.

3 RUN A QUICK TEST

Select the hard disk that you want to test and then choose Quick Test. On the next screen, click Start. Drive Fitness Test will now run a series of diagnostic tests on your hard disk to make sure it's working properly. If the software detects any errors, you'll be told at the end of the test; otherwise, you'll get a green completion message. Click OK to accept it.

With a brand new disk this should be good enough to show that it's working correctly. If you're testing a hard disk from an old computer, follow Step 4 for a more in-depth test.

4 ADVANCED TEST

The Quick Test doesn't give the drive a full workout. For this you need to run the Advanced Test. This will run more thorough tests and check the surface of the disk for errors.

As this involves checking every part of the disk, this test will take a lot longer to run than the Quick Test, but it's worth doing, particularly if you're checking an old hard disk. It's also essential if you think that your hard disk could be causing problems.

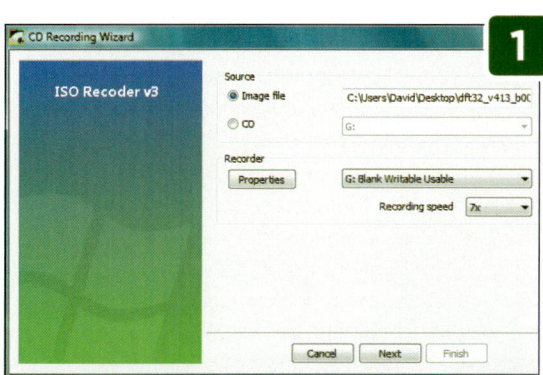

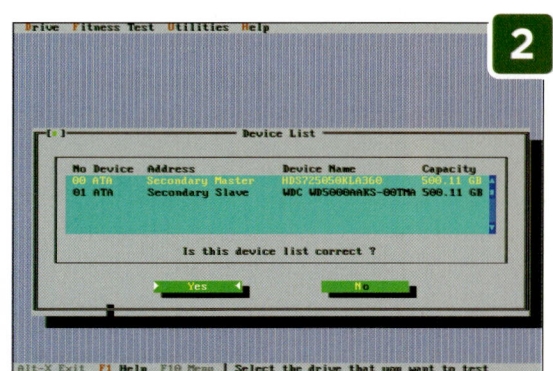

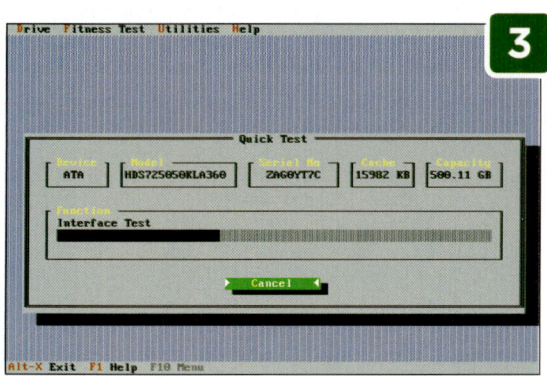

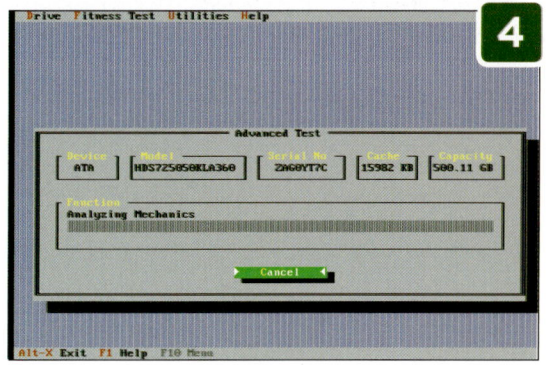

TIP
You should run Windows Check Disk on your hard disks regularly to find and fix faults before they become too serious.

Testing your PC for heat

EVERYTHING INSIDE YOUR computer generates heat to some degree. It may seem obvious that your processor does – after all, it has a giant fan and heatsink on top of it – but all components produce a certain amount of heat. Memory, hard disks, graphics cards and even your optical drive all contribute to the overall internal temperature of your PC's case.

Heat is a big problem inside computers. If your PC is too hot, you'll find that it will crash more often, as the components shut themselves down to prevent damage. In the long term, the effects of too much heat inside your system can cause your components to have a shorter lifespan. In the case of your hard disk, this could see it failing before its time, taking some of your important data with it.

MONITOR AND MEASURE

It's really important, therefore, to make sure that your PC is running at the right temperature. Keeping it cool will save you trouble and hassle further down the line. Our step-by-step guide on the opposite page shows you how to monitor your computer's temperature with the free utility SpeedFan. You can download this from *www. almico.com/speedfan.php*.

Click the download tab and click the link in the download section of the page. Once installed, it can monitor and help control the temperature inside your PC. Before you can set it properly, though, you need to know what should be expected from your system.

IDEAL TEMPERATURES

To get SpeedFan working properly, you'll have to set some maximum temperatures. These can be tricky to work out, but we've got some tips that should help. Hard disks, for example, shouldn't run any higher than 55°C, or they can be damaged. Overall system temperature inside the case should be kept below 50°C, but the lower the better.

Processors are harder to measure, as it depends on the type of chip that you're using. Generally speaking, AMD processors should have an external temperature of less than 40°C. Intel processors should have an external temperature of less than 55°C.

You may find that, depending on your system, your temperatures are either close to these figures or a lot lower. Much depends on the temperature sensors in your PC. Motherboard manufacturers use different types of sensors in different locations, which can cause a lot of variance between boards. As long as you're running your PC at temperatures less than we've highlighted, though, it will be fine.

MORE FANS

If your PC is running really hot, there are some things you can try to lower the temperature. First, reseat your processor cooler, making sure it has enough thermal paste on it to increase the efficiency of the heatsink. Make sure your case's fans aren't clogged up with dust. If you can control your fans manually, try turning them up.

Finally, if you haven't got any case fans or have enough space for more, then install some. They're easy to fit, and pretty much every case has mountings for them. Inspect your case's manual for full instructions on the size of fans you can install. Ideally, you want to get airflow moving through the case to extract hot air. So, if your fan at the rear is blowing out the back of the case, fit one in the front that blows into the case. This will bring in cool air from outside and help push the hot air out of the case. If you have one hot component, such as a hard disk, then you need to fit fans near it to help cool it down.

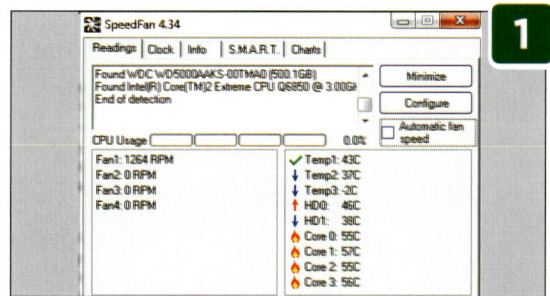

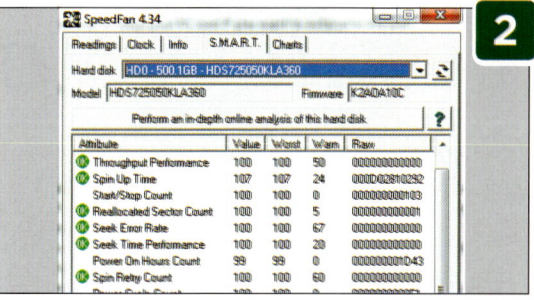

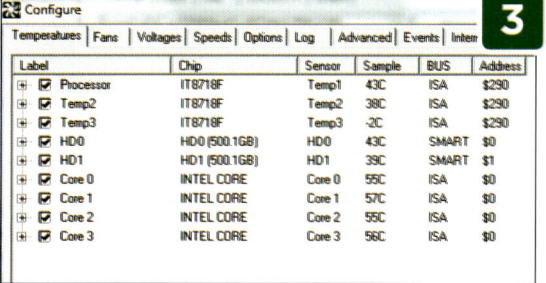

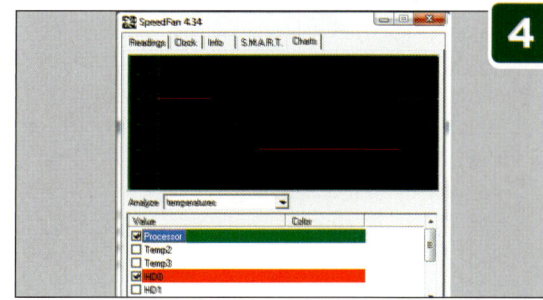

HOW TO...
Monitor system temperature

1 READINGS

SpeedFan automatically detects temperature sensors on the motherboard and displays their current readings. Unfortunately, it doesn't always give them recognisable names, so it can be hard to tell which one is your processor's temperature and which one is the system temperature. The easiest way to find out is to leave your system idle for a few minutes until the temperatures settle. Note down the temperatures, restart your computer and go into the BIOS. Its monitoring section will give you real names for the sensors – all you have to do is match the relative values you recorded.

SpeedFan places an icon next to each temperature reading, which is designed to show you the current status of your computer. A green tick means that everything's all right, arrows show whether the temperature is increasing or decreasing, while a fire means that it's too hot. However, SpeedFan doesn't always get the warnings right, so ignore them for now.

2 HDD AND CORE

As well as accessing the motherboard, SpeedFan can read the temperature of your hard disks using Self-Monitoring Analysis and Reporting Technology (S.M.A.R.T.). Each disk in your PC will be numbered (HD0, HD1 and so on) and have its own temperature. You can also get a report on

your hard disk by clicking on the S.M.A.R.T. tab. The core temperatures are the readings from inside your processor.

3 CONFIGURE SETTINGS

Click on the Readings tab and then on Configure. You'll see the list of temperature sensors. Click to select one, wait a few seconds and then click again. You can now rename the sensor to match what you identified in Step 1. Press Enter to set the name.

Click on a sensor and you'll see two readings: desired and warning. The first is an ideal temperature, while warning determines when a flame will be displayed. You only need to set the warning temperatures for hard disks and the processor, as defined by the limits opposite.

4 CHARTS

Click on the Charts tab and put ticks in the sensors that you want to measure. SpeedFan will then track temperatures over time. This is a good way to see how your system responds when you do different jobs. For example, if you play a lot of games and see that your PC's temperature is running very high during this activity, you'll know that you need to get some extra cooling. This can also be useful when running burn-in tests, such as Hot CPU Tester (see page 156).

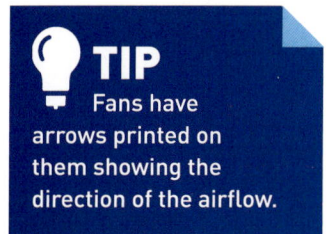

TIP
Fans have arrows printed on them showing the direction of the airflow.

Testing your processor

THE PROCESSOR IS just about the most important part of your PC. Without it, you'd just have a collection of components that wouldn't be able to do anything. The processor controls every single aspect of your computer, from loading and running the operating system to running the clever artificial intelligence in the latest games.

Processors are constantly being updated, and are also becoming more complicated. These days, it's the norm for a single chip to house at least two processors (called cores), but four cores are rapidly becoming more affordable. While this extra complexity means that computers today can storm through tough tasks such as video encoding quicker than ever, the result is that there's more that can go wrong.

A processor crashing will immediately freeze your computer, losing any unsaved work in the process. If the hard disk was being accessed at the time with an important Windows system file

open, a processor crash can even mean that you need to reinstall Windows. Here we'll show you how to test your computer for stability with the free Hot CPU Tester (available from *www.7byte.com*).

PROBLEM SOLVING

The free version of Hot CPU Tester doesn't run the full suite of diagnostics, which is available in the Professional version. However, there's enough there to make sure that your processor is running properly. Using its Burn-in test, you can find out how effective your processor's cooling is.

The most common reason for a processor to fail any of the diagnostic tests is overheating. Processors are sensitive to heat, and can start causing errors when they get too hot. Intel's processors try to deal with the problem by slowing themselves down, which makes your computer very sluggish until the core temperature has dropped. Alternatively, processors can shut themselves down completely, meaning that you'll need to restart your computer.

COOLING OFF

The essential thing with processors is to make sure that there's plenty of cooling. Follow our step-by-step advice opposite to work out how hot your processor is. If it exceeds the limits we set on page 154, you've got a problem. Take your PC apart and make sure that its fan is working and that there's decent contact between the processor and the cooler. You may need to reapply thermal paste.

If heat doesn't seem to be the problem and your processor is still failing diagnostic checks, make sure you're running it at the intended speed in the BIOS (see page 72). Running the processor faster than it is meant to can cause errors.

Finally, try taking the processor out of its socket (see pages 54 and 55 for full instructions). In Intel LGA-775 sockets, look for any bent pins. If you see any, push them gently back into place with a jeweller's screwdriver. For AM2 and AM2+ processors, make sure that you haven't bent any pins on the processor. Inserting a credit card between the rows should allow you to bend them back into shape. Take great care when doing this or you could cause more damage.

HOW TO...
Test your processor

1 SET THE TEST DURATION
Install Hot CPU Tester (*www.7byte.com*) and run it when the installation has finished. Click OK to skip the message about upgrading to the new version. Before you start, click on the Options tab and select the Test Modules item. You'll see that the test duration is set to six hours. While this will give your PC a thorough workout, it's probably too much for most people. We'd recommend setting it to an hour or slightly under.

2 RUN TEST
Click on the Diagnostic button and click Run Test. Hot CPU Tester will then give your processor a thorough workout. It will run lots of mathematically complex tasks to stretch your processor to its limit. It will use every core in your PC, so you'll be unable to use your computer for anything else during this time.

Once the program has finished the test, you'll receive a report telling you if your processor failed any of the tests. If it didn't, you know that it's working properly.

3 BURN IN
Click the Burn-in icon. This test will run your processor at 100 per cent load, and is useful for checking how temperature affects it. However, in the free version of Hot CPU Tester, which tests only a single core, you can run only a single thread. A workaround is to run Hot CPU Tester as many times as you have cores by double-clicking the program icon.

4 MEASURE
Before you start the Burn-in test, run SpeedFan (see page 155) in order to measure the temperature. Keep it somewhere onscreen where it will be visible. Start the Burn-in test on every open copy of Hot CPU Tester by clicking the Run CPU Burn-in button. SpeedFan may stop responding, as your processor is too busy to deal with it. Don't worry; just leave the test running for around 10 minutes and then stop all the Burn-in tests. When they've stopped, look at the temperature of the processor in SpeedFan. If it's exceeded the limits you set for it, you may have overheating problems.

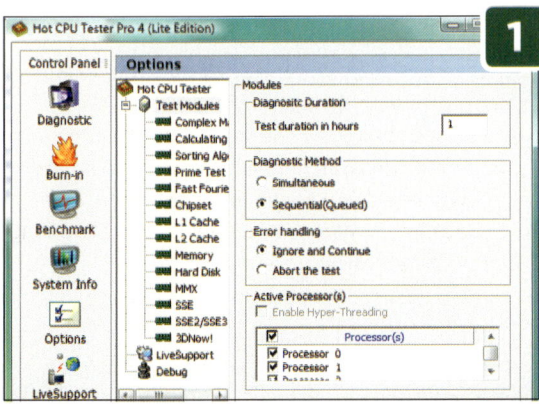

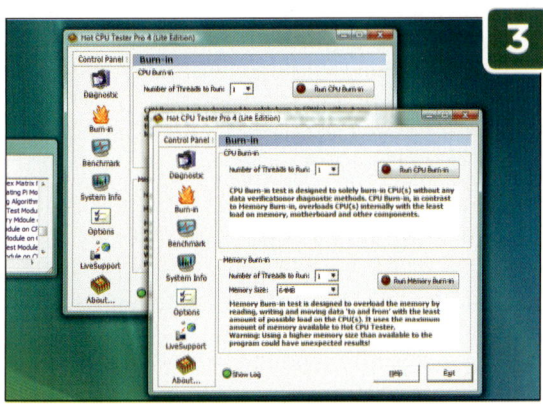

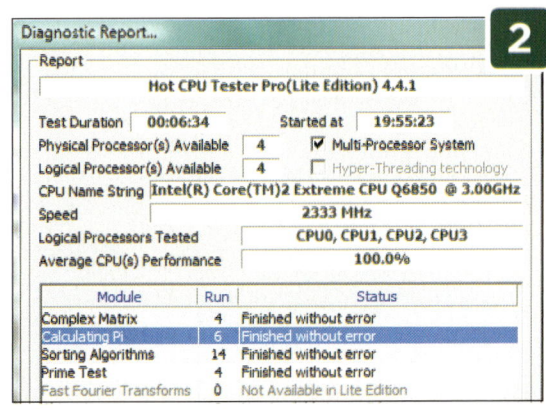

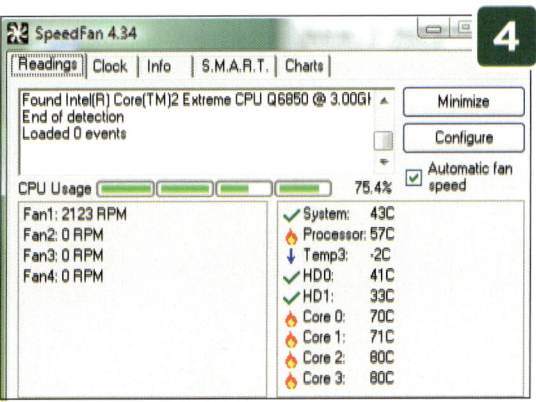

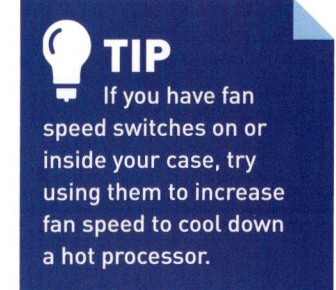

TIP
If you have fan speed switches on or inside your case, try using them to increase fan speed to cool down a hot processor.

Glossary

From ADSL to ZIF, we explain 100 key PC terms

10/100Mbit/s See Ethernet.

10BASE-T See Ethernet.

64-BIT 64-bit processors have an extended instruction set, allowing them to process more data at once and access more memory. Only software that supports 64-bit extensions will benefit.

802.11b, 802.11g See WiFi.

ADSL Asymmetric digital subscriber line, the commonest form of broadband. It works over existing BT phone lines, provided that the local exchange is ADSL-enabled.

AGP Accelerated graphics port, a slot for graphics cards. Several versions of increasing speed and decreasing voltage were launched. Now superseded by PCI Express.

ATA AT attachment. See IDE.

ATAPI AT attachment packet interface. See IDE.

ATHLON 64 AMD's current mainstream processor. Has been made for Socket 754, Socket 939 and now Socket AM2.

ATX POWER CONNECTOR This PSU connector supplies the PC's motherboard. It was previously a 20-pin connector, but a 24-pin version started appearing on motherboards in 2005. A split connector is commonly provided to power either version.

ATX See Form Factor.

BIOS The basic input/output system configures your motherboard at startup and boots your PC. It's stored on a flash memory chip and keeps its settings in the CMOS.

BLANKING PLATE Used to cover unoccupied PC case cutouts. You must remove one to install a PCI, PCI Express or AGP expansion card.

BTX See Form Factor.

CARDBUS The 32-bit expansion slot most commonly found on laptop PCs, equivalent to the PCI slot on desktops. Is now being superseded by ExpressCard.

CAT5, CAT6 See Ethernet.

CELERON Intel's budget processor. Current models are cut-down Pentium 4s, available for Socket 478 and LGA775.

CLOCK SPEED All computer components work in time with a clock signal. Each has a maximum clock speed, shown in megahertz (MHz) or gigahertz (GHz), at which it's designed to run. Running the clock faster (overclocking) boosts performance, but can cause a PC to crash.

CMOS Battery-backed memory where the BIOS stores its settings. Cleared using a jumper.

COMPONENT VIDEO A high-quality analogue video connection using three cables.

COMPOSITE VIDEO A basic-quality video connection using a single cable.

CORE 2 Intel's newest processor, available for LGA775 in mainstream Duo and premium Extreme versions.

CPU Central processing unit, also known simply as the processor.

CROSSFIRE ATI's system for combining the power of two Radeon graphics cards in a single PC. Also see SLI.

CRT Cathode ray tube. Refers to a conventional glass-tube monitor.

DDR The type of memory used in most current PCs, called double data rate because it runs twice as fast as SDRAM of the same clock speed. Comes in several speeds, including PC1600, PC2100, PC2700 and PC3200. PC3200 DDR runs at 200MHz but is called 400MHz DDR because of its doubled effective speed.

DDR2 The type of memory used in the newest Pentium 4, Core 2 and Athlon 64 systems. Available in speeds from PC2-4200 (533MHz effective).

DHCP Dynamic host configuration protocol. This allows PCs on a network to obtain their network configuration automatically from a DHCP server, often running on a router.

DIMM Dual inline memory module, a common name for the similar physical packages in which

SDRAM, DDR and DDR2 come, with 168 pins, 184 pins and 240 pins respectively.

DIRECTX Windows extensions from Microsoft that give games and other performance-hungry software fast access to hardware. Check that your PC has the latest version – currently 10 – installed.

D-SUB Analogue monitor-to-graphics-card connection, also known as a VGA cable.

DUAL-CHANNEL Capability of a processor or motherboard to access two DIMMs at once, improving performance.

DVB-T Digital Video Broadcasting – Terrestrial, a standard used by Freeview digital TV in the UK.

DVI Digital visual interface. A monitor-to-graphics-card connection that can include digital and/or analogue signals. The commonest form, DVI-I, has both.

ETHERNET Non-specific networking term, today used to refer to any networking hardware using RJ45 plugs and one of a number of compatible standards including 10BaseT, 100BaseT and Gigabit Ethernet (GbE). Older 10/100Mbit/s hardware supports only the two slower speeds, and runs reliably with the Category 5 (Cat5) grade of cable. The highest grade, Cat6, is a safe choice for Gigabit networks.

EXPRESSCARD Expansion slot found on new laptop PCs, equivalent to PCI Express on desktops. Incompatible with CardBus.

FAT32 See NTFS.

FIREWALL Software or hardware designed to protect networks from hackers or from software that they control.

FIREWIRE Also known as IEEE 1394 or i.Link. Fast data connection used by PCs, digital camcorders, external hard disks and more. The connector comes in four-pin and six-pin versions, the latter including pins to power one device from the other. A faster nine-pin version, known as FireWire 800, is backward-compatible.

FIRMWARE Software used by a hardware device and stored on a flash memory chip so that it can be upgraded, typically to improve compatibility.

FLASH A type of memory chip that stores data permanently unless it is deliberately overwritten, a process known as flashing.

FLOPPY POWER CONNECTOR A compact four-pin power connector for floppy drives.

FORM FACTOR Motherboards adhere to standards called form factors that dictate size and layout. The commonest are ATX and its compact relative microATX. BTX is Intel's newest standard. Cases will support one or more form factors, telling you which motherboards can be fitted.

FSB The frontside bus connects the processor and other parts of the system. On all but the latest motherboards, the memory runs at the same speed as the FSB – typically 133MHz, 200MHz or 266MHz.

GIGABIT ETHERNET (GbE) See Ethernet.

HEADER A group of pins on a motherboard where you can connect additional ports. USB and FireWire headers are the most common.

IDE A common name for the ATA disk connector, strictly called ATAPI in its modern form, which supports a variety of devices. All three are also known as PATA (Parallel ATA), to distinguish them from SATA (Serial ATA).

IEEE 1394 See FireWire.

JUMPER A plastic-enclosed metal contact used to connect two pins to configure a hardware device. Also see Master.

LGA775 Intel's current processor socket, with pins rather than holes. Used by Pentium 4, Celeron and Core 2 processors.

LINE-IN Audio input for signal of standard 'line-level' volume (louder than microphone input). Usually light blue and takes a 3.5mm jack.

LINE-OUT Audio output of standard 'line-level' volume. Usually lime green, and takes a 3.5mm jack.

MASTER Two IDE devices can share a single cable, provided that one is configured as a master and the other as a slave. This is done using jumpers on the devices.

MICROATX A compact mainstream motherboard form factor with a maximum size of 244x244mm.

MIMO Multiple-input, multiple-output: a way of improving the range and performance of wireless (WiFi) networks using multi-faceted antennas. A technology, not a standard. See Pre-N.

MOLEX Common name for the four-pin power connector used by hard disks and other drives. It has yellow (12V), red (5V) and two black (ground) wires.

NTFS Hard disk file system used by XP, Vista, Windows 7 and other advanced versions of the operating system. Replaces FAT32, as used by Windows 95, 98 and Me.

OEM Original equipment manufacturer. Used to describe products intended for PC manufacturers rather than end users. Typically these will have minimal packaging and manuals.

PATA See IDE.

PC100, PC133 See SDRAM.

PC1600, PC2100, PC2700, PC3200 See DDR.

PC2-4200 See DDR2.

PCI A motherboard expansion slot used for all kinds of upgrade cards except graphics cards. Internal modems, TV tuners and sound cards generally use PCI.

PCI EXPRESS (PCI-E) The relatively new expansion bus for all kinds of upgrades. Slots come in several lengths. Long, fast x16 slots are for graphics cards; short, slower x1 slots are for devices previously made for PCI. A slower card can be used in a faster slot.

PENTIUM 4 Intel's current mainstream processor.

PHENOM AMD's latest processor is designed for Socket AM2+ motherboards, but can work with some older Socket AM2 boards, too.

PHONO Hi-fi style interconnect, correctly known as an RCA jack and used for various audio and video connections. Red and white plugs are used for right and left audio channels, yellow for composite video.

POST Power-on self-test, performed by PCs when switched on, generating the text output that you see before Windows loads.

PRE-N A term used for wireless networking equipment based on the draft 802.11n standard, which has only recently been finalised. Uses MIMO technology.

PRIMARY CHANNEL Most motherboards provide at least two IDE connectors for hard disks and other drives. The PC will boot from the master disk on the connector marked as the primary channel. The secondary channel is typically used for CD and DVD drives.

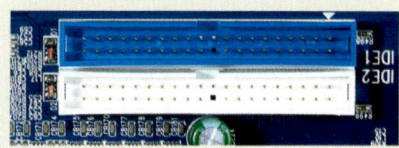

PS/2 CONNECTOR Used for keyboards and mice, although these now often connect via USB.

PSU Power supply unit. Refers to the device inside a PC that converts mains electricity and distributes it to the system's components, and also to the external mains adaptors supplied with some peripherals.

RAID Redundant array of inexpensive disks: a way of storing data on several hard disks to improve performance, or to provide a backup if one disk fails, or both. Modern motherboards support RAID on their PATA or SATA ports.

RAMBUS The company responsible for the expensive RDRAM type of memory used for a few years in Pentium III and Pentium 4 systems. Now obsolete, RDRAM came in modules called RIMMs. If your PC needs it, try eBay.

RCA See Phono.

RDRAM See Rambus.

RF Radio frequency, referring to the coaxial cable connection of TV antennas. An RF signal carries many video channels, while S-video and composite carry only one.

RIMM See Rambus.

RJ45 Plug used for Ethernet network cables, with eight wires. Larger than, but often mistaken for, RJ11.

SATA The Serial ATA interface is used for modern hard disks because it's faster and neater than PATA (Parallel ATA). The original SATA ran at 150MB/s, but the current standard has a 300MB/s mode, compared to PATA's maximum of 133MB/s.

SDRAM The memory type used by most Pentium II and Pentium III PCs. Common speeds are PC100 (100MHz) and PC133 (133MHz).

SECONDARY CHANNEL See Primary Channel.

SERIAL PORT Old, slow port rarely used today but still present on many motherboards as a nine-pin connector.

SLAVE See Master.

SLI Nvidia's system for combining the power of two GeForce graphics cards in one PC. Also see CrossFire.

SOCKET 478 Intel's previous-generation processor socket, still supported by a handful of new motherboards and Pentium 4 and Celeron processors.

SOCKET 479 Socket for Intel's Pentium M and Core Duo mobile processors, the predecessors of Core 2.

SOCKET 754 Socket used by AMD's early Athlon 64 and current Sempron processors. Only supports processors with a single memory controller.

SOCKET 939 Socket used by AMD's Athlon 64 processors, including dual-core X2 versions. Supports processors with a dual memory controller.

SOCKET A Also known as Socket 462, used by AMD's old Duron, Athlon, Athlon XP and Sempron processors. Now obsolete.

SOCKET AM2 AMD's processor socket, which supports DDR2. Used by Athlon 64, Athlon FX and Sempron processors. Very similar to Socket 939 with one extra pinhole.

SOCKET AM2+ AMD's latest processor socket, which supports PC-8500 DDR2 memory and Phenom processors. Backward-compatible with older CPUs.

S-VIDEO An average-quality analogue video connection with a four-pin cable.

TV-OUT Generic analogue output used for connection to a TV. Includes S-video and composite.

USB Universal serial bus. These ports are used to connect all manner of external devices.

USB2 The latest version of USB, which supports the Hi-Speed 480Mbit/s mode as well as older USB 1.1 devices.

VIVO Video in, video out. A compound connector on graphics cards that combines video inputs and outputs. Usually has a breakout cable that maps the pins to standard S-video or composite video connectors.

WEP Wired equivalent privacy. An encryption standard used to secure wireless networks. Comes in various strengths up to 256-bit, all weaker than WPA.

WIFI Name used collectively for the IEEE 802.11 wireless networking standards, including the 11Mbit/s 802.11b and 54Mbit/s 802.11g standards.

WPA WiFi protected access. An encryption standard used to secure wireless networks more reliably than WEP.

ZIF Zero insertion force: a processor socket where the chip is clamped using a lever.

BUILD A BETTER PC 2011

EDITORIAL

Editor
David Ludlow

Production
Steve Haines

Design and layout
Colin Mackleworth

COVER ILLUSTRATION
Ian Naylor

PHOTOGRAPHY
Danny Bird, Jan Cihak, Linda Duong, Pat Hall, Timo Hebditch, Andrew Ridge, Hugh Threlfall

Digital Production Manager
Nicky Baker

MANAGEMENT

MagBooks Manager
Dharmesh Mistry

Publishing Director
John Garewal

Operations Director
Robin Ryan

Managing Director of Advertising
Julian Lloyd-Evans

Newstrade Director
Martin Belson

Chief Operating Officer
Brett Reynolds

Group Finance Director
Ian Leggett

Chief Executive
James Tye

Chairman
Felix Dennis

MAGBOOK

The 'MagBook' brand is a trademark of Dennis Publishing Ltd. 30 Cleveland St, London W1T 4JD. Company registered in England. All material © Dennis Publishing Ltd, licensed by Felden 2010, and may not be reproduced in whole or part without the consent of the publishers.

ISBN 1-907232-62-1

LICENSING

To license this product, please contact Winnie Liesenfeld on +44 (0) 20 7907 6134 or email winnie_liesenfeld@dennis.co.uk

LIABILITY

While every care was taken during the production of this MagBook, the publishers cannot be held responsible for the accuracy of the information or any consequence arising from it. Dennis Publishing takes no responsibility for the companies advertising in this MagBook.

The paper used within this MagBook is produced from sustainable fibre, manufactured by mills with a valid chain of custody.

Printed by BGP